INTRODUCTION TO AFRICAN ORAL LITERATURE AND PERFORMANCE

INTRODUCTION TO AFRICAN ORAL LITERATURE AND PERFORMANCE

by
Báyò Ògúnjìmí and Abdul-Rasheed Na'Allah
2005 revisions by Abdul-Rasheed Na'Allah

Africa World Press, Inc.

Africa World Press, Inc.

P.O. Box 1892
Trenton, NJ 08607

P.O. Box 48
Asmara, ERITREA

Copyright © 2005 Báyò Ògúnjìmí and Abdul-Rasheed Na'Allah
First Printing 2005

All rights reserved. No part of this publication may be reproduced, stored in a retrieval system or transmitted in any form or by any means electronic, mechanical, photocopying, recording or otherwise without the prior written permission of the publisher.

Book design: Sam Saverance
Cover design: Roger Dormann

Library of Congress Cataloging-in-Publication Data

Ogunjimi, Bayo.
  Introduction to African oral literature & performance / by Bayo Ogunjimi and Abdul-Rasheed Na'Allah.
    p. cm.
Rev. ed. of: Introduction to African oral literature. c1991.
Includes bibliographical references and index.
  ISBN 1-59221-150-X (hardcover) -- ISBN 1-59221-151-8 (pbk.)
  1. Oral tradition--Africa. 2. Folk literature, African--History and criticism. I. Title: Introduction to African oral literature and performance. II. Na®allah, Abdul Rasheed. III. Ogunjimi, Bayo. Introduction to African oral literature. IV. Title.

GR350.O367 2003
398'.096--dc21

2003014747

Table of Contents

Acknowledgements	vii
Preface: African Oral Literary Performance in the Classroom	ix
Original Acknowledgement to Volume I	xv
Original Foreword to Volume I	xvii
Original Acknowledgements to Volume II	xix
Original Foreword to Volume II	xxi
Introduction	1

SECTION 1:
ORAL NARRATIVE PERFORMANCE

CHAPTER ONE: The Sources and Origins of African Oral Literature and Performance	9
CHAPTER TWO: Fieldwork Practice and Research Methodology in Oral Literature & Performance	31
CHAPTER THREE: Archetypes	47
CHAPTER FOUR: Myths	55
CHAPTER FIVE: Legends	65
CHAPTER SIX: Folktales	75
CHAPTER SEVEN: Proverbs	85
CHAPTER EIGHT: Riddles and Jokes	95
CHAPTER NINE: Stylistics and the Performance of Oral Narratives	101

SECTION 2:
ORAL POETRY PERFORMANCE

Introduction to Section 2	121
CHAPTER TEN: Religious Poetry	125

CHAPTER ELEVEN: Incantatory Poetry	147
CHAPTER TWELVE: Salutation or Praise Poetry	165
CHAPTER THIRTEEN: Funeral Poetry	183
CHAPTER FOURTEEN: Occupational and Heroic Poetry	199
a. Occupational Poetry	199
b. Heroic Poetry	205
CHAPTER FIFTEEN: Topical, Lullaby and Occasional Poetry	215
a. Topical Poetry	215
b. Lullaby	229
c. Occasional Poetry	234
CONCLUSION	241
Bibliography	245
Index	253

Acknowledgements

My students, friends, academic colleagues and scholarly reviewers in Nigeria, Canada and the United States all deserve my gratitude for being wonderful supporters since the original publication of the two volumes of *Introduction to African Oral Literature*. Most importantly, my former teacher, colleague and co-author, the late Báyò Ògúnjìmí, a rare gem, this revision and republication is dedicated to him. I remember all the days and nights we spent in rural areas in Nigeria, either researching or writing chapters for the two volumes. I am happy that this book will continue to serve his good name and be useful to students and scholars of African culture to whom the late Dr. Ògúnjìmí dedicated his life and energy. I thank Akíntúndé Akínyemí for marking the tones for the Yoruba texts in this book. I also thank the University of Illinois's Center for African Studies, whose 2000 Regional Africanist Fellowship gave me opportunity to start revising and converting the two volumes of *Introduction to African Oral Literature* into the present single cover, *Introduction to African Oral Literature and Performance*.

Preface

African Oral Performance in the Classroom

One of the most difficult things to do for a teacher of African culture is to teach African oral performances within the four walls of a classroom. How do you present a people's culture to students, especially when that culture has performances based on spontaneous renditions, community involvement and daily performances of life manifesting in social, political, economic, religious, scientific, metaphysical and other areas of human and cultural endeavors? Someone might say, "You should use video, audio tape or computer simulation." It is not as simple as that. While spontaneous video transmission of oral performances from one setting to another may prove particularly advantageous to the teacher of African oral forms, the audiovisual transmission neither convey the total sense of the spontaneity of the moment nor does it allow the type of participation that the teacher might want of his students. In other words, even with the most recent satellite support that modern technology can afford the teacher, the teacher may still not be able to convey the complete sense of an African oral performance to his students without their involvement in actual performance. As it is difficult for a teacher do this, in my opinion, so is it even more a gigantic task for a scholar to put on the pages of a book the meanings, lore and rudiments of African performances that are based more on words and actions than on written or graphical design. How does one present, as teacher and as scholar, oral performances of a continent so diversified through language and traditions as Africa without exaggerating or without leaving out many important areas and issues that are crucial to their existence? When we first wrote these books, our intention was to provide materials for Nigerian students studying African oral literature. I have since found myself teaching African and African Diaspora performances in America and confronted with enthusiastic students who want to enter into the world of Black performances. I have sent out students on fieldwork to several American communities to explore Black performance cultures or field materials from White or Hispanic traditions for comparative analysis. This revision is therefore intended to be sensitive to the needs of my American students and students and scholars around the world as it continues to cater for the aspirations of Nigerian and African students in Africa that want to study their own performance cultures.

It has been sometime since the two volumes of *Introduction to African Oral Literature* were published, i.e., 1991 and 1994. From comments received from many students and scholars that have used the volumes at the University of Ilorin, the University of Ibadan, to Bayero University, Kano, and to students, scholars and general readers who have reviewed them from around the world, especially the United States and Canada, we feel this has been a useful venture complementing existing excellent materials on oral literature and performance by such leading scholars as Ruth Finnegan, Isidore Okpewho and others. We intend for *Introduction to African Oral Literature and Performance*, like its earlier volumes, to be a book that can actually be used in the classroom as well as consulted in the library at all levels of education. Our intention with this project is to bring the scholarship of African performance to students and scholars and involve them in performance projects and exercises that will ensure that they gain experiences crucial to understanding African performance traditions. The current revisions and combination of the two volumes into one book will provide even greater opportunity for interested persons to explore African oral narratives and poetry performances from several cultures. I am adding a section on "Further Reading and Work" to relevant chapters so that interested readers may be provided with additional guidance for further studies in African oral performances. I have largely retained the structure of the earlier volumes. However, this new book provides more sources and information on recent materials on African oral traditions and is therefore more up-to-date. The exercises have been enhanced by a few more questions and project activities. Some chapters have been rearranged, and perhaps the most important one brought forward is what is now Chapter Two in this book, "Fieldwork Practice and Research Methodology in Oral Literature and Performance."

Preface: African Oral Performance in the Classroom

From teaching a university course on "African American Folklore" in regular classes as well as on the web and sending students to do fieldwork across the United States, it is certain that research methodology is an important area that any book on oral performances of people of African descent must address. It is most interesting to hear reports of difficulties faced by students even in places where, in the United States, one would think Western education and literacy would ensure a greater cooperation for the collection of data by student researchers. To cite a 2003 example from one of my web students whose frustration led her to request for my approval to abandon important aspects of her fieldwork on church performances:

> I am having some serious problems here. I have called various churches and synagogues to ask permission to camcord various aspects of their ceremonies. I explained who I was, my school, etc. I told them I was doing a research paper on how oral performance plays a key part in religion (I am trying to keep it basic). I offered to let them see what I taped and let them read and edit my paper (their part in it). No takers. The Jewish synagogue doesn't allow any sort of recording on the Sabbath. The American Baptist minister wanted "no part in it" and thought his congregation would think he was "leaving," go figure! Others told me to call the Pastor, Reverend, Priest tomorrow but they expressed doubt. They are even hesitant on audio recordings and still photos. I will still push in this direction because I feel Jewish, Roman Catholic, American and Southern Baptist, and African Methodist Episcopal are key aspects in what I am trying to accomplish. BUT, if no one will let me tape, would you allow me to use photos from other sources to illustrate my paper? I will do a full bibliography as not to plagiarize. Pretty please?

(in an e-mail letter of January 20, 2003)

What more methods should this student or others who want access to similar venues as researchers of a traditional custom and performance adopt? Should they take the easy way out in their studies and rely on still pictures (or re-circulation of photographs from old and outdated reference books) in an age when electronic advancement makes it possible to have a simultaneous transfer of motion pictures and performance images from one setting to another? Yet, is there anything different in the impediments that students and scholars encounter in their fieldwork in North America or Europe than in Africa, the Caribbean or Latin America? When should oral performance researchers make use of a particular method or gadget, and when is a prior physical consultation better than snail mail or e-mail contact even when researching in the West? Chapter Two has been revised to answer many new questions that researchers may face exploring oral traditions of people of African descent from both continental and Diaspora Africa. In general, this book presents two important sections. Section 1 on Oral Narratives, with three generic introductory chapters on sources and forms of African oral performances, research methods and archetypes, and seven others, ending with Chapter Nine on "Stylistics and Oral Narrative Performance." Section 2, introduced by a general introduction, is on Oral Poetry Performance, dealing with different topics, from religious poetry, incantatory poetry, funeral poetry, occupational poetry, topical poetry to lullaby and occasional poetry, from Chapters Ten to Fifteen. Section 2 also has, in every chapter, a subsection on "Stylistics and Nature of Performance."

Performance Studies scholars as a whole must begin to take a different approach from anthropologists' whose Participant Observant strategy in African oral traditions have not always led to a better understanding and interpretation of African oral traditions and performances. It is old information to say that early anthropologists, through what they regarded as scientific method of Participant Observant, sometimes imposed preconceived notions on their renditions of what they observed on the field. Contemporary scholars of African oral performance often got lost at the moment they interpreted oral materials they collected from the field, perhaps because when they participated in actual performances, they were busy observing the steps instead of being spirited participants themselves who were able to enter into and lived the actual world of the performers. It seems to me that the moment a participant claims to be an observer, he or she is either becoming over or under sensitive to the actual performance steps that are crucial in entering the actual performance world he is observing. The process of observation would drag him or her away from the total involvement in and process of performance. It is for this reason that I have insisted (Na'Allah 1997) that Participatory Performance is the most important fieldwork tool for the African oral performance scholar, and

Preface: African Oral Performance in the Classroom

indeed all performance studies scholars as a whole. Performance Studies should have its own inherent method instead of relying too much on anthropologist perspective that may not satisfy the primary concerns of contemporary performance specialists: understanding a performance from its contextual reality. Participatory Performance method can be called a methodology of double performance, i.e., participate and perform, both focusing on one and the same thing, entering the world of the performance and being the same with indigenous performers! Being at the same level with them is necessary in achieving the same mood that any other performer may attain so that after the actual performance, the fieldwork scholar of performance can realize that he or she has gone through about the same experience and attain about the same understanding with the indigenous performers.

It is for the importance of performance to African oral traditions that this new volume is titled, *Introduction to African Oral Literature and Performance*, and that every Section has important areas discussing performance styles and features. From the very moment that the late Báyò Ògúnjìmí and I started this project, we were certain that ours was an effort to presenting African performance to scholars, students and all interested members of the public.

Finally, there cannot be African Performance Studies without the community tales and stories and the poetry, and the drama or theatrical performances. But more importantly, dramatic art alone, written or oral, does not constitute African performance even in the twenty-first century. Important as African traditional festivals, rites and rituals are, poetry performance of incantation, praise, spiritual and other chants and invocations provide their platforms. In Nigeria, the *Ègbá Alárìnjó* performance in Abeokuta, the *Kwa Hir* performance among the Tiv, or the *Egwugwu, Egúngún* or *Ìgunnu* (masquerades) performances among Igbo, Yorùbá, and Nupe all involve active poetry performances. Wole Soyinka's rendition of a Yorùbá dance ritual in *Death and the King's Horseman* would not be complete without the involvement of Olóhùn-Oyin, the Elésin-Oba's praise poet. The poet or the griot in Africa supplies memory and cultural direction to all people involved in ritual performance.

This book is, therefore, adopting its stance from the root of African performance when it presents to all scholars, especially the performance studies scholars, students, teachers and scholars of African oral literature, cultural studies and African traditions as a whole, and to librarians and the general public, two Sections: Oral Narratives and Poetry Performances, as an important gateway to understanding African performance. It is hoped that soon a new volume on African oral drama performances will follow.

Abdul-Rasheed Na'Allah
Macomb, IL

Original Acknowledgements to Volume I

The success of a pioneering project like this is a collective effort of associates and well-wishers. We want to give accolades to all those involved morally, financially and in other ways in the production of this volume of *Introduction to African Oral Literature*. Our elders say that a river does not forget its fountain. Therefore, we pay homage to all our teachers who have equipped us intellectually in this discipline. Messers Adéolá Awóyalé, Fàtáì Ekùntakòró, Àlí-Àgan, Àkànbí II, Sa'adu, Làmídì, Abdul 'Razaq, Dr. Adémólá Ògúnjìmí and Mrs. V.A. Àlàbí have contributed immensely to the success of this book. We want to recognize the relevance of our oral literature students, whose fieldwork has influenced the logic of our reasoning and presentation. We appreciate the cooperation of Dr. G.G. Darah, President of the Folklore Society of Nigeria, who readily accepted to write a Foreword to this book.

Our dear ones, Mrs. Jérin Ògúnjìmí and Miss Rahmat Tóyìn Kamal have given us the necessary morale booster. We appreciate their love and cooperation.

Original Foreword to Volume I

The study of African oral literature is beset by a number of problems, one of which is the dearth of appropriate texts. It is therefore a great delight to have the *Introduction to African Oral Literature* by two scholars who have had considerable experience in teaching and fieldwork. Academic interest in the African tradition of the oral literature began in earnest following the publication of extant texts by scholars in the mid sixties. Most of these works were by foreign scholars and researchers whose knowledge of the literature was inadequate. But the materials available in print had great potential as examples of oral literature and it needed the intervention of literary scholars to begin to examine their aesthetic features.

In this endeavor, much insight gained was gained from the original research and theoretical perspective of Milman Parry and Albert B. Lord who opened up fresh fields of textual analysis based on the context in which the piece was performed. This approach has been adopted and improved upon by African scholars, such as Isdore Okpewho. We can now speak of a poetics of oral texts without reference to the feature of written analogues. Bayo Ogunjimi and Abdul-Rasheed Na'Allah have made an important contribution to the evolving discourse of oral narratives. The main strength of this book is the learner-based approach, which is useful for teaching and fieldwork purpose. Many texts on oral literature assume a stated knowledge for the users, which is often exaggerated. Many students who take courses in oral literature know very little of the culture from which the literature comes. The method adopted by the authors is to take the reader through a *process*, from generic names, definitions, samples and analysis. The pedagogical utility of the book is further enhanced by the questions and exercises at the end of each chapter.

The generic classifications and typology in the second half of chapter one are not without problems. The authors are close to Ruth

Finnegan's *Oral Literature in Africa* (1970) whose limits they acknowledge. There is a great deal of emphasis on functions of the various types identified. This is understandable because each context of performance determines the aesthetics and meaning of the material. Ropo Sekoni's work on Yoruba prose narratives has revealed the complex nature of the tales as instances of literary experience. Although the authors are aware of these developments, they have chosen to adopt the more familiar approach of functionalist criticism. The Sekonian method is very influenced by semiotics and studies in performance. Ògúnjimí and Na'Allah attempt a simplified form of this approach in Chapter Seven [now Chapter Nine] which treats stylstics and performance of oral narratives.

It is an axiom in oral literature scholarship that the texts live in performance. This performance can be stretched to mean that the aesthetic grandeur of oral material in translation is revealed in good analysis. That is what Ògúnjimí and Na'Allah have achieved here. The book will serve the interest of the teachers, students, researchers and librarians who are part of the growing team of specialists on African oral literature and traditions.

Dr G.G. Darah
Senior lecturer in Oral Literature,
Obafemi Awolowo University, Ile-Ife.

Original Acknowledgements to Volume II

The accomplishment of this second volume of *Introduction to African Oral Literature* has been due, partly, to the encouragement, support and challenge from our friends, colleagues and students. We are grateful to Mrs. V.A. Àlàbí, Mr. Adéolá Awóyalé and Dr. Efurosibina Adégbìjà. We remember our friend and brother, Late Dr. Adémolá Ògúnjìmí, who had been a strong supporter of our scholarship venture. Our oral literature students deserve great commendation for constantly cheering songs from our "awoko" mouths. This has encouraged us to forge ahead.

We appreciate the cooperation of Professor Olátúndé O. Olátúnjí, Professor of Yoruba Literature and former Dean of Arts, University of Ibadan, for accepting to write a foreword to this book despite his very tight schedules.

Our parents, Late Amos Ogúnjìmí, and Wúràólá Ògúnjìmí, Ahmad and Bilqees Na'Allah, for giving us the knowledge to venture into life which itself archetypally is a creative process.

Original Foreword to Volume II

This volume is the second in the series by the authors on Africa oral literature. Though information in the discipline is available in rare books and research findings, students in primary and secondary institutions do not often have access to these materials. The authors have therefore set for themselves the task of providing books on African oral literature for students at these levels. They have dealt with prose narratives in the earlier volume; their focus in the present volume is poetry.

The authors have derived their classifications of African oral literature largely from Ruth Finnegan's (1970) with its attendant problems and shortcomings, but for heuristic purposes, it is adequate. They display experience of oral literature research, as is evident in the attention paid to field methodology and in the volume of materials collected by themselves (for so I consider all unacknowledged texts). A wide area of the continent is skirted, and the authors have succeeded in making some of the information locked up in rare books and journals available to students.

I believe Dr. Bayo Ogunjimi and Mr. Abdul-Rasheed Na'Allah have in this volume taken a bold step towards establishing the study of African oral literature as a discipline at the secondary school level. I look forward to a short anthology of oral literature texts to complement this series so that a robust intellectual exercise can accompany this pedagogic venture.

Olátúndé O Olátúnjí
Professor of Yorùbá Literature
University of Ibadan

 *Introduction*

The educational syllabus on literature in Nigeria and Africa as a whole, even to the twenty-first century, has virtually continued to neglect a vital and fundamental aspect of the traditional literature of the people. This is still an achievement for the colonial education, which aimed solely at eroding African traditions, customs and culture generally. It is quite a tragic circumstance of history that almost five decades after independence, Nigeria can still not boast of a well-articulated syllabus on the traditional literature of the various ethnic groups that form the components of the country. Given this circumstance within Africa itself, how much can one regret the insufficient attention accorded traditional African literature and performance in the African Diaspora! Happily, the study of traditional Black oral literature and performance is today spreading across the globe, especially to the universities in Europe and the Americas, and teachers, students and researchers need a book such as this to give them a strong background into African performance and to guide and complement their fieldwork activities on performance in Africa and the New World.

Haphazard attempts are made to rescue the Nigerian traditional cultures from the demise of colonialism, instead of inculcation in the developing generation elements of rudiments of culture via a genuine pedagogical process, a process properly entrenched in the Nigerian educational system. FESTAC 1977 in Nigeria, in spite of its elegance (Apter, 1996; 1998: 134-8), could not perform a meaningful function of creating a cultural renaissance that will orientate the culturally starved generation into a fertile avenue of cultural education.

This book we have embarked on is still viable and lucrative for another tangential reason. The study of oral tradition in Africa as a whole has ever been the prerogative of only the intellectuals in the ivory towers. Even at the advanced colleges of education, only superficial and insignificant attempts are made to emphasize oral literature.

A brief inventory of the books available on this subject indicates that books written by academic stalwarts are only available on shelves and in the markets. One can only think of the European scholar Ruth Finnegan's *Oral Literature in Africa*, which seems to be the catechism for the study of Africa oral literature. Scholars of oral literature in Africa worship Finnegan, even with her Eurocentric outlook. Thanks to the likes of Isidore Okpewho, a versatile and prolific oral scholar has produced educative, well-researched materials on African oral literature. Some of his books include *Epic in Africa, Myth in Africa, African Oral Literature,* etc. Several authors from Kenya and Nigeria, including those from Tanzania, South Africa and a few other African nations particularly paid attention to presenting largely oral narratives from a few ethnic cultures. Several scholars in American and European academia also analyzed their fieldwork materials on oral griots and griottes. Other scholars like Karin Barber, focused on specific aspexts of an ethnic group's oral performance traditions. While we pay tribute to this scholarly venture, our problems are still not yet solved. This is because books are still not yet available for pupils and students in the primary, secondary and tertiary institutions on this subject. Our task is to bridge this gap.

Though it can be argued that there are creative works such as short stories and poetry books that recall elements of traditional African literature, we still believe that these lack the focus which we embark on in this project. It is even obvious that some of these are so heavily loaded with particles and mannerisms of written literature that they become hybrids of various and assorted cultures. Our approach is quite different. We have provided students and scholars the essential tools for the creation, appreciation and evaluation of the traditional literature of African people.

To some extent our project is kind of cultural renaissance aimed at developing a well-equipped generation, mentally and physically alert to the socio-political and economic realities of their time through the institutions, mores, norms and artifacts of their people. It is then that culture can perform its functions as the life-wire of any social system. The innovative, susceptibility of culture to changes will even inervate the socio-culture in a dialectical and radical manner. The heroic eforts at changing the colonial literature curricula in higher educational institutions in Kenya (see Laban lo Liyong's *Popular Culture in Africa: Oral Literature*), Nigeria, Tanzania and many other African countries seem to have dwindled in the twenty-first century when globalization threats have made them even more crucial. The twenty-four hour Global electronic media now threatens the inclucation of traditional African performances values in young Africans and now serve with greater efficiency as the new colonial power of the twenty-first century. It is the massive colonial power that constantly intrudes into African homes through the remote control. This is also massively completemented by cyber-jungs available unhindered all minutes through the Internet.

Our ambition in this book is to make the syllabus on African oral literature and performance in all levels of our institutions, active and operational, and avialable to students and scholars in Africa, the African Diaspora and the world as set out below.

THE METHODOLOGY OF TEACHING ORAL LITERATURE

General Empirical Methods Introduction:

Our lessons in this book are not intended to be mere memory work as has been traditional of language and literature learning in our schools. In line with the mood of the National Policy on Education in Nigeria, and most especially with the secondary school syllabi (junior and senior) as regards English Language and Literature-in-English (which) have been integrated at the junior secondary school level in Nigeria, and in line with the existing culture with practical courses in tertiary institutions around the world, our teaching methodology here is learner-based. The learners are expected to be actively involved, while the teacher serves simply as a guide.

Aim:

The fundamental relevance of this learner-based method is to ensure that the learners have performance experience in all lessons involved, since the basic essence of oral literature is performance. The teacher is only to serve as a model and to set up situations. The teacher in these lessons should "become more like the skillful conductor of an orchestra, drawing the music out of the performance."

Teaching-learning situations:

It is clear truth that we cannot separate literature from the totality of true cultural experiences in society. A teaching of African oral literature without relevant situational or contextual touch is, therefore, incomplete. Our methodology here, in other words, is also situational-based. The central premise of *Introduction to African Oral Literature and Performance* is therefore learners- and situational-oriented.

In line with our teaching and scholarly methodology, this book has not preoccupied itself with the provision of every tale, poem or drama needed. What it has done is to provide models and to give learners effective exploring and appreciating skills and to encourage them to go to the field for more materials. To help the learning, research and fieldwork program for students and scholars, we have provided in every chapter a short list for further reading and work. Every chapter is therefore expected to be broken into (I) lessons, (II) class activities that include (a) teacher's roles and (b) learner's roles, and (III) exercises that consist of (a) in-class exercises and (b) field activities.

A major performance aim of every lesson is to ensure that students acquire performance experience, appreciate the literary and performance aesthetics, and identify and imbibe the necessary moral lessons contained in the works. The exercises immediately after every lesson are therefore focused at evaluating the successes of these objectives. Every lesson is incomplete without appraising the exercises.

Framework of Teaching-Learning processes (Narratives):

I) Lessons:
   A) Passage(s) or heroic (etc.) tales.
   B) Analysis or breakdown of the story into necessary functions and explanation of the functions.

II) Class Activities:
   A) Teacher's roles:
      1. Teacher presents the passage for students to read.
      2. Teacher makes sure the students pay particular attention to the use of words and cultural references in the narrative- tale, legend, myth, etc.
      3. Teacher creates situational atmosphere relevant to the thematic and aesthetic experiences presented in the passages.

Introduction

    4. Teacher guides students to derive some narratives of folktales, legends, and myths known to them, which are relevant to the one(s) in the passage.

B) Learner's roles:

    1. Students read the folktales, etc. in silence and aloud (as directed by the teacher).

    2. Students examine the use of language and other stylistic/aesthetic elements in the narrative.

    3. Students discuss the narrative in class bringing out its theme(s) and moral lessons(s) and supplying possible alternative headings to the stories.

    4. Students produce drawings and other diagrammatic impressions of selected scenes in the folktales, legends, myths, etc.

    5. Some students dramatize the stories.

III) Exercises:

A) In-class exercises: Students are to attempt some simple questions or carry out some activities contained in the exercises at the end of the lesson, e.g.

    1. Write a story of about 20 lines similar in theme.

    2. Write a short explanation of what you think three of the important images contained there stand for.

    3. What are your impressions of the theme of the folktale first read?

B) Field activities: Students are to go out to the field to collect oral materials, which are later analyzed in line with the guidelines prescribed by the teacher. Usually, such materials are to be recorded by the students on tapes or and video. Students are to put down records on paralinguistic elements and musical instruments that accompany oral narratives, songs, and dramatic performances. Students are to ensure that they follow such questions that are provided to the letter. Examples:

    1. Get to the elder members in your family and collect as many folktales as you can.

    2. Try the community near your own village or town (where they speak a different language from yours). Collect some oral tales and identify areas of similarity and differences with yours (you may need an interpreter).

    3. Try to determine how frequently songs accompany the folktales you collect.

Further Reading and Work
(read and compare materials with those in this book)

Miruka, Simon Okumba. *Studying Oral Literature*. Nairobi, Kenya: Acacia Stantex Publishers, 1999.

Petrilli, Susan and Augusto Ponzio. "Telling Stories in the Era of Global Communication: Black writing—oraliture." *Research in African Literatures*. 32.1 (2001): 98-109.

Yai, Olabiyi Babalola. "Fundamental Issues in African Oral Literature" in *Ife Studies in AfricanLiterature and the Arts ISALA*. 1 (1982): 4-17.

References

Apter, Andrew. "Death and the King's Henchment: Ken Saro-Wiwa and the Political Ecology of Citizenship in Nigeria." *Ogoni's Agonies: Ken Saro-Wiwa and the Crisis in Nigeria*. Ed. Abdul-Rasheed Na'Allah. Trenton: AWP, 1998.

---. "The Pan-African Nation: Oil-Money and the Spectacle of Culture in Nigeria." *Public Culture* 8.3, 1996: 441-66.

Section 1

ORAL NARRATIVES

Chapter One

 **The Sources and Origins of African Oral Performance**

We want to be systematic in our approach. We do not want to plunge students and other interested readers into a vacuum where it will be very difficult for them to trace the beginning, the middle and the end. We want them to know the origin and sources of what we shall later identify as various elements of traditional African literature and performance. In this case, we want the students to be familiar with the organization of the African Universe and how this has affected the formulation and production of literary and performance cultures that are not written but passed from generation to generation verbally. We are, afterward, dealing with the literature of non-literate societies not yet contaminated with the world of technology.

THE NATURE OF THE AFRICAN UNIVERSE

What then is the setting of the African Universe? How does this affect the creative process of the traditional African mind? What are these fundamental factors that produce the intellect, the wisdom and the creative potentials of our ancestors? How were they able to sustain the harmonious rhythm of their existence without having the advantage of using mechanical gadgets, e.g. radio, television, videotape, paper and books?

The organization of shaping of the African Universe is in a pyramidal structure. Philosophy seems to form the anchor on which the existence of the people depends. Philosophy is the perception of the people about their universe and existence in general. Philosophy explains the world outlook of the people. It also embraces supernatural and natural elements. By supernatural, we mean all those invisible and unseen forces that influence and affect the existence of the people, for instance, philosophy and the belief in supernatural forces give birth to religion. Religion itself embraces rituals, sacrifices and other routine activities that sustain the existence of the people.

THE SUPREME BEING

Earlier, we had compared the nature of the African Universe to a pyramid. At the apex of the pyramid is the position of the Supreme Being—the creator. The Yoruba refer to this as "Olodumare" or "Eleda." He is the creator of the whole world and he has the power of omnipresence, omnipotence and omniscience. Among the various peoples of Nigeria and Africa, he is called various names. The table below contains some of these.

PEOPLES	DIFFERENT NAMES FOR GOD
Yorùbá	Olódùmarè
Tiv	Aondo
Ibo	Chukwu
Hausa	Ubangiji
Oromo	Rebi
Amharic	Igziaber

Since this creator is the controller of the Universe, all other elements in the pyramidal framework are under him. He caters for their existence, survival and needs. Therefore, there must be a way of appeasing him and soliciting his assistance all the time. This brings about religion, which involves sacrifice and rituals. As we go further in our discussion, we shall be able to see that there is a constant correspondence between the supernatural and the natural worlds, especially for the sustenance of the latter. Since it is this Supreme Being that created the Universe, people of different societies have stories of how they were created. These may or may not be true, but they form basic beliefs for the daily performance of the people. These, as we shall see fully later, are referred to as *myths*.

GODS AND GODDESSES

Between this Supreme Being are lesser gods and goddesses who also have their various names among different peoples of Nigeria and Africa. These gods and goddesses, such as Obàtálá, Ògún, Sàngó (Amadioha in Ibo), Sòpònná, and Èsù, are next in rank to the Creator in Yoruba mythology. It is believed that some of these gods, especially Obàtálá, were even involved in the process of creation. Ògún, the god of iron and war, paved way for the other creatures after creation.

Human beings, therefore, pay great obeisance and respect to these gods, who are at times referred to as the messengers of the Supreme Being. These supernatural forces serve as the intermediaries or mediators between the Supreme Being and Man. Rituals and sacrifices, which assume dramatic forms, are involved in the process of man's attempt to appease and solicit the help of these gods. Verbal utterances in various forms, such as praises, incantations, etc., are integral elements of this ritualistic phenomenon.

These gods have their own respective roles to play in the life of man. Hence, they are associated with different phenomena. In the Yoruba creation myth, Obàtálá was respected for being the first creative artist—creator of man. Ògún was the pathfinder god. Sàngó (or Amadioha) is associated with the climatic rhythm, and therefore, his help must be solicited by farmers. Among the Igbos, Ani—the goddess of the earth—is associated with fertility and production. Èsù (Satan) is associated with the acceptance of rituals and sacrifices, but not like the Biblical and Koranic Satan. Praises, songs, chants and costumes form parts of these rituals.

SPIRITS

In the pyramidal framework, there is that realm or sphere inhabited by the spirits. Unlike some other inhabitants who are stable in their settings, spirits roam about, not only in the cosmos. They invisibly interact with the human world. They influence the physical and psychic formation of those with whom they have dealings. Spirits include gnomes, fairies, "ànjònnú," etc. At times they appear in the guise of human beings. "Àbíkú" or "ogbanje" is a typical example of these. These are children who, after their birth, refuse to stay in the world. They are immediately nostalgic about the world of their "kindred spirits," so they desert the human world. Elements of magic and consultations with traditional religious priests must be made before they eventually stay or decide not to come again.

Spirits influence the belief systems of the African world. For example, pregnant women are advised not to walk in sunny afternoons, the most likely time that these spirits roam about. At times, it is believed that the mother of a newly-born deformed child must have faced the wrath of the spirits. We can recall the "jinni" in Urling Smith's *Tales from the Arabian Night*. One fact still remains that all the strata in the African Universe interact and influence each other positively or otherwise.

ANCESTORS

Below this ladder is the world of ancestors, who are the progenitors of those who are still living. Before, they too were human beings, but they have now exchanged their world for that of the cosmic. Africans believe strongly in life after death. It is also strongly held that reincarnation is followed by deification, at least for heroic characters. The dead is transformed into a new life in another realm, from where they cater for those who are still living.

Ancestral belief and worship has become a kind of religious activity in Africa. Masquerades (Egungun) are the ancestors that came back to life. Their voices are guttural, different from that of the living. Almost every family in Africa worships ancestors in one form or the other. Children are given the names of their ancestors. The respect accorded the dead illustrates this. Some of the activities involved during burial ceremonies develop into elaborate dramatic forms. Songs are composed to express the sense of loss and achievements of the dead. This will be categorized later into funeral poetry.

MAN

At the center of the pyramidal pattern is Man. In the African Universe, Man is at the center of the Universe and he is the linking force for all the elements in the hierarchy of African values. Unlike the supernatural forces, Man inhabits another realm or world entirely. He lives on earth, but his survival and performance on earth hinge on the cooperation from the cosmic forces at the upper realms. Man deals with these supernatural forces with respect and a level of mutual correspondence and understanding exists between them.

Man also finds in the cosmic world exemplary forces to emulate in his attempt to organize his world. A spirit of heroism may grow in man due to his encounters with his "god-head" in the supernatural world. This produces a form of literary process called *epic*. The link between the supernatural forces and man fosters a harmonious and functional man-cosmos organization.

OTHER ELEMENTS OF NATURE

Below man are other elements, animate and inanimate. All these are under the control of man. Man can use them in his attempt to maintain a harmonious rhythm in his universe. For instance, animals, plants, and virtually all other elements of nature are mobilized in the process of rituals and sacrifices. Communal festivals and ceremonies are given the sumptuous performance by the use of these various elements of nature in their various forms.

Some of these natural elements are developed into complex magical forms to reinforce the community or the individual. J.S. Mbiti refers to this potential of natural elements to boost the mental, psychic and physical morale of man as the "vital force".[1] Several beliefs we have in totems and taboos are woven around these natural elements. Animals, birds, etc. become symbolic phenomena in the existence of the people. These elements are crucial in the creative process.

Apart from their symbolic aesthetic values, they are used in all forms of art, including sculpture, painting, plastic art and ceramic. All these provide cultural artifacts which are very relevant in our understanding of the content and form of African oral literature. In traditional literary genres of narratives, drama and poetry, these elements perform roles as characters, etc. especially in folktales.

We have been able to discuss the various components of the African Universe. We have also suggested, in passing, how these components are relevant in the composition of traditional African literature in terms of content and form. The relevance of the African Universe in the creative process of traditional literature will become clearer later in our discussion.

RELEVANCE OF COSMOLOGY TO AFRICAN TRADITION

It is necessary to mention the relevance or influence of this African Universe in the creation of a socio-cultural model, which serves as a *sine qua non* for the existence of Man in dealing with his material and immaterial problems. Scholars of sociology, such as Taylor and Auguste Comte, define culture as the life scheme of a community, through which the people are able to create a model of sustenance.[3] Culture is the life wire of any people. Culture exists before a society; a society only services culture. Culture embraces the mores, institutions, rules, and artifacts accumulated over a long period of time.

In a simpler form, culture embraces all the activities through which a harmonious scheme is forged in human society. These include religion, modes of dressing, respect, and customs. African philosophy, as we have earlier on mentioned, is somehow a basic determinant for these cultural activities expressed in artistic models.

TRADITIONAL VERSUS MODERN SOCIETIES

The creative process and the production of African literature generally are usually affected by the socio-cultural and philosophical setting. Beliefs, customs, traditions and modes of communication determine or influence such a creative process. Therefore, the nature and complexity of any society at a particular point in time affect the nature of the literature produced in that society.

It will therefore be interesting to ask our readers or students to study and examine carefully the differences between traditional and modern societies. How many of us as students are born and bred in and are familiar with traditional societies? What is the nature of the activities that go on in the rural communities? How do people interact, communicate and pass information to each other in this cultural setting? Those of us who are familiar with the traditional societies know that such societies are quite different from urban societies like Ilorin, Kano, Lagos, Enugu, Kaduna and Jos.

How then can we differentiate between traditional and modern societies? It is necessary to find out these differences because the types of literature produced in these two settings are quite different from each other. We are concerned with the literature produced in traditional societies or rural communities in Africa.

How many of us have followed our parents, relatives or friends to traditional settings? What is the nature of the relationship and organization of existence in such societies? Or what can we define as traditional societies? Traditional societies are those that are not yet contaminated or influenced by foreign cultures. People organize their pattern of existence according to the cultural beliefs passed to them by their ancestors. The existence of the people is greatly influenced by what we had earlier on discussed as the hierarchy of African values.

COMMUNAL INTERESTS

In traditional societies, there is a spirit of collectivity. This is otherwise called communalism. People do things together. The survival of the society is determined by the collective participation of members of the society in any social process or activity. Love, kindness and popular interests are also manifested. Daily activities reflect a sense of purpose that links the people of the community together. The rhythm of social activities, such as naming, circumcision, religious and cultural festivals, is expressed through artistic composition. To the traditional people, these activities are creative and at the same time functional.

CULTURAL SETTINGS

Traditional societies can be distinguished in terms of their settings. Traditional societies are noticeably closed. By this we mean that the time and space that constitutes the setting are not so enlarged as in modern societies. The geographical setting is so circumscribed or limited that members of any community know each other.

They do not only know each other, but they also show much concern and interest in the cultural survival of the community. Again, the nature of the setting influences what we had earlier referred to as communalism. Cultural activities are organized together. Noticeable within the general communal settings are the family compound (referred to as "agbo-ilé" among the Yorubas or "Ilo" among the Ibos), religious shrines and market places. There are other traditional settings where communal and religious expressions are given to the lives of the people. These include mythical settings such as that of river Òsun.

All these settings are reflected in the creative process since the function and content of art are properly integrated with its beauty, the artistic.

MODES OF COMMUNICATION

This is an important aspect in the discussion of traditional African literature and performance. What do we mean by modes of communication? These are the various ways by which information, ideas and interests are conveyed to people in any society. The circulation of news, ideas and social activities is necessary for the healthy survival of the society.

We can then look around and ask ourselves whether the modes of communication in the traditional societies are the same as those of modern social settings? Definitely, the answer is no. In their own traditional environment, our forefathers create functional, effective and practical modes of communication.

Fundamental to this is the idea of verbal communication. Ideas and information are orally transmitted from individual to individual, from group to group and from community to community. Verbal or oral communication is therefore fundamental to traditional African literature.

Parents narrate stories of supernatural powers, demigods, heroes (legendary), animals, trees and all the elements in the African

Universe to their children by mouth. Praise singing to a family, to traditional rulers and to heroic individuals is rendered verbally. Rituals, sacrifices and dramatization of beliefs, customs and ideas are displayed in terms of verbal correspondence and verbal utterances, symbols, signs and codes.

Modes of communication in the traditional societies are further conducted through the use of other materials, which are not necessarily extraneous to the world of traditional art but are a complementary and integral part of it. Dissemination of information is made through communicative gadgets, such as drums and flutes. A person who is familiar with the Igbo society hears the symbolic information passed by "Ogene" in the early hours of the morning. Talking drums, "bàtá," perform the same function among the Yorubas. The multi-voiced flutes of the Angas of the Plateau State of Nigeria is a reputable medium of communication. So also is "Kàkàkí" in the traditional Hausa palaces. We shall be able to discuss in a more comprehensive manner later, the importance of these accompaniments in the rendition of traditional African literature.

PHILOSOPHICAL BELIEF

One basic feature of the traditional societies is the philosophical beliefs of the people. We have discussed this extensively at the beginning of this chapter. There is the link between the supernatural world and the world of the living. Man at the center of the universe must pay necessary homage to the cosmic forces above him for the stabilization and effective functioning of his universe. This inevitably involves rituals, sacrifices, conceptualization and symbolization of beliefs.

The presence of magic, charms, juju, wizards and witches explain this cosmic model of the African Universe. The faith and survival of the traditional people are anchored on these beliefs. It is therefore not surprising that religious poetry, funeral poetry, incantations, ritual and magical displays are derivations of these philosophical beliefs.

MODERN SOCIETIES

Major features of traditional societies discussed are philosophical beliefs, communalism, claustrophobic settings and modes of communications. As young people, most of us belong to the budding generation and unless with some of us modern Africans occasionally follow our parents to the rural settings or villages, it is doubtful whether we are familiar with our cultural origin. Africans in Diaspora and others who have never experienced traditional communities in Africa or anywhere else may find such a concept a bit far fectched since the metropoli may be their only basis for measuring sophistication. But then, we can still get a clearer picture by setting the features of the traditional settings against those of the cities or urban set-ups with which we are familiar.

Then we may wish to ask ourselves these questions: What is the nature of social relationships in the urban sectors? Can you compare the settings in the urban areas to those of rural areas? What are the modes of communication in modern social structures? What is the general belief of the people in the world about technological development? Is the acquisition of computer skills, cyberwealth and the use of its technology enough in defining community's values for greater humanity? Our proven ability to answer these questions will show clear differences between our understanding and projection of the concepts of traditional and modern societies.

First, the world of technological rationality has greatly devaluated the belief of the people about their universe. Based on the world of fact-findings, experiments and empirical involvements in laboratories, people tend to disbelieve what they regard as the "unscientific African Universe." Many of us today who perform experiments in our physics, chemistry and biology laboratories are gradually initiated into the modern scientific world of technology. Then it may be difficult for us to believe supernatural or magical powers. This is the root of the controversial debate between the exponents of traditional and modern medicines. For the scientifically oriented minds, religious poetry, rituals and sacrifices may not be meaningful for a harmonious organization of the universe.

This scientific perception of the universe changes the modes of thinking and perception of the contemporary urban-based African children or budding generation. Instead of listening to narratives such as myths, legends and folktales, they like to watch movies on television or lost their hearts into Playstations or Nicktendoes. Children's games, which used to be the source of moral education in the traditional societies, are downgraded. Children play with toys, ludos, scrabbles... all these are alien to their culture.

This leads us to the modes of communication in complex modern societies. We had identified the verbal-oriented modes of communication in the traditional societies. Can readers recall some of these and discuss with interested others the relevance of such traditional means of communication in modern societies? You may come to a rapid conclusion that does not need any deep pondering.

Introduction To African Oral Literature & Performance

In modern societies, information, news and ideas are disseminated through the print or electronic media. Ideas are conveyed through the electronic media via radio, television and videotapes. This implies that oral literature is almost virtually eroded by the world of technology. Even when oral materials are recorded by these modern gadgets, there are problems with distortion and inadequacy of information. For instance, no matter the efforts put up in the "Tales of Moonlight" on television, it is difficult to really capture the traditional setting, characterization and aura.

Another important difference between the traditional and modern societies is in the sphere of human and social relationships. Harmonious social culture is achieved in the traditional social settings because everybody believes that he is his brother's keeper. This fosters the sense of communalism and a functional social rhythm. However, modern societies are characterized by European individualism. What the Hausa rightly call "Kowa da nasa." You are not concerned with the plight of your neighbors whose babies are weeping or who are fighting. This brings about separation of relationship and social disintegration. Most of these unsavory tendencies of individualism are recreated in modern African literature with which many of us are familiar.

EXERCISE 1

1. Can you prepare a diagram to show the pattern of arrangement of the African Universe? Discuss the various elements of the diagram with your classmates.
2. Mention at least four ways in which the pattern of the African Universe has affected the production of oral literature in Africa.
3. Consider the major differences between the traditional and modern societies. How have these affected the survival of African oral literature?
4. Differentiate between the ways ideas are communicated in traditional and modern societies.
5. How has the communal nature of traditional societies assisted in the production of oral literature?

CLASSIFICATION OF TRADITIONAL AFRICAN LITERATURE

So far, our discussion hinges on the origins and sources of the African oral literature. Our reader should not take this exploration as another indulgence in African sociology or anthropology. Our

The Sources and Origins of African Oral Performance

discussion is not an end in itself. It is a means to an end. We have been able to relate these source materials to the formation of the functions and artistic components of African traditional literature.

We have equally provided a necessary background study, which will be useful later in our discussion of the various genres of African oral literature. For the sake of recollection, let us draw the link between this general background already discussed.

The exploration of the features of the African Universe and the examination of the differences between traditional and modern societies are very basic to the formation of literary materials we shall be discussing later. Various components of literature are derived from this background exploration. Myths, legends, folktales, proverbs and ritual dramatic forms have their origin in the hierarchy of values of the African Universe. Characters like the supernatural, the spirits, fairies, humans and animals have their abodes in the same universe. The settings may be in limbo, in the world of the spirits or in the natural and social habitat.

All these are synchronized by communication media rendered poetically either verbally or by musical accompaniments. The relationship of elements of literature, such as actions, characterization, setting, themes and subject, will be fully explained in our consideration of each of the genres. Meanwhile, we shall attempt a broad categorization of the forms and types of traditional literature.

I.) ORAL NARRATIVE FORMS
   A) Myths
   B) Legends
   C) Folktales
   C) Proverbs
   D) Riddles and jokes

II.) ORAL POETRY FORMS
   A) Praise or salutation poetry
   B) Religious poetry
   C) Funeral poetry
   D) Occupational or work poetry
   E) Heroic poetry
   F) Topical poetry
   G) Incantations
   H) Lullaby

III.) ORAL DRAMATIC FORMS
   A) Religious rites and rituals

B) Traditional festivals
C) Children's games
D) Miscellaneous traditional performances

TRADITIONAL ORAL NARRATIVES: GENERAL STYLISTIC FEATURES

Literature is a discipline that performs cultural, moral and social functions. It also entertains. Literature appeals to the sense of beauty through the stylistic devices employed by the artist. Therefore, two elements are basic in the discussion of literature: one, the functions it performs and two, the stylistic devices through which beauty is evoked. Traditional African literature effectively integrates these two functions, that is to say, it is functional and at the same time artistic. All along in this introductory section, we have been discussing the various aspects that determine the functions of African traditional literature and performance, but it is meaningless to discuss such functions without considering the ways employed by the traditional artist to communicate his or her ideas.

In this section, we want to consider the various artistic devices used by the traditional artist. We can simply define style as those elements that are the ways by which the artist communicates his ideas to the audience/listeners or readers. These may involve the narrative technique, the use of words, the modulation of voice and tone to recreate a particular event and the wisdom of the narrator in choosing words and witty sayings, such as proverbs. The artist's choices of relevant images and attendant actions to his narrative are equally important. All these are further aided by elements such as setting, action, characterization and audience. For the sake of clarity, we shall first consider how these elements are used in prose.

ORAL NARRATIVES

Students should refresh their memory to recall those aspects that make the traditional African oral narratives. All these elements are identified by their narrative trend, i.e. they are in form of stories. What then are stylistic features of traditional narratives?

Plot

In any storytelling or narrative, the plot is important. Plot is the sequential arrangement of actions and ideas in the story to make meaning and sense to the listener. Performers cultivate an effective opening method to command the attention of an audience. Actions of various characters are dramatized to recapture the reality of the moment. Performers' choice of words and images, the wavelength movement of the voice and the general use of language compliment the strength of the plot or the story line.

In traditional narratives, actions that constitute the plot may be from the world of the supernatural, spirits, ancestors human beings, even animals and plants. Actions in traditional narratives show that there is a fluid interaction of these various constituents of the hierarchy of African values.

Settings

Traditional stories based on myths, legends, folktales and at times proverbs have various settings. A setting is the physical environment or the location in which the actions of the story take place. In traditional stories, actions may take place in abodes of gods, goddesses, spirits and ancestors. At times, actions take place in the world of man, animals and even plants, hills and oceans. At times, the setting is stable with actions taking place in only one world. And at times, actions involve all these worlds.

It is essential to note that there is a close relationship between the plot and the setting. It is common in traditional folktales to hear of settings such as the abodes of the spirits, cave of fairies, wilderness of animals, villages and market places of human beings and some others. It is therefore essential and important for students to be able to locate the setting of any action, why that setting is chosen and its relevance.

Language of Narration

We should bear in mind that oral narratives aim at creating meaning and beauty, performing functions and educating. Therefore the narrator who, in the traditional setting, is always an elderly person must be full of devices to involve an audience consisting mostly of children.

In Yoruba folktales, the most popular way of calling the attention of the children is by his opening remark, "Àló o." The children will respond by saying, "Ààlòò." In Hausa it is "Gatanan Gatanan Ku". The narrator then practically removes the children out of their own world to fascinate them. He continues to say, "Nigba lai lai, nigbati oju wa ni oruken, ti ori wa ni ibadi"—"In those days when the eyes were on the knees and the head was on the waist." Definitely, the children will like to know of this strange world and time.

At times the narrator may even start off with riddles to initiate the children into full participation. He may even start with a short song and ask them to clap while singing. All these make the children mentally and physically alert for the interesting stories to be told.

We should remind ourselves that the traditional artist has no dictionary to look up meanings of words. He has no televisions, radio or videotape to store his ideas. Yet he has a magical memory bank that stores all his ideas, which he passes from generation to generation. In the process of storytelling, the narrator makes use of words that are from the womb of tradition, thereby educating the children in the language of their people. He draws apt analogies, comparisons and allusions to describe events, characters and settings. The African Universe is opened to the children in various ways. Images are products of the immediate environment of the narrator and the audience. It is therefore easy for them to grasp various elements mentioned in the process of storytelling.

Performance

Traditional storytelling is incomplete and even meaningless without practical participation by both the narrator and the audience. It is quite unlike modern written prose forms which the individual reader has the joy of reading. The storyteller must be able to develop the potential of mental and physical displays to recreate the actions in his story. He mimics the voice of the masquerade, the roaring of the lion, the wailing voice of the spirit, the meaning of man suffering in pain and the clapping action of the thunder. He raises his eyebrow, stands in akimbo, jumps like the frog, walks majestically like an elephant, demonstrates the cruelty of the lion.

All these dramatic actions consciously or unconsciously provoke his audience to action. The participation between the performer and the audience is an essential aspect of the traditional narrative rendition. At times, the narrator's story culminates in a song, thereby making for soloist-chorus relationship. The performer is the soloist while the members of the audience constitute the chorus.

The audience of the traditional storytelling is not passive. The audience makes corresponding remarks to display the actions mentioned or dramatized by the narrator. In a moment of agony, the audience laments "o-o-o-o!" In a moment of joy, they clap and laugh. They make occasional remarks to complement the narrator's performance. They even punctuate the narration by occasionally asking questions. All these elements make for entertainment, which always makes the children interested and fully involved. Besides, such elements teach children moral lessons and contribute towards their emotional, mental and physical stability. Even the art of indigenous discourse, the verbal and the non-verbal traditional African discourse are deeply rooted in performance (see Okepewho, 1990).

MUSICAL ACCOMPANIMENT – ORAL NARRATIVES

All genres of oral literature—oral narratives, poetry and drama—have musical accompaniment to their performance. By musical accompaniment we mean drumming and other instrumental beatings that go along with the rendition of oral tales. Music and its instrument, we must emphasize, are part(s) of the principal performance features that make prose, poetry and drama oral.

However, prose narrative has what can be described as the lightest musical involvement. As we shall see later in our textual discussion, folktales, legends and myths, songs and dance are notable elements of prose narratives.

Among the Hausas and Fulanis, a kind of Hausa guitar called Kutigi is used (the type adopted by Dan Maraya Jos in his oral performances). Traditional flutes are also used. Among the Yorùbás, it is usually the flutes that are employed (the type in D.O. Fagunwa's *Ìrìnkèrindò Nínú Igbó Elégbèje*). We also have instances in all African cultures where the tale itself signifies the particular type of drum instrument being used in storytelling.

We see this in a Yoruba tale where Tortoise is saddled with the responsibility of tricking Elephant to town to be killed. An elephant's flesh is required for a ritual sacrifice. Tortoise tells Elephant that the entire people have recognized Elephant's might and charm and have resolved to make him king over them. Elephant is very happy about this and then agrees to come to the town for installation. On the day he sets for the town, "gbedu" drums are beaten and beautiful songs are rendered by Tortoise and other members of the community:

Tortoise:	A ó m'érin joba
Audience/Chorus:	Èwè kú ewele
Tortoise:	A ó m'érin joba
Audience:	Èwè kú ewele
Tortoise:	We shall install Elephant our king
Audience/Chorus:	Èwè kú ewele
Tortoise:	We shall install Elephant our king
Audience/Chorus:	Èwè kú ewele.

Elephant is very pleased with this song. He jumps, dances and moves his hands up and down in all directions in appreciation of the beautiful songs.

What we are interested in here is that we are told specifically in the tale that *gbedu* drums are used. The students of *Introduction to African Oral Literature and Performance* should try to know what a gbedu drum is. Normally, when the tale is told in the night, the gbedu drum is not there.

Nevertheless, the narrator and members of the audience provide an imitation of the sound of gbedu drum from their mouths when the songs are rendered. Other musical elements that accompany Yoruba folktales are whistling, hissing and rhythmic beatings of simple sticks on empty tins, bottles or simply hands or any object around.

In Igbo prose narratives, "Oja" (flute) and "ubo akwara" (Igbo guitar) may be used. Even the "Igbo," a kind of leather drum beaten either with fingers or small sticks, is employed. The musical instrument common to all African prose narratives is the palms. The narrator and members of the audience clap frequently when songs are rendered in the narrative sessions.

The teacher of oral literature should try to improvise ideas and be creative on the musical instrument to be adopted in prose performance in his lessons. The instrument should normally be suitable to the culture from where an oral narrative is picked. To realize in full impact and to ensure that the students get the best from *Introduction to African Oral Literature*, musical accompaniment must not be underplayed wherever they are relevant.

We shall discuss musical accompaniment more comprehensively when we get to Oral Poetry drama, where they are more relevant.

WHO ARE THE ARTISTES?

General Introduction

We must have been wondering who these people are who perform and sing, both in public and private places, for our entertainment. We know that we call them "alágbe" or "Òsèré" in Yorùbá and "Mawaki" or "Maroki" in Hausa. They are called Artistes in English. We should note the differences between Artists and these Artistes we are talking about. Note the difference in the spelling of the two words. Artists, on one hand, are people who produce works of art, especially paintings. We must, however, bear in mind that sometimes people do not make distinctions between them, especially when the word artist is used. It can refer to both professional entertainers and those who produce works of graphic art. The term "artiste" is however exclusively used for the singers and the oral entertainers.

The populace as traditional poets

Everybody is an artiste in a traditional African society. Women sing lullabies to pet their babies. Market men and women sing to advertise their goods. Farmers compose fine tunes while tilling the land. We also have those we call the alágbe or Maroki—beggar poets—in Yorùbá and Hausa cultures respectively. There are poets in courts and public singers who go about singing for money. There are also modern oral artists who, having introduced electronic gadgets to their musical instrument, have become big artistes.

In the evenings, children also gather round an elder to listen to tales under the moonlight. These tales are often marked with songs and choruses. Africans sing at festivals, at child-naming, burial and house-warming ceremonies. Africans sing at peace and at war. Various other traditional performances, like Egúngún, Ìgunnun, Bori and so on, are accompanied by dance and songs.

The three genres of poetry, prose and drama are clearly represented in African culture. Most often, the genres come together in African oral performances. Music, dialogue and dance collectively make up the African oral art. Let us see the arts we have identified above under their different genres:

I) Poetry:

Lullabies, songs used to advertise products in the market/community arena, work songs used by farmers/laborers at work, songs used to praise different professions and to highlight their qualities, music used for entertainment during festivals and ceremonies, folksongs that accompany our stories and tales, war songs, funeral songs and religious songs used during rituals and divinations performances to praise and appease gods. Among the artistes there are children, market men and women, farmers, laborers, traditional priests, local bards and court singers.

II) Narratives or tales:

Folktales, legends and myths, stories and accounts of wars and harvest. The artistes here are elder members of the community like grandfathers, grandmothers, parents and elder children.

III) Drama:

Traditional performances like Egungun, Igunnu, Kwa Hir and Bori displays. The drama artistes therefore include festive dancers and traditional acrobats like the Atilogwu dancers, Kwa Hir performers, Yan Tauri performers and Eré Olómoba dancers.

We can see that our earlier assertion that every one is an artiste in a traditional African society is very true. This is enhanced by the communal life of African society. Mothers, fathers, laborers at work and children enjoying lullabies are artistes in one form or the other. Sometimes these eventually grow into traditional artistes and performers. There are the professional, the freelance or non-professional and the modern artistes. Let us see those who occupy these categories one by one:

I) Professional Artistes:

A) The religious artistes.

The professional artistes are those who Isidore Okpewho rightly describes as restricted artistes. We can also call them specialized artistes. This category of performers is culturally destined to be artistes. The traditional African society does not expect them to do anything else. In fact, most of them inherit the art from their parents, and their household is identified as the traditional family house of the art concerned. These include those who perform for traditional religious rituals like those who Babalola refers to as "Ológùún"—Ìjálá chanters among the Yorùbás. Such religious performers get inspiration from their gods. They are seen as mouthpieces of the gods. They are unlike most other traditional artists, highly respected among the traditional religious circles. It is the gods who appoint them to sing. For example, the Ológùún, according to Babalola, are appointed by Ifá itself and whosoever is so pointed out must take to the art. To respect such people, therefore, is to respect the gods who appoint them.

B) The palace or court poets.

Another set of professional artists is the court minstrels. They are those who sing for traditional chiefs, obas, emirs, obis and other traditional title-holders in the community. These artists are restricted to the palace and other traditional chiefs' houses. They sing to boost the pride of the chiefs. They make historical accounts in their songs to remind their patrons of important historical points that are necessary for their rule. They also serve as checks to the chief as they occasionally rebuke and correct him when he goes astray.

We can see that both the religious poets and the court singers (also called griots or court minstrels) are specialists in their areas.

The Ijala chanter, whose example we gave above, cannot go outside Ijala chanting. Also, the court minstrels cannot sing for anybody else but their patrons, chiefs or obas. The Mawaka in palace of the Emir of Ilorin, for example, sings only for the emir. He cannot go outside to sing for other people or perform during marriage, child naming, house warming and funeral ceremonies, except when such occasions belong to the emir. The court singers are thus not as popular as those we shall soon identify as public poets. However, we easily see them when we visit palaces. Daba, in 1981 said that the father of one Nigerian popular singer, 'Dan Maraya Jos, was a court artiste in Jos.[4] In those days of strict traditional culture in Jos, 'Dan Maraya would be nothing today but a court poet taking after his father. Let us go round palaces to know who some of these court artistes in our localities are. We can investigate from elderly people who they are.

C) The freelance or non-professional artistes.

(i) The freelance.

These are people who do not take art as a daily job. Though they too perform in both private and public places, they do this only at their convenience and interest. Their performances are not always regular. They are normally full-time farmers, butchers, traders and calabash designers who sing usually as a hobby. All Africans who we say sing and perform during one occasion or the other can therefore be described as freelance artistes. Also, specifically, beggars like *almaqirai* among the Hausas who go about singing to appeal for assistance from people are freelance artists. These types of people exist in almost every African culture.

Maimouna in Ousmare's *Gods Bits of Wood* is a very good example of a poet-beggar in Senegalese society. Other freelance artistes include occasional poets like the "asa" in the Ilorin community or those who the Yorubas call "alulu gbomi eko"—"one who performs only for begging." Such poets are seen wandering from one ceremony to the other, performing and seeking favors from guests. These freelance poets are not usually formally invited to occasions they attend. They impose themselves through their music on the guests around and sing their praise names and boost their pride and ego. They make sure they earn monetary or materials gifts before they leave.

(ii) Modern professional artistes.

Still under non-professional artistes are the modern singers like Sunny Ade, Ebenezer Obey, Kollinton Ayinla, Bala Miller and Victor Uwaifor in Nigeria. Mariam Makebe in South Africa fits in this category. These artists develop their artistic forms from modern religions and modern European cultures. Even though these artistes also use traditional songs and poetic ingredients, their musical equipment is largely foreign made. In fact, their musical patterns are even largely foreign. They are non-professional and non-restricted in the sense that they have no cultural or traditional attachment to their art. They are the kind of singers who Abdul Kadir Dandatti calls "Public Poets".[5] They pick from all forms of poetry and sing for all sorts of people on all occasions. We may as well call them freelance artistes. In the African culture, such artistes have no place greater than the "almajiri" and "the alulu gbomi eko" in both Hausa and Yoruba communities respectively.

EXERCISE II

1. Give a vivid description of an evening session when an oral narrative is rendered to the young ones.
2. Describe the relationship between the storyteller and his audience in terms of performance.
3. What are the differences between the audience of traditional or modern narratives? What do you think is responsible for these differences?
4. Discuss the artistic strength of the narrator in the process of storytelling in the traditional setting.
5. Mention some musical accompaniment you can identify with storytelling? Tell your classmates how you came about these.
6. Mention the various categories of artistes in traditional societies and the role they perform.
7. Assuming you are the storyteller, create an appropriate scene and tell your classmates an interesting story.

Further Reading and Work

Besmer, Fremont E. *Hausa Performance.* New York, Garland Pub., 1998.

Ebron, Paulla A. *Performing Africa.* Princeton, NJ: Princeton University Press, 2002.

Furniss, Graham and Gurner Elizabeth. *Power, Marginality and African Oral Literature.* Cambridge University Press, 1995.

Hale, Thomas A. *Griots and Griottes: Masters of words and music.* Bloomington, Indiana University Press, 1998.

Okpewho, Isidore. *African Oral Literature: backgrounds, characters, continuity.* Bloomington: Indiana University Press, 1992.

---. *The Oral Performance in Africa.* Ibadan: Spectrum Books, 1990.

---. "The primacy of performance in oral discourse" in *Research in African Literatures.* 21.4 (1990): 121-28.

---. *The Epic in Africa: Toward a Poetics of the Oral Performance.* New York: Columbia University Press, 1979.

Seitel, Peter. The *Powers of Genre: Interpreting Haya Oral Literature.* New York: Oxford University Press, 1999.

Yai, Olabiyi Babalola. "Tradition and the Yoruba Artist" in *African Arts.* 32.1 (1999) 32-5.

Notes and References

1. See J.S. Mbiti. *African Religions and Philosophy* (London): Heinemann, 1969.
2. This diagram is constructed on the basis of Mbiti's discussion and our own analysis and stratification of the African Universe.
3. Taylor and Auguste Comte were pioneering fathers of Sociology and their definitions of culture are very important in this type of interdisciplinary study.
4. Daba, H.A. "The case of Dan Maraya Jos: A Hausa Poet" in *Oral Poetry in Nigeria*, Lagos: *Nigeria Magazine*, 1981.
5. Abdulkadir Dandatti: "The Role of an Oral Singer in Hausa-Fulani Society. A case study of Mamman Shatta" Ph.D. Thesis, University of Indiana, 1975.

Chapter Two

 ## Fieldwork Practice and Research Methodology in Oral Literature And Performance

INTRODUCTION

Is it really possible to study meaningfully any unwritten literature in the classroom, even in Electronic Classrooms with opportunities for Power Point presentations and chances for manipulation of slides and images? The answer is obviously no. To be really involved in the activities of the non-literate societies, from where the raw materials for oral literature and performance are tapped, students and scholars in this area of scholarship must be empirically involved. By this, we mean that practical efforts should be made in collecting materials from the original source. African oral performance as a field of study calls for such thorough fieldwork activities because of its unwritten nature.

The fact that such literature has a verbal composition necessitates the need to go into the setting that produces the formation and practice of such literature. Probably, the traditional African man or woman is more original, more articulate and more inquisitive at this state of raw contact with nature. This he or she displays by his or her spontaneous and constructive intellect of composing music and creating all forms of art. All these make it necessary and important for the researcher to really penetrate the resource center of his area of study.

Let us ponder a while and ask, how and where are the materials that make oral literature made? What is the source of the creativity of the traditional artist? What are the raw material resources of oral literature? Materials through which oral projects in the traditional societies are composed are by nature inherently practical. People operate by the physical involvement of their intellect, mind, hands and brain. The traditional man applies his potentials and resources in the process, creating existence from nature for the historical, cultural and social development of the society.

The maxim that necessity is the mother of invention is more tenable with the traditional rather than the modern African man. People are necessarily motivated by the spiritual and material demands of their environment to cultivate the modalities for existence and survival. Therefore, creativity in all its ramifications is an essential factor of existence in the traditional societies. People, because of their nearness to nature, interact and harness nature through their potentials to create their means of existence, among which is art.

Apart from the socio-cultural conditions and the need for survival, man in traditional cultures is naturally creative. His logic of reasoning, his mental attributes and the cumulative assertiveness of his intellect are practically visible in his naturally cultivated doctrines of craftsmanship. It is also important to disabuse the false claims by Eurocentric scholars of various disciplines that perception in the traditional cultures are only metaphysical not scientific.

Magic, like mysticism, is inherently a scientific exercise of the mind. The knowledge of the traditional man to coherently create a mutual correspondence between the material and immaterial resources of his universe is rooted in scientific logic, the complexity of which is difficult to unravel. The need to study the potentials compels the scholars of orature to go to the field and study the metaphysical and scientific situation in which the mind of the traditional artist works.

It is necessary for the student of African orature to penetrate the heart of the primordial to experience the dynamic thoughts of the traditional man. These dynamic thoughts develop into the oral structures of myths, legends, folktales, archetypes and others. The researcher needs to locate and interact with the traditional man in his natural, social and cultural habitat. This will enable the researcher to know the strengths and forces that motivate the creativity of the traditional artist.

Primeval values are translated into reality depicting the performance of the resourceful mind and body in the traditional setting. Objects that represent the spiritual and material worlds need to be created to link the forces in the hierarchy of African Universe. This is the logic that promotes a functional socio-culture. Artifacts are the cumulative aggregation of people's intellectual and spiritual struggle with the forces of their environment. Artifacts are the end products of culture that systematically organize towards more permanent structures of civilization.

The indigenous technology through which people construct complex, conducive and functional architectural designs and the science that created the Nok Culture and the Egyptian irrigation system are dynamic potentials in non-literate cultures. The same technology facilitates the traditional arts of painting, sculpturing, carving and pottery. All these constitute the practical elements that the researcher in oral literary traditions needs to evaluate and appreciate.

The various issues we have discussed place a researcher in oral structure in the stream of all other disciplines, such as anthropology, sociology, ethnology, ethnography, history, politics and science. Our students need to know these disciplines and what they represent to grow in knowledge and perception of the reality of their environment. Of course, like the traditional man, the researcher in oral literature is necessarily a man of many disciplines.

It must be emphasized that a field researcher in oral performance has the target of locating the traditional elements of cultural arts. The end products of his fieldwork are directed towards the realization of the creative and critical perceptions of the literature of the traditional setting. In the words of Ropo Sekoni, he is only concerned with the verbal and non-verbal structures through which creative process in prose, poetry and drama can be designed and discerned.[1] But of course, he needs the extra resources of these other disciplines to consolidate the gains of his specialty. This point can be explained by the numbers of oral literary theories, which are products of the amalgamation of these other disciplines.

WHY THE NEED FOR FIELDWORK?

At this juncture, it is necessary for us to outline the reasons why a scholar of oral literature and performance must essentially be involved in fieldwork.

I) Traditional cultures, patterns or ways of existence are not formulated by mere dogmatism or armchair thinking. In fact, in the traditional society, theory does not precede practice, both are interlinked and emerge in the day-to-day philosophy that governs and sustains the society. This is not the logic of modern or even postmodern science, which merely operates on hypotheses that are easily falsified. In other words, there is no demarcation between theory and practice in Africa. The traditional person interacts with the forces of his or her environment to systematize them into a body of thoughts to foster the effective functioning of the structure. To study the creative potentials of such dynamic minds cannot be achieved only in the classroom or simply by using electronic technology in the lecture hall. The researcher in oral art must be practically involved with them.

II) The survival of any culture can be achieved by how much of the components of such culture the subsequent generations can grasp and recall through mental recording. Therefore, the sustenance of culture precludes a systematic and organized fieldwork activity to provide a useful memory bank for traditions and to achieve what Carl Jung regards as "psychic residue". This means permanent thoughts built into the memory force of an individual or community and tapped consciously or unconsciously from time to time from the preomodial of culture and society. This permanent rudiment facilitates archetypes and dynamics of mental, social and economic development. Students of oral literature must be practically involved in identifying these archetypal structures.

III) If we may ask, is it possible for learners and scholars of African orature to gather materials for their subject without going to the field? Since oral literature is verbal in nature, the texts for the study of the performances can only be gathered on the field. Materials gathered from the field now replace the written texts studied in modern literature.

IV) Do we think that mechanical aids can be totally relied upon by a fieldworker? Can such equipment effectively capture the sensibilities of tradition? For a more scientific data, the scholar needs to go to the field him or herself to crosscheck the anomalies technical aids may impose on the traditional talents and potentials.

V) Oral structures derive their true meanings from the verbalizations and oral performances that really give them the aura of originality. The need to have properly written and memory records of the rendition patterns and the exercise of the power of repertoire and dramatic performances in the course of creating traditional arts make it imperative for an oral scholar to go to the field. The gestures arising from the conceptual framework can be properly grasped on the field. It is the researcher himself who can perceive the nature of the setting, the composure and comportment of the audience, the nature of musical accompaniments, and when they are used, the melding of costumes into the actual structures of performances.

Oral structures in prose, poetry and drama are concrete emanations of some residual philosophical frames of thought and idyllic perceptions stored in the traditional reservoir of knowledge. To understand the structure of the praise poetry of Sango, Ogun or lineage of any town, the underlying myths and legends ritualized in drama must be known. Eyewitness and authentic information about these oral elements can only be gathered on the field. A meaningful critical evaluation and appreciation of oral literary materials can be achieved by some extra-literary documents that are verbalized and stored in the minds of the custodians of the culture. Electronic storage can only serve as a compliment.

VI) Researchers in various disciplines of the social sciences believe that a thorough familiarization with and understanding of the literature of non-literate cultures can only be possible by learning the language of the people. Claude Levi-Strauss is a strong exponent of this. Language is the vehicle and promoter of culture. Issues which the researcher needs to unravel are buried in the womb of language. Taboos, norms, ethics and traditional cultures have their vitality and strength in the language of the people. In *Structural Anthropology*, Levi-Strauss emphasizes the role of language in the functional operations of the systems of the Social Structure. He perceives language as the linking force for traditional institutions, such as kinship. Fieldwork therefore affords the researcher the opportunity of understanding the language of the people among whom he or she works. This advantage of language must be stressed as a means to comparative study of oral literature and performance.

TRADITIONAL MASS CULTURE VERSUS POP-CULTURE

We have somehow discussed the importance of fieldwork to the study of oral literature and performance. We can summarize this important section by pointing out the effect of the ever-increasing urban structures on the study of oral literature, but as students or readers, do you feel you are separated from your cultural roots? If so, ask who and what are responsible? As you are involved in some critical probing on this issue, you may wish to have a discussion with your teacher or professor on it.

The budding generation, which is to serve as the safety valve and promoter of cultural continuity, are in most cases uprooted from the traditional environment. This is a serious impediment for the study of African oral literature and the practice of African culture in general in contemporary Africa and in the New World. Many youths are not born in the traditional setting, and it is an asthmatic injury for people to mention the village in their hearing. Even many adults do not want to have any dealings with tradition again. The hip-hop generation in the New World, and even those now forming in Africa, are fast adopting a basterdization of urbanity enhanced by electronic garget to represent a new cultural identity.

The factor of the urbanization of intellect, psyche, physique and total existence is more tragically displayed in the acquisition of the pop culture psychology. The pop culture mania is a product and demise of other cultures. Acculturation, or the suppression and subjugation of African culture, is a tragic phenomenon of history that is fast destroying the original cultural complexion of not only the budding African generation but even the adults.

It is necessary to pose questions here for a dynamic study of African orature in Africa and the New World. Is there any link between the traditional mass culture and modern pop culture? Can we isolate and neglect the impacts of foreign cultural values on the study of African oral literature? Some scholars in and outside the discipline of oral literature do not really see the relevance of pop culture to the discussion of African traditional literature and performance. To them, such a neophyte is totally outside the scheme of study of literature in general. To discuss oral literature from the perspective of pop culture means lack of focus to such people.

Literature is an offspring of culture. Therefore, culture is literature and literature is culture. All those forces that influence, negate, contradict and moderate the traditional African culture must be brought to bear on the discussion of both traditional and modern African literature. We can study traditional literature by what it is not or by that which negates and destroys it. This is where pop culture is central to a meaningful and dynamic future study of African orature and performance.

Pop culture is an appendage of bourgeois aesthetics, which is elitist and anti-tradition. Omafume Onoge discusses how traditional cultures are impoverished or demeaned to satisfy the class egoism of the ruling class. C.W.E. Bigsby and Max Adereth discuss the ideological terms the conflicts between traditional mass culture and pop culture. The former is the authentic culture that informs nature and permanent structures of growth and development, while the latter impoverishes them. For proper ideological orientation and dynamics, scholars of African literature and African performance need to battle with this cultural aberration called pop culture. Is it the same culture called the hip-hop culture in the New World society, and now spreading to urban Africa, which some would prefare to even call a hybrid culture? Such a pop culture, spreading like a wild fire around the world through global electronic media, challenges the scholar of African tradition to consider the threat of this electronic culture on the traditional values of African oral performance.

The link between the need for fieldwork and the crisis of pop culture should be clear to students and scholars of African oral literature and performance. The practice of traditional culture in developing nations is zeroing down into crisis and extinction because of the interest in pop culture products by adults and youths alike. The budding generation in these regions knows more of the customs, norms and ideas of America, Britain and France than those of their own countries. They are detached from their own immediate environment by the "beauty" of the Western cultures and the jet age. Fieldwork is the only rescue valve to understand and protect the culture of any race from total collapse.

TECHNIQUES OF FIELDWORK

Having established a strong case for the importance of fieldwork, it is necessary for us to grasp the tools essential for the practice. It is not just easy for a fieldworker to walk into the area of performance to collect his primary materials. Even if the researcher is able to dodge the task by merely recording materials, the materials are still not useful to him. The proper channel of seeking knowledge has been side-tracked, therefore proper knowledge cannot be attained.

For instance, how will the researcher interpret his "stolen" materials? How does he get over the problem of language, assuming he is not working within his own language? Even with his language, how does he solve the problems of generic words and constructions? How does he get into the heart of the issue raised in the material? Who will explain to him extra-literary materials through which the content and form of his collection can be thoroughly analyzed? Definitely, the fieldworker needs more than possession of materials. The search for true knowledge implies the search for a solid approach.

We want to place before the students and scholars of orature guidelines through which a fieldworker can extend his vision and practice of this essential aspect of his discipline. These include:
I) Planning for Fieldwork
II) Primary Sources
III) Secondary Sources
IV) Data Structuring

I) Planning for Fieldwork

We have argued earlier on that the researcher in oral performance or a scholar of African orature has got no prescribed texts to read. He cannot go to the bookshop to buy his primary texts. It is not proper either for him to be briefed about a traditional performance. All these cannot compensate for his personal construction of a text based on his fieldwork practice. This, of course, necessitates his close interaction with the custodians of such literature and performance.

A committed and organized fieldworker should first identify his frame of reference. He should program the necessary issues surrounding his specimen of research and organize a program of action on how to set about them. We want to use our own fieldwork experience and encounters for illustration. Since the researcher has got his aims and purposes for setting on the fieldwork, he needs to have direct or indirect consultations with those in charge of the materials he is searching for. It is not advisable for the researcher, because of his age or cultural attitude, to make direct consultations especially in Africa, but perhaps also when researching in the African Diaspora. He may not be taken seriously. This makes it imperative for the researcher to conduct him or herself in a way not to betray his or her intention and purpose. A researcher can therefore employ or solicit the help of those in the age group of the custodian of the materials in question. If the sample is religious poetry, the researcher can approach the target through the members of the cult or religious belief, the owners of the materials. However, there are some fieldwork activities that may not be as risky as to demand this type of approach.

The researcher must be able to articulate coherently and convincingly his or her subject of research and purpose. Emphasis should be made to convince the intermediary that the research is not to ridicule or condemn tradition, but to enhance it. It is also important for the researcher to conduct perfect rehearsals that will enable him or her to effectively operate the mechanical aids on the field.

What the authors of this book did on such an occasion of research was to contact associates who are close to the King of the town where the research was conducted. The ruler, after being convinced about our intention, asked us to come on the seventh day. As we did on that occasion, a fieldworker must prepare functional mechanical aids, such as tape recorders, videotapes, cameras. These aids, as we shall show later, may be problematic.

II) Primary Sources

This simply is a situation in which a fieldworker himself goes to the field and he is physically involved in collecting the materials. We shall use our research involvement discussed earlier to further elucidate this point.

On the seventh day, we met the King and his traditional chiefs conducting rituals at the entrance of the palace. We immediately joined them and identified ourselves with the liturgical drama of the ritual. Here, we should emphasize that a serious researcher should mix freely with the people among whom he conducts his findings. His cultural comportments, mode of dressing and language of communication must be those that would be readily accepted by the people. They may not be forthcoming if the cultural attitude of the researcher is so different from theirs.

In our fieldwork activities, we always operate at the level of the indigenous performers and identify with their cultural attitude. At the occasion in question, we tasted what they tasted and performed as they performed. The traditional drummers, who provided musical accompaniments of "Dùndún," "Omele," "Aaro" and "Sèkèrè,"[2] were also identified with. We were able to obtain first hand information on the relevance of these cultural artifacts.

At the completion of the ritual in the King's palace, the traditional ruler asked our intermediary to take us to another setting undeclared to us. Certainly, there are risks, dangers and horrible experiences in fieldwork, but a cultivated sense of courage, ability to interact freely with the people and work on their psychology will surely allay these dangers.

When we got to the setting, it was a large open arena, synonymous with the contemporary theatre and stage. There was a mammoth crowd of Sàngó worshippers and the audience flowing together in the continuum of communal rapport. The setting of traditional rituals and sacrifices is always communal, providing a milieu conducive for the cosmic forces, their adherents and the general community.

Our intermediary took us to the chief priest, who was obviously in the ritualistic mood of celebration, well appareled in the costumes of Sàngó, with other habiliments, such as "àdó," cowries and various types of charms hung on the costume. He held his "osé" and "ìrùkèrè" for blessing people. He was enraged to see us. We definitely looked like intruders. It is obvious that there is a communication and cultural gap between the owners and custodians of tradition and those in search of it. A researcher who seeks for meaningful end products and knowledge has the Herculean task of breaking this barrier created by the cultural intrusion from the West.

Our intermediary immediately interceded and spoke that "Kábíyèsí," meaning the King, blessed our coming. Unknowingly to us, a messenger was sent to the King to confirm this. When we were proved right, he immediately hugged us and said:

> E seun omo dáadáa
> Àwon baba mi ó gbè yín
> Irúu yín là wá n fé.

> Thank you, good sons
> My ancestors will support you
> It is people like you we want.

But he confessed to us the cause of his suspicion about these researchers from the city and the ivory towers. They are bundle of liars and deceivers, who collected "our" ancestral materials to display on the television and radio without adequately acknowledging and compensating "us." Anybody who does that now is seeking the wrath of "Olúkòso," meaning "Sàngó." We pledged our total commitment and sense of responsibility.

Without wasting any further time, we joined the teeming worshippers, mainly women, in dancing to the rhythm of "bata." We also sang and chorused songs with them. We even pasted money on their foreheads to acknowledge their performance. Consciously or unconsciously, we were fully embraced in the circle of performance.

It was easy for us to position our mechanical gadget for fieldwork, the tape recorder. We were specifically warned not to take pictures. But even with the cooperation of our primary indigenous performers, lack of composure, good knowledge or effective operation of the recorder would have turned the whole exercise into a failure. It is therefore necessary for a researcher to have a good knowledge of his mechanical instruments.

The last stage of our research even exposed the more the danger of fieldwork. To show that we were fully accommodated, the Sàngó Priest, our primary indigenous performer, invited us to a very dark room, which is probably the shrine and the consortium of the various cultural artifacts associated with Sàngó. Each of the images in the room has a "Praise Poem." A female religious poet was already there to introduce to us by way of poetic renditions all these images associated with Sàngó. A fieldworker who is unable to command the full support of his indigenous performer may not be able to withstand the tense atmosphere of the shrine.

It is necessary for us to give one or two more examples to educate the researcher on the type of socio-psychology he should cultivate before going to the field. Our research into the Dadakúàdà poetry also gave us some relevant experience. Despite the familiarity of the researchers with the Dadakúàdà poet in question, there were untouchable areas. While the Dadakúàdà poet agreed after consultations that recording could be done at any of his performances, he warned that no pictures or videotaping should be done. We felt we needed pictures to complement our research reports. We approached those who were close to him, who advised us to make a trial. We did, but nothing emerged. We respect the honesty and open-mindedness of this traditional artist. This further confirms our position that a conscious approach must be made to gather information and materials from the field.

We also want to cite the example of Ziky O. Kofoworola of the Centre for Nigerian Cultural Studies, Ahmadu Bello University, Zaria, whose reputable research in the Emir's palace culture reflects the need for patience by a researcher. It is obvious that he needed knowledge of spoken and written Hausa language and probably other local languages to be able to operate effectively. We are impressed by his ability to apply his research in oral structures to influence an operatic drama of class struggle. The performances of the Kufena Group of Arts and Cultural Centre, Kaduna, at the Festival of Arts in Edinburgh, Scotland, in 1987 showed this brilliant management of the oral structures of the palace settings.

So far, we have described the activities of a devoted and committed field researcher in an attempt to obtain primary sources and information for his study. However, this technique may take another dimension. It may involve a situation where the main researcher himself does not really go to the field, but employs research assistants who do this on his behalf. The inability of the main researcher to get to the source of the materials may be a reason for this approach. It may also be possible that the main researcher plays a coordinating role and oversees the activities of his research assistants working on different issues.

But this seems problematic, since the main researcher himself has been deprived of eyewitness account of the resource materials. This means that the main researcher is distanced from his primary sources. Probably, a way of normalizing this crisis is to employ as many research assistants as possible on a specimen, the results of which can be collated and crosschecked, but using and financing such an approach may be a major obstacle as will be discussed later.

We propose that unless there are chronic problems, the main researcher must be directly involved in the collection and production of his materials. There are some practical activities or some obscure ideas that the informant may not be able to clear. The presence of the main researcher at the scenes of oral performance may solve this problem.

III) Secondary Sources/Indigenous Performer Services

This technique is relevant not in the collection of raw materials for the researcher's text but in interpreting and explaining some issues in the primary materials already collected. The informant who is an indigen at this juncture is not necessarily concerned with the cultural performance and activities compiled into the researcher's primary text. He or she may be or may not be an outsider to such a performance on which he is being interviewed, but must be a competent and knowledgeable individual with vast insight into the culture and traditions from which the primary materials have been gathered.

He possesses the "psydric residue" for interpreting implied myths, legends, maxims, words and their origin. He is capable of providing information on the genealogical tree, historical, anthropological or ethnological records. His information corroborates and complements the primary texts. We may argue further that such person, at times freelance performer himself, provides extra-literary materials on which the researcher bases his or her critical evaluation and appreciation of a particular specimen, but as already argued, such an approach may involve more than one performers or knowledgeable indigenous persons who may not be primary performers to be able to test and reaffirm issues at stake.

IV) Data Structuring

Fieldwork does not end with the successful or unsuccessful collection of materials from the field. The experimental test for the researcher really lies in his ability to translate the products of his research into concrete meaningful thesis. The endproduct of any research is to expand the intellectual scope in the discipline concerned. Therefore, the success of the research lies in making his investigation relevant to universal scholarship. Also, materials from the field can be arranged, appraised and structured to tackle a problem or issue on a specific concern.

To achieve these objectives, materials from the field must be properly translated. In oral literature, this is to prevent the isolation of knowledge, but this also has its own problems. All the extraneous materials not part of the performance must be brought to bear on the total study and evaluation of the specimen.

PROBLEMS OF FIELDWORK

Dealing with the custodians of traditional literature or performance may be at times very difficult. Apart from secrecy in opening up the lobes of culture, the basic fact is that the custodians of oral art, like other aspects of culture, are suspicious of the researcher, who has been remolded by the Western education, religion and civilization. The researcher is thus perceived as an intruder or betrayer who wants to incite cultural bastardization in the name of academic research.

At times, those who own the materials may be furious to the extent of exposing the researcher to some threats of survival either by disease or death. They may invoke the wrath of their gods or ancestors to deal with the researcher. We have already proferred solutions to this. The field researcher must be tactical, diplomatic and must make consultations.

If we do not know, we have researchers even among the traditional people. They embark on perilous adventures. The seven hunters created by D.O. Fagunwa in *Ògbójú Ode Nínú Igbó Irúnmalẹ̀*, the venture of Èjìgbèdè on the way to heaven, are all in the traditions of field research. Contemporary researchers should tap from the fountain of knowledge of these traditional fieldworkers.

Another problematic area of fieldwork culture is finance. To embark on fieldwork, the researcher must be financially strong. He needs to make many trips to his place of research. With the psychology of materialism pervading the contemporary society, the custodians of the resource materials may even charge some money to mount a traditional specimen the researcher wants. The researcher has to pay for his survival in the course of his trips. Mechanical aids to do appropriate recording may be too expensive to purchase. Developing his research findings into a concrete document if he can scale through these hurdles becomes more problematic.

Research activities in underdeveloped countries are subjected to the whims and caprices of the ruling class. The crisis of the educational system itself is enough to account for the drifting of research activities. It is always a paradox that European scholars have resources that make them more accessible to traditional materials in Africa and other continents of the Third World. They utilize relevant aspects of their findings to buttress the development of their cultural technology. Some other aspects are used to denigrate Africa, properly described as ethnocentrism.

A fieldworker who does not possess the knowledge of the language of the people among whom he works is at a great disadvantage. It is most unlikely that he will achieve meaningful results. There is little that a translator or interpreter can do. Oral performances and some cultural attitudes fade away in the process of interpretation and translation. This reminds us of the crises mechanical equipment can create. Operational materials may not be readily available where the researcher is, since many African villages are yet to taste the impact of modern technology, such as electricity, etc. Materials recorded may lack clarity of vision and audibility. This may be waste of energy and resources for the researcher.

A crucial problem rocking cultural continuity in Africa is the ever-increasing scholarship in translation. While translation is an inevitable strategy of comparative studies, it is more organized towards the extinction of the oral or verbal art. We have emphasized before that oral materials lack originality in translation. This explains the reason why oral literature should be recognized, performed and communicated in its original language of production. Linguists have argued that the meaning and usage of a word cannot entirely be the same in two different languages. Hence, the socio-cultural contents of traditional literature, which are rooted in the traditional concept of the 'word,' cannot be appreciated outside the context of that language. The implication is that the process of translation is the process of erosion of the contents germane to that cultural background. Aesthetic realization in the materials in terms of language and stylistic performance cannot be properly appreciated in translation.

Critics may even raise the issue that the process of data collection itself may be incomplete or even prostituted. It can be argued that a researcher is on the field to collect materials for critical appreciation and analysis. He is not a traditional performer who is an actor and critic at the same time. The incomplete aspects of his research are left for further investigation. Research is meant for the discovery of an unexplored content or value by previous researchers. Therefore, the damage done to the original materials through translation cannot be synonymous with the supposed incompleteness in the research process itself.

CONCLUSION

By a way of summary, we want to restructure the major issues in the field research process and experience as working principles for a fieldworker. These field researchers must understand, embrace and practice. The field researcher must bear the following in mind.

There must be clarity of perception as regards the subject matter, aims and purposes that have motivated the researcher into the field.

- It is more tactical to consult the custodians of the literature and performance through reliable intermediaries who in a way can still be regarded as traditional experts.
- A fieldworker must be cultured in terms of discipline, emotional composure, close rapport and identification with the cultural practices and behavior of the people among whom he or she conducts his or her research. The creation of an "alien" indifference may not produce fruitful research results and the deserved knowledge.
- Courage, patience and hard work must be guiding moral and ethical pillars of a fieldworker. He or she must be able to stand against all odds
- A field researcher must possess the dexterous skill to operate his or her research equipment, mechanical and others.

EXERCISES AND FIELDWORK

1. What is primary text in oral literature?
2. What do you consider as the differences between the primary text in oral literature and modern literature?
3. Suggest some of the settings where the primary oral performance materials can be collected.
4. What is the importance of fieldwork?
5. What are influences of electronic age on fieldwork culture?
6. Identify some techniques of fieldwork. Discuss the importance of these techniques for a successful fieldwork.
7. Address some of the problems that confront a fieldworker.
8. Discuss the relevance or otherwise of the use of technical gadgets in the fieldwork.

Further Reading and Work

Bukenya, Austin, et. al. *Understanding Oral Literature*. Nairobi, Kenya:Nairobi University Press, 1994.

Miruka, Simon Okumba. *Studying Oral Literature*. Nairobi, Kenya: AcaciaStantex Publishers, 1999.

Okafor, Clement Abiazem. "Research Methodology in African Oral Literature. " *Okike*, 16, 1979: 83-97.

Okpewho, Isidore. "Oral Literary Research in Africa" in *African folklore: an encyclopedia*. Ed. Philip M. Peek. New York: Routledge, 2004, Pp. 303-310.

Notes and References

1. Ropo Sekoni "Literary Pragmatology in Postcolonial Nigeria" in *International Semiotics Spectrum* Toronto, 1989
2. "Omele," "Aaro," "Sèkèrè," and "Bàtá" are all Yoruba traditional music accompaniments.

Chapter Three

 **Archetypes**

In this chapter, we shall attempt to view the discipline of African Oral Literature and Performance from the point of view of a concept that is fundamental to the study of traditional literatures and arts generally. By reviewing the major issues and elements of nature that we will study in later chapters of this book, we shall explore the concept of the archetype.

DEFINITIONS

As usual, approaching the issue by direct definitions may not be totally meaningful to the intellect and scholarship of our reader. It will, of course, amount to a superficial or shallow study of the issue at stake. We shall therefore, in a relaxed and resourceful manner, perceive an archetype by a more meaningful method.

Let us trace human development to the origin and imagine the various cultural, physical, psychological and natural attitudes cultivated and developed by man. Modern developments are patterned along these layers of growth. In terms of the internal operations of the human mind, certain issues and phenomena present images that continue to repeat themselves in our imaginative perception. When we link the present to the origin of human civilization, certain events or phenomena persistently emerge in our thoughts and cultural life from generation to generation. What we are saying, in effect, is that such thoughts and cultural patterns recurring can be traced back to the remote past and the genesis of man in his natural and social environment.

Maud Bodkin perceives archetypes as narrative designs, character types, or images which can be identified with varieties of literature, myths, dreams and ritualized modes of social behavior.[1] What must be properly emphasized from these definitions is the essence or importance of archetypes in the creative process and imaginative literature.

The relationship between oral literature and archetypal structures cannot be far-fetched. Oral literature holds the creative skills and potentials of man in non-literate societies. It is a literature that identifies with cultural patterns deriving immediate motivations from the origin of human civilization. Such literature is an aggregation of the beliefs, mores, institutions, artifacts and practices not yet contaminated by the complexities of modern societies. In the same sense, archetypes as earlier defined have their roots in remote cultures and civilization. Thus, archetypes are continuous remodelings of the ancient attitudes, activities, materials, cultures, without necessarily changing their inherent meanings or the ideas they symbolize.

We therefore examine in this chapter the appearances of these primordial structures in the creative imagination of traditional cultures. We explore the various types of oral narratives as discussed in previous chapters and how they are lined by these recurrent structures. Our concern is to locate the creative potentials in archetypes as they appear in myths, legends, folktales, proverbs, riddles and jokes. In addition, we explain archetypes as strong creative elements that sustain traditional literatures.

Such actions, images and phenomena that repeat themselves in the course of human development are regarded as archetypes. Let us take for instance the attitude and the general portrait of Tortoise, "Ìjàpá Tìrókò Oko Iyánníbo." If we take samples of stories where this animal appears as a character from different parts of the world, there is one thing that can be identified with him and that is "Trick." Hence, we can identify the archetype of Tortoise the trickster.

Within the cosmological setting of the African Universe, rituals and sacrifices are essential ingredients for sustaining the relationship between man and the forces above him or her. In the history of religion and philosophy, certain items are used for sacrifices as a means of compensating for the irrationality of man. Such objects are the means by which the sins of men are expiated. Jesus Christ died on the Calvary to carry away the sins of man. Dog is sacrificed by the Ògún worshippers for appeasing their god during Iléyá festivals, rams are killed, the blood of which is believed will redeem the sins of man. These various objects used in the process of rituals can be regarded as archetypes of "Scapegoating".

We can summarize our discussion so far by considering Carl Jung's definition of an archetype as "the primordial image of a figure, whether a demon, man, or process that repeats itself in the course of history, where creative fantasy is freely manifested."[2] Jung regards archetypes as emerging from the experiences of our ancestors. Such experiences are stored in human memory and they constitute aspects of the creative force and imagination in man.

More importantly, we evaluate and appreciate the positive total effects that oral literature and archetypes have on the modern creative process. Functionalism appreciates the cumulative effects of these elements in the sustenance of culture, maintaining and servicing human values that determine the development of any social structure.

UNIVERSALITY AND ARCHETYPES

Archetypes can be explained in relationship to the concept of universality in art. Universality in art explains that any creative piece has relevance in any age, and society. George Orwell's *Animal Farm* was written many years ago, but the issues raised by the novelist are those that plague contemporary societies. Universality therefore implies the ability to identify common denominators in the literature of any age and social setting. Such denominators may be in terms of themes, characters, events, settings and even artistic formations. This is the meeting point between archetypes and universality. Both have motifs or impressions that have their roots in the history and culture of the past, but they are still relevant today. Thus, like universal literary models, archetypal patterns have dialectical relevance. They move in time past, time present and time future.

FUNCTIONS

We shall discuss archetypes as literary phenomena and consider their relevance in the framework of content and form in literature.

a) Since archetypes have their origins in the remote past, they initiate concrete creative potentials in the artist.
b) Creative sensibilities are informed by the patterns of culture and human development through ages for a comparative analysis in literature. This is made possible through archetypes.
c) Archetypes afford the artist the opportunity of having varieties of motifs, themes, characterization and stylistic components to fashion a model and work of art that can withstand the test of time.

d) Built from a cumulative or aggregation of human endeavors, experiences and traits, archetypes have the potentials of initiating in art changes and development in human societies.
e) Archetypes are given validity because of their permanence.

TEXTUAL STUDY OF ARCHETYPES

For consistency and to allow students to recall various issues and illustrations discussed in the previous chapters, we shall draw our examples for this discussion on texts already used. But definitely, such texts, ideas and issues are to be viewed from a new perspective. It is therefore necessary for students to have a thorough revision by relating examples of prose narratives, discussing them with their colleagues to prepare them for the exercise in the study of archetypes.

For the sake of organization, effective analysis and understanding by students, we shall base our study of archetypes on creative and critical elements such as subject, themes, characterization and setting. Apart from using the texts or narratives already examined in this work, we shall extend our study of archetypes to have a wider scope to broaden the knowledge and intellect of our reader.

I) Subject Matter

We can briefly define subject matter as the core of action that provokes issues, ideas and function in any work of art. Examples of these include birth, coming of age, death, guilt, a quest, scapegoating, rites of passage and a phenomenal occurrence. For example, in the legend of Moremi, there is the archetype of the quester. Throughout human history, we have heard about human beings, heroes or epic characters who decided to go on dangerous adventures to bring peace to their communities. The seven hunters in D.O. Fagunwa's *Ògbójú Ode Nínú Igbó Irúnmalè* are good examples. Moremi's legend implies a quest motif. She made a journey to the Igboland to find a solution to the problem of her people, the Ifes.

Actions of seduction are commonplace subject matter in human experience. Solomon in the Bible sent Uriah to the battlefield to be killed so that he could marry his wife. Koranche in Armah's *Two Thousand Seasons* kills Ngubane to seduce Idawa, his wife. It is this archetype of seduction we find in the folktale "Banjankaro and his Dija." The ruler who wanted to seduce the beautiful wife of Banjankaro meets a catastrophic end.

We also encounter in human experiences about why and how certain things happened, whether to human beings or other creatures. We give this the name "phenomenal archetype." The folktales of why Cricket's teeth got burnt, why Tortoise's shell cracked and why Emedike in Mbaise has no stream belong to this category. We also have archetypes of natural disaster, eruption and earthquake as reflected in some of the folktales. We have archetypes of mysterious disappearance, as seen in myth of Olófin in Ìdànrè and Oba Konko in Asegbe in Sakí. These are analogous to the Biblical myth of Elijah who went to heaven in a chariot of fire.

II) Themes

Themes in any work of art are the ideas or the vision that in the first instance motivated the writer to write. Themes have varieties of meanings, including messages, preoccupations and vision. Themes may include certain human traits that are good or detested, moral and ethical issues, general social criticism and the need for social change. In literature, these general themes may be broken down into conflict between parents and children, rivalry among brothers, maternal affection (Oedipal complex), etc.

In our own present day life, there are instances of when two brothers or friends are at war with each other. This is illustrated by the folktale of "The Duel Between Rain and Fire." In the same tale we see the recurring issue of suitors competing for the hands of a lady.

This at times involves a protracted fight, tournament or going on an adventure. This archetype is dramatically recreated in "Sharro" among the Fulanis. This archetype of romance dated back to the Medieval Ages when the idea of courtly love was practiced. Men worshipped their ladies and went on perilous adventures to gain their affection.

This archetype is similar to that of confrontation between the ruler and the ruled as seen in "Banjankaro and his Dija." Contemporary social organizations still amply manifest this in the motif of the oppressor versus the oppressed. In this way, archetypes may produce the radical psychology of class struggle and social revolution. This archetype explains that of Evil and Good, which we see in the Hausa myth of Bayagida. The Biblical myth of creation identifies "Snake" as an archtype of Evil. It is the same motif that the Snake in the myth of Bayagida represents. On the other hand, Bayagida stands for Good.

One common theme that is strongly archetypal in nature is that of betrayal. This is ironically depicted in the story of "Tortoise and Squirrel." Squirrel, though making a wise decision not to kill his mother like other animals, betrayed the collective decision. Tortoise committed a more criminal act of betrayal by taking other animals to collect food from Squirrel's mother in his absence. Here, deceit is complementary to betrayal. Betrayal has a more disastrous consequence in "Asegbe." The brawl between the two brothers is a betrayal of the ancestoral communal love. This made for the loss of original link with their ancestor Oba Konko.

It is not only in myths, legends or folktales that we have archetypes. They are also found in proverbs. For example, in the proverb of "Àrèmo Aláseju," we find the recurring theme of stubborness and the attendant dastardly repercussion. This type of archetype is recreated in Achebe's *Things Fall Apart*, when the stubborn wrestler decided to go to the land of the spirits to fight. He went and was destroyed by his own "Chi."

The proverb, "a nursing mother does not hear the cry of her child and continue to sleep" explains the inherent motif in the Oedipal complex archetype. Maternal affection is described by psychoanalysts in terms of the archetype of Oedipal complex. Throughout history, experiences of the inherent intimacy between the mother and the child recur. This is seen in the story of Emenike in Elechi Amadi's *The Concubine*.

Traditional African proverbs also explore the archetypal theme of predestination. This is a philosophical issue that deals with the theme and myth of creation. A Yoruba myth has it that every man had chosen his fate on the day of creation and no matter his efforts on earth, it cannot change. Hence the proverb "ritual, sacrifice and charm cannot change the course of destiny." Such an archetype of predestination explains the philosophical irony of man's life on earth. This is contained in the riddle "immediately a child is born, he comes out of a house and immediately moves towards another house." The answer combines "womb and tomb." This implies that man must die. This is the major problem raised by the existentialist philosophers.[4] "Why is man created to be destroyed?"

III) Characteriztion

Characters are very important in translating actions into reality in the plot of any narrative, whether oral or written. Because of their vital roles in articulating social, political and philosophical images, characters may have archetypal meanings. Characters in this case are not only restricted to human beings but also include demons, spirits, animals and even rocks.

We have earlier on discussed Tortoise as an archetype of tricks and deceit. Fox is also noted for its cunning. Characters like Moremi, Bayagida and Awon possess archetypal features of a messiah. The concept of messianism goes back to the period when the Israelites were in Egypt. God sent Moses as a redeemer to take the Israelites out of bondage. Jesus Christ of Nazareth had to bear the agonies of the Cross to redeem people from their afflictions. Precisely, this was the role performed by Moremi. Bayagida performed a heroic fit of a protector and a messiah. He rescued the people of Daura of the past from the archetypal serpent that threatened their existence. As a healer/warrior, Awon also performed the archetypal role of a messiah.

The ruler in "Banjankaro and His Dija" is ruthless, representing the archetype of villainy that recurs in history. Olúorogbo in the myth of Morèmi is an archetype of "scapegoating," associated with messianism.

IV) Setting

Setting is very fundamental to the plot pattern of any narrative. It is the locale where the actions of a narrative take place and the characters dramatize their will, emotions and actions. Setting in traditional narratives may have archetypal relevance because they can still be traced to the mythical or historical past. Physical nature may have archetypal meanings as we see in the case of the cave in the Basaori myth. The well in the myth of Bayagida becomes an archetype of a setting forbidden to human beings because of some dangerous creatures like snakes and other ferocious animals. The mountain setting in the legend of Olófin recalls the setting of destruction in classical myths.

Generally, archetypes perform relevant functions in contemporary literary forms. Various creative strategies in subject matter, themes, characterization and settings re-emerge in a more refined from in the modern creative process, but the ability to recognize archetypes in literary form needs a critical perception and intellect.

EXERCISES AND FIELDWORK

1) Are there big names in your family who have performed heroic feats? Do you see the need to emulate such people? How then can you describe the recurrent features that develop from this?
2) Collect at least two specimens each of myths, legends, folktales and proverbs. Compare them with the examples of archetypes discussed in this book.
3) Compare experiences in stories from various places and explain the relationship between archetype and universality in literature.

4) Pick some major archetypes from the textual discussion and draw more examples from them.

Further Reading and Work

Brooks De Vita, Alexis. *Signatures and signs: reading diaspora and continental African Women's mythatypes*. Ph.D. Diss., University of Colorado, 1998.

Euba, Femi. *Archetypes, imprecators, and victims of fate: origins and developments of Satire in Black drama*. New York: Greenwood Press, 1989.

Jung, C. G. *Four Archetypes; mother, rebirth, spirit, trickster*. London: Routledge and K. Paul, 1972.

Chapter Four

 **Myths**

DEFINITIONS

In Chapter One, we identified types and forms of traditional oral narratives. It is necessary for us to recall these types. We must also remember that oral narratives tell stories about experiences and the nature of characters, actions and settings involved. It is these various functional elements that actually determine the differences in these types of narratives. But one thing is also basic, the reader, watcher or participant in actual oral narrative session can perceive a story line, actions and dramatis personae involved.

In considering myths, it may not be proper to approach the discussion through definitions. Our emphasis will be more on the experiences that build the definitions. This approach makes our understanding of myth more permanent, practical and involving. To get to the root of myths, can you imagine the time when you were not yet born? Can you imagine what experiences were at the corridor or origin of human civilization? Can you imagine a situation when various elements of the hierarchy of African Universe discussed in Chapter One played their games of survival?

In the pyramidal structure, myths deal more with forces above man and of course man himself. The world of myth has the Supreme Being, the lesser gods and goddesses, spirits, ancestors and human beings. These forces relate to Man and the forces below him to make for a harmonious order in the regions above and the regions below. From this point of view, myths can be perceived as experiences and actions that link the worlds of the supernatural and the world of man. The survival of man depends on how he can rationally explain the interrelationships between the cosmic and human forces.

Because of the role played by these forces at the genesis or origin of man, man feels that his existence is incomplete without summoning these forces. Myths therefore recreate experiences of man's interaction with the forces above him. The movement of man's self and his "inner man," (the mind), its stability or otherwise are influenced by the forces beyond him. Man tries every moment to expose the crises within him through mythic experiences. Of course, myths constitute rational explanation by man to justify his living in relationship to the world of the supernatural.

From this perspective, Bolaji Idowu defines myths as:

> ...explanatory answers to the question posed to Man by the very facts of his confrontation with the physical universe and his awareness of the world which though unseen, is yet sufficiently palpable to be real to him[1].

The question of the unknown poses problems and confrontation for man and his solace is in the world of myths.

There is one basic opinion that myths deal with an attempt to explain some metaphysical phenomena in the life of man in society. In this guise, myths are closely related to religion and philosophy. Religion deals with the faith of man and the cosmic forces that govern his universe, while philosophy attends to the total issue of man's survival and existence. We can argue further that social norms, institutions, mores and artifacts, the totality of which is termed culture are traceable to myths of a particular community or society.

Myths, however, are not static experiences and phenomena. As they link man to his root, so also they connect man with the future. Whether they are true or false experiences, they are moulded to create a system of social growth, development and change. The view of Thomas Knipps is tenable here: "History is Myth. It is the reorganization of the past according to the needs of the present."[2] It is this innovataive essence of myths that is being referred to as diachronic. Social norms, political attitude and societal organizations borrow from experiences in myths. It is therefore not surprising that modern African artists use myths in the process of creativity. We can recall the Agikuyu myth of creation and inheritance employed in Ngugi's novels and the Agurumo myth in Olu Obafemi's *A Night of Mystical Beast*. This is the point made by Kofi Anyidoho of Ghana when he talks about "mythmaking and mythbreaking" in African oral scholarship.[3]

We must however, stress the imaginative potentials in myths. The oral artist, despite the fact that he has a model on which to pattern his narrative, makes his own creative inputs in terms of embellishments. His characters, setting and actions are painted with imaginative touch. Such creative inputs make myths to survive for ages. Issues that recur in myths include the creation of the Universe, religion, divinities and rites of passage, such as birth and death.

We can therefore uphold the thesis that despite the fact that many myths originated in the remote past, they are very fundamental in the link between man and the invisible forces, important in creating a socio-psychology of existence and strategic in fostering social changes.

FUNCTIONS

The following are the major functions of myths:

a) Foster man's understanding of his universe and the conduct of his own existence.
b) Mix the real and the unreal to create a balanced spirit of survival.
c) Contain the sources of intimations about the cosmological components of human existence.
d) Give historical solutions to human contradictions and create patterns of development from epoch to epoch.
e) Provide psychological comfort through cosmic activities integral to myths, such as rituals and sacrifices. Mircea Eliade describes rituals in terms of their therapeutic values.[4] By this, he means that rituals allay human worries and so disburden the troubled mind.
f) Myths provide modalities for dialectical or radical innovations in human society.
g) Because of their cognitive and aesthetic values, man emulates the fictional components of myths such as characterization, actions and behavior.
h) Myths have didactic values: they have the potentials to teach ethics, morals and general attitude.
i) Myths provide sessions of entertainment, leisure and relaxations.

TEXTUAL EXPLANATION OF FUNCTIONS

Any discussion on literature is incomplete without relevant illustrations, evaluation and appreciation of ideas from the existing body of available materials. We shall therefore engage our readers in a discussion session with illustrations on the functions of myths listed above. As students, we must cultivate the habit of discussions of ideas on literature with full illustrations that are properly explained. We shall therefore select samples of myths for this discussion. Through the explanation of such myths a clearer picture and meaning will be given to these functions.

The Myth of Bayagida

As already pointed out, myths go back to the primordial times and, as such, they may relate the experience of the creation of Man, a lineage, a rock, or any monumental phenomenon. The Hausa myth of Bayagida relates the origin of the Hausas.

Bayagida was the progenitor of the Hausas as related by the myth. As a wanderer, he came to a place called Borno. He was noted for his intelligence and bravery. The king gave him his daughter in marriage. However, a crisis of confidence set in and the king was jealous of the growing fame of Bayagida. As it happens in many cases of jealousy, the King planned to kill him. His wife revealed the secret and Bayagida escaped.

After wandering for a long period, he came to a place, hungry and thirsty. He asked for dinking water from an old woman he saw but the woman could not give him the water because they could not fetch water. A mysterious snake would not allow them.

Bayagida displayed bravery and defied the terrible monster. He lowered the calabash for drawing water into the well. He pulled the calabash with a strenuous effort, and a snake appeared to see who the intruder was. Bayagida then cut off the snake's head. The Queen wanted to compensate him with money, houses, horses, etc., but he refused. He wanted to marry the Queen. They married and gave birth to seven children who later founded the seven Hausa states.

COMMENT: Apart from being a creation myth, the narrative teaches a lesson in bravery. It also exposes the symbol of evil that the snake represents in its relationship to man. As members of a growing generation, the audience of this narrative would surely like to be as brave as Bayagida.

The Myth of Awon Shao

Myths, we should not forget, in most cases involve supernatural characters. In the case of the origin of Shao, a town in Kwara State, the role of AjakiboObo spirit was very important. He could be described as the founder of the present day Shao. When he came to a place where Shao is now located, he saw some settlers/people and approached them as a human being. He introduced himself as Awonhin. He embarked on a healing mission and gave barren women children. He made everybody comfortable. However, he left them and promised to come back to settle with them because of their hospitality.

During his second coming he brought two other spirits namely 'Moro' and 'Asa.' He settled down as an herbalist and Moro and Asa became his assistants. He made the barren productive, healed people's ailments and made them prosperous. He also created peace and harmony. He became the symbol of guidance and protection to the people. The god "Awon" received whatever was given to him as reward, no matter how small.

Awon mooted the idea of a festival to celebrate his importance, a celebration to which people readily agreed. It was agreed that the festival should coincide with marriage ceremonies in Shao. Initial rites are performed at the shrines while major ones are performed by the Awon river. The Alawon wears white clothes as a symbol of purity. "Awon" as a god is represented by a carved wooden image flanked on the left by Moro and on the right by Asa. They all have tribal marks and their body. From the shoulder to the ankle they are wrapped separately in white cloth and multi-colored beads are used as ornaments for their necks. Their faces are painted blue and the whole of the body is painted red. Up 'till today, "Awon" is still solicited to solve societal problems.

COMMENT: The myth of Awon related the intimacy between human beings and the cosmic forces. The festival fosters communal solidarity. People have the fervent belief in the efficacy of Awon's mythical healing force. Cultural artifacts that represent the image of Awon, Asa and Moro are also symbolic codification of oral literary elements. Such creativity shows the creative skills and potentials of the traditional artist in carving.

The Basaori Myth in Saki

Basaori is the name of a mythical cave situated among the hillocks of Otun in Saki. Saki is located in the Oyo North of Oyo State. It is believed that Basaori has the setting of a house with rooms, passage and a backyard. In size, Basaori is not very large, the entrance would hardly take a full grown adult. It is widely upheld that during the dry season when all rivers should have dried up, Basaori gives water that comes from the mouth of the cave but is not frequently done.

Basaori itself is a big python with a mythic origin. When culture was at its virginity and marriage customs were respected, people used to go to Basaori to seek for solace, respite and marital blessings. If the family of the bride cold not raise the dowry, Basaori would be solicited for assistance. Five days to the marriage, people would go back to the cave and they would find the materials needed for the marriage in a basket placed on the top of the cave. Such materials included clothes, necklaces, shoes, beads etc. Basaori was addressed not in person or through any medium rather they talked to him by speaking to the cave.

Between the ninth and 13th day after the marriage, the materials had to be returned. However, on one occasion, a woman failed to return the materials. In the thick of the night, she was forcibly raised from her sleep by Basaori, who stared at her but did not harm her. The following morning, she confessed her sin to everybody. She died of body ache. Basaori is still worshipped by the Apeki family together with Aganran, another god of the hill.

COMMENT: The myth of Basaori depicts the benevolence and generosity of the python god. Certainly, it portrays some human beings as monsters of ingratitude. There is a link between the African cosmology and culture as evident in the myth. Functionalist anthropologists like Malinowski perceive totem in non-literate cultures in terms of what J.S. Mbiti regards as the "vital force."[5] As an anchor of belief, Basaori stabilizes the society and protects/provides for people and their needs.

The Myth of How Emedike Has No Stream

The myth narrates how Emedike in Mbaise in Imo State failed to have a stream. The myth has it that Emedike failed to have a stream a long time ago because of ignorance. In the olden days, Emedike people suffered from acute shortage of water. They then pleaded with the giver of stream, Imo, with a ritualistic song:

> Onwa – na – agba n'ogo gba n'egedepe
> zabgari-m
> On wa n-agba n'ogo gba n'egedepe
> Zagbari-m
>
> Mighty Imo give us a stream
> Mighty Imo give us a stream
> Mighty Imo give us a stream

Mighty Imo saw their affliction and decided to give them a stream. On one bright Eke afternoon water surged out from an area of land called Ogwugwu Nnabe between the boundary of Emedike and a neighboring town Mbutu. The stream dug a very deep rift. The stream stayed for four days, Eke, Orie, Afor and Nkwo. The inhabitants of Emedike sent to the town crier to summon everyone to the village square because they had an important visitor who had come for good.

They were happy to see the stream, but the stream said it would only stay if they could bring two-day old white and black living creatures. This baffled the people and they argued among themselves about who would bring his two-day old child for sacrifice.

The argument dragged on for a long time, until the stream shifted and surged up in a neighboring village called Ife, also in Mbaise. The Emedike people lamented and consulted the god Alugbage on what to do. Alugbage laughed at them and told them that the stream did not ask for any children. What it demanded fro were a two-day old white chicken and a two-day old black chicken. The people of Emedike blamed themselves for consulting the god late. People of Ife provided the sacrifice and had the stream. Emedike people always went to fetch water from the Ife amidst insult, taunting and laughter at their ignorance.

COMMENT: Various elemental forces like fire, water, sun, air and basic cosmological features link the celestial realm of the cosmic forces and the terrestrial realm of Man. Occupations such as agriculture and fishing are determined by the stability of these forces as indicated in the myth of Emedike people. The cosmic forces provide for man but demands for compensation to make man realize their worth. Here, rituals and sacrifices are soothing mechanism to grease the relationship between the supernatural forces and man to effect what Wole Soyinka refers to as a functional man-cosmos organization. It is crystal clear that man must reckon with these powerful forces above him.

THE IGBO CREATION MYTH[6]

When death continued to plague man on earth, man wished to be immortal. He sent Dog and Toad to God and told them that God would accept the message of whomever of the two got to Him first. Man then told Dog to tell God: "Let man die no more," and he told Toad to tell God "Let man continue to die."

When Toad and Dog set off for God's abode, Toad went and passed a heap of a stool on the way through which Dog would pass. When Dog reached there, he began to eat the stool. As he was doing this, Toad ran off and reached God's abode before Dog and told

God, "Let man continue to die." When Dog finished eating the stool, he ran off to God and told Him: "Let man die no more," but God replied, "God listens to the first words and not the second." This is why men have continued to die.

COMMENT: This myth is similar to the Zulu myth of creation, with a little variation.[7] In the Zulu myth, Chamelion represents God, while Salamander represents Toad. The failure of Chamelion, like Dog, to get to the creator in good time, makes man mortal. Ironically, while man hates Chamelion today, the Dog has become one of the intimate pets of man despite his original mistake. What is fundamental to the two myths is the African belief in the omnipotent Spirit of the Supreme Being, the Creator of the Heaven and Earth. Unlike in other myths, the central actors are animals interacting with God, while man, the focus of the issue, is at the periphery. The essence of attending to collective responsibility is the didactic valve of the myth.

CONCLUSION

We have just taken some samples of myths to illustrate their functions. The ability of students to identify with their subject matter will be determined by the degree of personal efforts they put in collecting more of such myths during their fieldwork. We can conclude that inspite of their elements of fantasy, fictitiousness and probably falsity, myths play meaningful roles in the growth, survival and existence of man. Man's psycho-social behavior and comportment are partly accounted for by his emotional and philosophical attachment to these cosmic environments which oversee his existence.

EXERCISES AND FIELDWORK

1. Can you think of some other myths different from those in this chapter? Consult elderly persons around you for this assignment. Do additional fieldwork in your community.
2. Mention the major features or characteristics of myths and comment briefly on them.
3. Stage the performance or actions of the characters in the myths collected during your fieldwork.
4. Enumerate the various functions or myths and illustrate them with good examples.
5. Consider the roles of these characters in some myths you have collected.
   A) The Supreme Being
   B) Lesser gods and goddesses

C) Spirit
D) Ancestors
E) Man
F) Other natural elements.

Further Reading and Work

Okpewho, Isidore. *Myth in Africa.*Cambridge: Cambridge University Press, 1983

Parrinder, Edward Geofree. *African Mythology.* New York: P. Bedrick, 1986.

Notes and References

1. Bolaji Idowu. *Olodumare: God in Yoruba Belief.* (London: Longmans, 19620, p. 7.
2. Thomas R. Knipp. "Myth, History and the Poetry of Kofi Awoonor." In *African Literature* Today vol. 11 (ed.) Eldred Jones (London: Heinemann, 1980) p. 58.
3. See Kofi Anyidoho, "Mythmaker and Mythbreaker: the Oral Poet as Earwitness" in *African Literature in Its Social and Political* Dimensions. Ed. Eileen Julien, Mildred Mortimer et:al. (Washington: African Literature Association and Three Continents Press, 1983).
4. Wandell C. Beans & William C. Doly ed. *Myths, Rites, Symbols: A mircea Eliade* Reader (New York: Harder & Rex, 1976) p. 64.
5. See J.S. Mbiti. *African Religions and Philosophy* (London: Heinemann, 1969).
6. This Myth is taken from Asonye, Uba-Mgbemena, "Ifo Prose Narratives as Bearer of Beliefs of Traditional Igbo Society." A paper presented at the Second Annual Conference of the Folklore Society of Nigeria, Ilorin, 1982.
7. See Mazisi Kunene's *Anthem of the Decade* (London: Heinemann. 1981).

Chapter Five

 # Legends

DEFINITIONS

Our discussion in the last chapter on myths has some relevant bearing to our discussion and explanation of legends. Myths and their associated elements are placed on the high ladder of the African Universe. If you can recollect, myths deal with the cosmic and invisible forces, those powers above man. However, with legends, we need to go down the ladder of arrangement of elements in the African Universe.

Legends primarily concern and involve man at the center of the pyramidal structure discussed in Chapter One. Legends embrace the world of Man and those forces below him. This does not imply that legends do not have some cosmic or supernatural features. The historical features of legends imply political, military and cultural actions related to messianic feats. Despite the fact that the characters involved in legends performed historic and heroic roles, they may not necessarily be classified as gods in the real sense of it, even if they are deified.

It is necessary to make some clarifications on the classification of Okpewho. He identifies two types of legends in his diagrammatic illustration: historic legend and mythic legend in *Myth in Africa*.[1] There is a possibility of establishing a causal effect to link the two. In the process of the historical character performing some heroic functions or perilous adventures, he interacts with the world of the supernatural, which reinforces him or destroys him. It is also possible to argue that in their lifetime, such legendary figures possessed some supernatural powers either through magical potentials or some other factors. Sango as a legendary character during his lifetime simultaneously performed heroic political and magical feats. The latter seemed to elevate him to the level of a demi-god.

It is also relevant to discuss legends in relationship to epic. In its original conception, epic is a heroic narrative in poetic forms, embracing myths and legends. Epic characters can as well be regarded as legendary figures. They performed historic and heroic roles relating to the survival of their various communities or tribes. In a larger political sense, epic deals with the national destiny of a race and the legendary figure is the central figure. The idea of mythic legend comes in when a hero's actions are influenced by supernatural forces or when he himself transforms into a demi-god.

Legends can also be explained in terms of the cult of ancestors or ancestral worship. The individual, be he the head of a clan or a tribe, a warrior or a traditional medicine man, is deified. He moves into the world of the ancestors and saints to protect those who are living. This explains the African concept of apotheosis. Such legendary characters serve as the bridging link between the worlds of the living and the dead. It is possible to argue that the cult of masquerade is an extension of this legend of the ancestors. Negritude, which is a literary philosophy, has legends of the ancestors at its roots. However, it must be emphasized that it is not all ancestors are legendary figures. It is only those who performed heroic feats.

Legends are always associated with events such as wars, rules (dynasties), migration and settlement. We also propose that it is not only human beings that performed legendary or heroic roles. Animals, trees, rocks and streams may also be involved.

On the whole, we want to stress the imaginative and creative qualities of legends by citing the authority of B. Fieldman and R.J. Richardson. According to them:

> ...true history or real life is the legend which for practical purposes...means a story that strains back at a real event but in which the historical details cannot—thanks to the oral mode of transmission—avoid the taint of fictive coloring.

FUNCTIONS

a) Legends give people some historical accounts of the past of their ancestors and their remarkable performances.
b) Such accounts afford the present generation the opportunity of developing some typical traits, modes of behavior and practices identified with some legendary figures.

c) Legends give fundamental information on the origins of a dynasty, a settlement, a historic phenomenon or natural features.
d) Legends, because of their historical potentials can set modalities for political and social organizations, thereby enhancing human development.
e) Like myths they have diachronic features. This implies that legends can inform the present with the past and project the future. This is the spirit of dialectics in African orature.
f) Legends enhance the spirit of historical continuity.

TEXTUAL EXPLANATION OF FUNCTIONS

The Legend of Olófin: Agbalaagbogun Akin

This is a case where we are almost tempted to label the narrative a myth because of the heroic feats of the legendary characters, but the fact still remains that we cannot label this a myth. It is the feat of a human, not a supernatural being. The legendary narrative of Olófin is from Ìdànrè. Though a mystical figure, the fact that he was a human being before turning to a spirit made him a legend. He lived in Ìdànrè in time immemorial and he was reputed a gallant warrior. Our sources confirmed that he was a descendant of the Great Odùduwà, who so loved him that he gave him a crown. The crown was so mysterious that it was always brought to the public once in a year.

A brave warrior, he was a strong safety-valve for protecting his people. On one occasion, the battle was so fierce that he fought in all directions, but he was beheaded. However, as was typical of him, he immediately beheaded another person to replace his head and he continued with the war. At a time, people wanted to install him as king. He confessed that he wore a woman's head and that a woman does not wear a crown in Yorùbáland.

Also, on one occasion when enemies were to attack Ìdànrè, Olófin conjured a big mountain to become a plain, grown with varieties of fruits. The enemies sat down on the plain eating fruits. Unexpectedly, the mountain resumed its normal position and all the enemies were trapped. Tragically, since the death of Olófin people could no longer conjure the mountain, because they defied the god of the mountain.

His legendary feat was more acclaimed by the way he died. Olófin told people that when he died, nobody would know his burial ground. After his death, he was dressed according to the customs and rituals of the people. People were waiting for him to fulfill his promise. Some even chanted some incantations. Suddenly, a loud and alarming sound in form of an earthquake rocked the ground. People were thrown helter-skelter. In the midst of the confusion, Olófin rose from where he was laid, wrapped himself in the white robe and took the 'opa' lamp with him and started singing a historic and oracular song. As he was going away his body touched a person, who died instantly. He continued his journey to an unknown destnation. Later, he appeared for three months in the sky before he finally disappeared.

He was deified and worshipped. Initially, a human being was used for sacrifice. With modernization this was replaced with cows and other items. The celebration always lasted for seven days. His praise poetry was always sung thus:

> Abalaagbogun Akin
> Olupese temitemen,
> Elegunre Soromoyen
> Elegunre Tekunebu Jeun
> Oloposina ginangiren
> Olopemiriwo peyan
> Olope yo wo sugbo mole
> Domudi d'owo lorun de din kounge.

This is about was his bravery and gallantry. Also, one of the songs in form of prayer and praises always sung during the festival is:

> Solo   Aba jàre o
>   Father Please
> Chorus Aba jàre momo luka ko mi bi ee
>   Father provide me with good children
> Solo   Oye wa sodon o
>   All of us have celebrated this year.
> Chorus O ye wa sodon o awa su umodon ee
>   All of us who have celebrated this year
>   will celebrate the next one.
> Solo   E ho utitu o
>   Good money.
> Chorus Eho itutu wa pese ko mi mi ee
>   Father provide me with cool money.

Legends

This song goes on as long as the performers want.

COMMENT: The legend of Olófin can be classified into the category that Isidore Okpewho terms the "mythic legend." The legend of Sàngó, one of the Aláàfins of Òyó, also belongs to this category. In the legends human characters with historical and heroic feats were elevated to the level of supernatural characters. Olófin's political activities reduced him to the level of human performance. However, his ability to magically conjure the mountain and the manner of his disappearance after his death had supernatural strength. He combined human and supernatural qualities to protect his people. The nature of the dramatic rituals during his death and the profuse use of incantations and praise poetry consolidate the supernatural force in him. The innovations in ritualistic patterns emphasize the influence of modernity and civilization.

The Àsegbé Legend

"Àsegbé" originally means one who does something and gets away with it. History has it that if any criminal entered Àsegbé, he would be forgiven his sin and nobody would question him again. Àsegbé used to be a compound at Ayétòrò in Sakí. Àsegbé had a legendary and historical origin. Oba Konko, the son of Olú Otun, was the major dramatis personae behind the Àsegbé legend. It is claimed that while he was alive he had a lot of charms and amulets. He was a very strong medicine man, just like Sàngó. He was feared and revered by all and sundry. This magical power was not restricted to him alone, but extended to all the members of his family.

At the zenith of his power, he buried himself alive. When he buried himself, he did so with a long chain hanging from his neck. Each time any member of his family wanted to consult him, the chain would be pulled. However, on one occasion, there was a clash as to who should talk to Oba Konko between two brothers. In the fight that ensued, the chain got broken so they lost touch forever with Oba Konko. However, up till today, people can still identify the place where he entered the ground.

Things have changed. The family does not want to be called "Àsegbé," but "Àselà" — one who engages in a venture and is successful.

COMMENT: This legend depicts some historical tendencies. While the individual that loomed large in the legend is very important, the legend seems to be more embracing in that it involves a family. Thematically, the repudiation of the name "Àsegbé" for

"Àselà" implies that culture is not static. When people identify some faults or anomalies in any custom and tradition they adjust to make the society functional. Also, the two brothers in the narrative learned their lessons in a hard way for their brawl and uncompromising attitude. It is certain that this would be a part of reference in history and social development to check conflicts and discontent.

The Legend of Morèmi

All along, emphasis has been on male characters in the creative world of myths and legends. Moremi was a legendary woman who played a gallant role in rescuing the Ife people fro destructive and incessant raids by the Igbos. In those olden days of inter-clan and inter-ethnic wars, the Igbos ruthlessly invaded Ife once in a year. People would be enslaved and their property taken as booty.

Morèmi was not happy with this. She decided to consult a river goddess, Èsìnmìrìn to get a solution to this horrible annual experience. Èsìnmìrìn advised her in the right direction that she should allow herself to be captured by the Igbos. Being a beautiful woman who could easily attract any man, Morèmi could use her natural talent to get the secret of the power of the Igbos.

The plan worked accordingly and Morèmi was captured during a raid by the Igbos. She became a focus of attraction for all the Igbo warriors. She was taken to the palace of the King of the Igbos. She used her beauty to entice the ruler, who revealed the secret of their power to her. The King informed her that in the next two days the Igbos would invade Ife. The King added that the Ifes should prepare grasses for thatching roof called "Oguso." When the Igbos invaded their place, they were to set the grasses on fire and put them on the bodies of their enemies. Having heard all these, Morèmi decided to escape back to Ife before the next Igbo raid.

After two days, the Igbos invaded Ifè. Morèmi had prepared her people for the attack. They set grasses on fire and put them on the bodies of the enemies. Their bodies were burnt and they were taken into captivity. It is believed that up 'till today there are still some Igbos in Ifè called Olùyaré.

After the victory over the Igbos, Morèmi went back to the river goddess to pay homage and fulfill her covenant. Moremi gave all sorts of presents and gifts to Èsìnmìrìn. At every moment the gifts were thrown into the river, they were returned to Morèmi. The only present that Èsìnmìrìn wanted was Morèmi's only child, Olúorogbo. Morèmi sacrificed her child for the survival of her people. Since then,

Morèmi became the mother of the Ifè people. An annual festival still holds in Ife today to celebrate the legendary feats of Morèmi.

COMMENT: The Morèmi legend has shown that in traditional settings, it was not men alone who embarked on Herculean tasks to rescue their people from attack and exploitation. African oral literary tradition has many female characters who sacrificed a lot for their people. We can mention legendary Agikuyu women who went to the battlefield with their male counterparts. In the Zulu orature, Mhudi was a distinguished heroine who went on perilous adventures to rescue her race from the Boers.

Morèmi's legend has historical elements. Tribal, ethnic and clan wars were prevalent in the past. Many settlements were totally destroyed or taken into captivity. The legend was based on the heroism of an individual who embarked on a mission to rescue her people. The emphasis in the traditional society was the collective force. Supernatural activities are seen in the legend as shown by the ritualistic exchanges between Èsìnmìrìn and Morèmi. This also confirms that there was always interaction among the forces in the hierarchy of African values.

Individuals like Morèmi left their footprints on the historical record of her society. Elaborate festivals are always conducted to commemorate her heroism. Like Mumbi of the Agikuyu people, she became the mother of her race. Individuals today wish to identify themselves with the heroic feats of Morèmi. Human beings and public places are identified with Morèmi. The legend's didactic value is indisputable. People must be ready to make sacrifice for the collective survival of the society.

The Crocodile Legen in Yenagoa

This legend is from the Yenagoa area of River State. There ws an incident involving two brothers when their families went fishing along the down stream of river Nigeroff, river *Wun* and were drowned. No sooner had they spread their nets than a heavy thunderstorm, just like hurricane occurred. Daylight gave way to darkness. Their canoe sank, but the two brothers swam to safety. However, members of their families had disappeared. All efforts made to rescue them proved abortive. There was gloom and lamentation in their village. However, on the seventh day, the women and children were found at the beach along the Wun. When interviewed, they said they were brought to safety by "seven crocodiles." The villagers were full of joy and Ebenekien (chief) resolved that no village should kill or eat the meat of crocodiles again. The villagers believed that crocodiles are not animals but "gods". The 'Ogilagba Festival" (New Yam Festival) was a period of celebration in honor of these river creatures. People who disobeyed by eating crocodile meat have their tongues swollen and inflamed. Members of the family of such people would be sick if Adiafa was not performed.

COMMENT: The legend has proved one strategic or crucial point. All the elements in the African cosmology are relevant in the sustenance of the interrelationships between the cosmic and social realms. In this case, animals, classified to be under man have performed a benevolent and Herculean task of rescuing man from danger. The legend explains further the relationship of man to the natural forces around him. Among the riverine people of Nigeria, there seems to be an intimate correspondence between humans and water. Water itself has almost assumed the status of a human character. The legend goes a long way to explain the traditional ways of life of the people. For instance, the audience is informed that fishing is the main occupation among the riverine people.

CONCLUSION

Legends constitute essential elements of the African traditional narratives. Their contents have thematic meanings that inform the survival and existence of the present and generations to come. Heroism is a remarkable feature common to all the legends discussed in this chapter. Heroism paves the way for messianic roles through which individuals imbued and talented with charismatic traits rescued the larger society from abysmal destruction.

Legends like myths assume some supernatural force that serves as the belief system of any community or a group of people. They serve as checks and balances in the conduct of the constituents of the society and the society itself. The functional and aesthetic relevance of legends cannot be underestimated.

EXERCISES AND FIELDWORK

1. List at least five differences between myths and legends.
2. Look around you, do you foresee any of those you know becoming a legendary figure in the future? Why? Interview seleced others and hear what they think.
3. Explain the difference between historic legend and mythic legend.
4. Explain the relationship between legends and epic.
5. Locate any function(s) of legend really occurring in or affecting your society now.

Further Reading:

Arnott, K and Joan Kiddell-Monroe. *African Myths and Legends*. Oxford University Press, 1989.

Tembo, Mwizenge. *Legends of Africa*. New York, NY: MetroBooks, 1996.

Notes and References

1. Isidore Okpewho. *Myth in Africa* (Cambridge: Cambridge University Press, 1983) pp. 66-71.
2. B. Fieldman and R.D. Richardson. *The Use of Modern Mythology* (Bloomington: Indiana University Press, 1972) pp. 412-413.
3. Taylor and Auguste Comte were pioneering fathers of Sociology and their definitions of culture are very important in this type of interdisciplinary study.
4. Daba, H.A. "The case of Dan Maraya Jos: A Hausa Poet" in *Oral Poetry in Nigeria*, Lagos: *Nigeria Magazine*, 1981
5. Abdulkadir Dandatti: "The Role of an Oral Singer in Hausa-Fulani Society. A case study of Mamman Shatta" Ph.D. Thesis, University of Indiana, 1975.

Chapter Six

 Folktales

DEFINITIONS

Folktales in African oral narratives are in most cases told by elders to children. Emphasis in folktales is on the physical and natural world. Characters in the tales include man and all the forces below him such as animate and inanimate objects like trees, rocks and waters. Folktales manifest regular interaction between the world of imagination and that of reality. They have strong creative potentials.

There are three basic types of folktales in Africa. These are dilemma tales, moral tales, and fairy tales.

I) Dilemma Tales

In dilemma tales, the audience is usually left at the end of the story to pick from many alternatives as resolutions to the conflicts in the tales. Questions such as the following are then raised: "if it were you, what would you do?" "Who among the wives should the husband pick?" "Who do you think actually loved this farmer, his wife or his mother?"

II) Moral Tales

Moral tales teach mainly moral lessons like goodness to parents and orphans, hardwork, hospitality to strangers, good relationships with one's children, step-children, husbands/wives and neighbors.

III) Fairy Tales

These are tales in which spirits and ghosts are also characters. This type of tale is different from the other two types discussed above.

FUNCTIONS

The most important function of African folktales is the teaching of moral lessons, since they are directed mostly at young children. Folktales constitute a kind of "catch-them-young medium" in which certain important qualities of life are inculcated into children. We can therefore identify the following functions of folktales in our society:

a) Folktales introduce children to the cultural practices of their society, including customs, institutions, mores and beliefs of the people.
b) They inculcate society's basic philosophy of life in children.
c) They introduce to them the African view about the universe, especially the African cosmology.
d) They develop in children the power of rhetorics and repertoire.
e) They develop in children the sense of communal responsibility.
f) They give children knowledge and skills on how to solve instant problems and riddles of life.
g) They make them develop meaningful psychological and physical traits.
h) Because folktales deal with rural and peasant cultures, they expose children to the physical phenomena of their environments. These include the sounds of birds, movement of waters, times of the season, voice of rain, thunder, etc. Therefore, nature becomes a functional part of the child. The study of nature through folktales prepares children for future profession such as fishing, farming and carving.
i) They inculcate in children the sense of social organization and collective sensibility.
j) They serve as cosmic relief and provide entertainment and relaxation after the day's hard work.
k) Folktales sharpen the intellect and power of memory of the elderly ones.

TEXTUAL EXPLANATION OF FUNCTIONS

Our intention in this part is to pick on some African folktales and explain how they play the roles we have identified above.

A Duel Between Rain and Fire

Once upon a time, Rain and Fire were friends. They loved each other dearly. In those days, they were human beings and were both handsome and powerful. One day, a misunderstanding arose between them over a beautiful lady. There was a clash of interest over who should marry the lady. Fire approached the lady's father over his intention of marrying his daughter. The father would not want to dictate to his daughter whom to marry: He asked Fire if he had discussed with her. He said if he had not he should first ask her. If she agreed then everything would be settled. Rain also came forward with his proposal to marry the same lady. The father was surprised because he knew that the two suitors were cordial friends. He answered the second suitor the way he answered the first. He should first of all ask the lady. Then he told the two to come in seven day's time to a specific place and whoever arrived first would likely win the hand of the lady in marriage. Everybody knew that in a situation like this, the two suitors would have to fight it out in a duel to determine the ownership of the lady. On the seventh day, the duel ensued and many people left their places of work to witness the fight between the two suitors.

Fire was the first to come, and when he saw Rain coming, he changed from a human being to a reddish, hot wild burning air, challenging Rain to come forward if he thought he was capable of withstanding his power. Rain too quickly changed to cloud and made the entire sky dark. In the twinkling of an eye, water started dropping from the sky. Before Fire could make any move, Rain overpowered him, killing him instantly. During the fight, the lady was placed in their midst. She was actually terrified by the degree of wrath displayed by the two suitors. She then started singing, and the people around (Spectators) were chorusing "ara n ta." We should practice this song ourselves.

Lady:	Iná rèé arére
Spectator:	Ara n ta
Lady:	Iná rèé arére
Spectator:	Ara n ta
Lady:	Ina pupa félélé
Spectator:	Ara n ta
Lady:	Ojo dúdú mìnìjò
Spectator:	Ara n ta
Lady:	Mba féná, ma fójò
Spectator:	Ara n ta
Lady:	Iná pupa félélé
Spectator:	Ara n ta
Lady:	Ojo dúdú mìnìjò
Spectator:	Ara n ta
Lady:	Mba féná ma fójò
Spectator:	Ara n ta.

And so, Rain won and carried the lady away. Rain, however refused to change back to a human being in readiness for any day that Fire may challenge back. Rain loved the beautiful lady very dearly and did not want her snatched from him.

COMMENT: In the Yoruba tale above, we can see how the two hitherto intimate friends became enemies. Fire lost his life just because of a woman. If they had allowed maturity and good reasoning to prevail between them, one of them would have still married the lady and their friendship would have grown from strength to strength. This tale also tries to show us the kind of conflict beautiful women cause among men. However great the degree of intimacy between men, women can bring about separation among them. There is a solid belief in African traditional culture that a woman's excessive beauty is a potential distraction to peace, success and unity among menfolk.

Banjankaro and His Dija

This tale was narrated by Al-Amin Abu-Manga in his article, "The concept of Woman in Fulani Narrative."

Once upon a time, a ruler sent his messenger to inform all the people in the surrounding villages about the deterioration of the life of the community and to ask them to come and settle in the city. The messenger, however, reported back to the ruler that one Banjankaro living in an isolated hut in the bush did not recognize his authority and would not move to the city.

The messenger also reported that this Banjankaro had an extraordinarily beautiful wife. According to him "I have never seen in my life a woman like her." The ruler immediately dispatched a brigade of 4,000 soldiers to go and kill the husband and bring the woman to him. However, Banjankaro was able to kill all the soldiers except two, who quickly carried the bad news to the ruler.

One strong man who possessed some mystic powers and who had been noted for successfully facing and conquering such tough enemies was sent to confront Banjankaro. The instruction actually was that he should bring Banjankaro and his wife to the ruler alive, but he was also mutilated. Finally, Banjankaro decided to go by himself and meet the aggressive ruler. On his arrival with his wife, the ruler jumped over the wall and escaped, thus leaving the throne for him.

COMMENT: This Fulani folktale definitely shows to us a greedy and terribly over-ambitious tyrant ruler. Instead of seeking the opinion of his people and asking for their consensus on important matters, he opted for forcing ideas on them. The ruler could have just appealed to those people in surrounding villages to move to the city and of course left anyone who felt he preferred his original settlement to continue to live there. We can see that this authoritarian ruler later met his doom.

Another important issue in the tale is the ruler's ambition to snatch Banjankaro's wife. Like the Yoruba tale we have considered earlier, the reported beauty of Dija intoxicated the ruler. He even ordered the murder of Banjankaro so that he could take his wife. This, definitely, is greed and lust. Again, the ruler's excessive love for beautiful women had brought about his downfall.

Cricket and the Sand

This is a folktale among the Ijaw people. It explains how Sand always maintains its position below water.

In the olden days, Cricket and Sand were friends. One day, they went fishing in a river. After getting one big fish, they roasted and divided it between themselves. Cricket said he was the elder and gave himself the lion share. Sand disagreed. He also claimed he was the elder and demanded the lion share.

Then Cricket, who thought himself wise, said that they should swim across the river and the first person to get to the other side of the river would be declared the elder. Sand agreed and they started swimming.

As they were swimming along, Cricket looked back and could not see Sand. He called out, "Sand are you coming?" Sand answered him, "I am coming." As they were swimming on, Sand was all the while dissolving into the water. Cricket kept on swimming and kept calling out again and again, "Sand are you coming?" However, Sand's voice became fainter and fainter. Sand eventually dissolved totally into the water. Cricket swam to the other side of the river. He looked back and did not see Sand at all. He started laughing. He was actually very happy.

Suddenly as he was standing, he noticed an old woman who had already made a fire. Cricket realized he was feeling cold. He got to the fire and was warming himself there. He was enjoying it and kept lowering himself closer and closer to the fire. He fell on the fire and burnt his teeth. This was how Cricket, who had a very fine set of teeth became toothless.

COMMENT: This tale clearly shows that both Cricket and Sand were greedy. They could not resolve the simple matter of age. If we may ask, what has age to do with sharing a fish? Why couldn't they share it equally? In a true African setting, it is even usually the younger person that is given a lion share in such instances. This is because it is he that does most of the work. He carries the utensils and washes knives and plates after usage. At the end of the day, neither Cricket nor Sand is able to actually eat the fish. They both lost out completely.

Spider and other Animals

This is a Hausa folk narrative. It is very popular among the Hausas, especially in Nigeria.

Once upon a time, there was a serious famine in the entire community. All the animals gathered and decided to embark on massive farming to produce enough food for the coming season. All of them except the Spider went back to the farm. All other animals had a determination to work hard, and they actually labored day and night till they successfully planted seeds in all their farms.

Hare noticed that Spider did not join in the work. He went to inquire from him why he did not farm, but Spider replied that he knew what he was doing and that he would never starve whether he farmed or not.

The crops were soon ripe for harvest. Everybody was anxious to eat the new crops. Suddenly they started noticing that some of their farm products were already being secretly harvested. It was particularly pronounced in Hare's farm. Hare and others reported the case to the king who made public appeals to the thieves to desist from their devilish acts. However, the more the king appealed, the more they noticed that more and more crops were still being harvested by the thieves.

One night, the king asked one of his messengers to secretly erect a doll in hare's farm. In the middle of the night, spider and his children, as usual, went there with baskets, calabashes and many other containers. That day they were going to take as much as possible to last their family for the season. Suddenly, one of the children saw the doll. She screamed and, with other children, ran quickly out of the farm. They did not stop until they reached home. Spider, however, was very brave. He approached the doll and demanded, "Why are you disturbing us? What do you want here? Why should you terrify my children? Will you answer or will you not so that I slap you?" Spider did not know that it was a mere doll.

He was very annoyed and slapped the doll, first with his right hand. The hand glued to the doll. He shouted at the doll to release his hand and slapped it again with the left hand. That also glued to the doll. He kicked it with the right, then the left leg and knocked it with his forehead and his legs and forehead glued to the doll. He shouted for help but nobody came to his rescue. He was afraid then.

He remained there till early morning when the king, Hare and all other animals gathered to see who the thieves were. Everyone who went there exclaimed in surprise "So its you, Mr. Spider!" They mocked him, rebuked him and threw stones at him. After parading him naked throughout the length and breadth of the community, the king ordered that Spider be given ten strokes of the cane. He was also to remain naked throughout his life.

COMMENT: Spider definitely felt that he was the cleverest of the animals, yet he ended up being publicly disgraced. This tale shows us why it is not good to be greedy and fraudulent. Spider would have lived well and be respected if he farmed like others and if he recognized that there was no shortcut to success. He learned his lesson in a hard way: however long a thief does not havoc, one day his nemesis will catch up with him.

Tortoise and Squirrel

This is an Ibo tale. We are likely to observe that this tale has a version in our different communities, too. This is so with most tales in Africa. Tortoise, for example, has been occurring again and again in our different tales. He is always the cunning, trickish and overly ambitious animal. Let us examine this Igbo talk about Tortoise and Squirrel.

Once upon a time, the animals gathered and said they would all kill their mothers and bring their skulls together to be used for musical drums. All the animals brought their mothers' skulls except the Squirrel. He secretly hid his mother very high in heaven.

He got a breadfruit, removed the edible part and washed and moulded it very well so that it had the shape of this mother's skull. He took it to the animals and they received it thinking that it was really his mother's skull. As time went on, the animals were hungry as they ran out of food. The Squirrel was not affected because his mother was still alive. He regularly climbed up to her to eat delicious food and come back.

One day, Tortoise said to him "Squirrel, you look so fresh, you don't look like others who are dying of hunger." Squirrel replied that it was the same with him and that he was also dying of hunger. Tortoise insisted that Squirrel was lying. He appealed to him to please show him where he gets his food always and that he would go with him. Squirrel then felt he should assist Tortoise since he was a good friend. He asked Tortoise to get ready.

So one day, Squirrel took Tortoise to where his mother was and sang. He always did this before his mother threw down a rope. Now let us sing the song. While a person acts like Squirrel and sings, others should be chorusing with 'tutu ucho.'

Let us begin:

> Mother throw down the rope o
> Tutu ucho
> Mother throw down the rope o
> Tutu ucho
> Your child is dying of hunger o
> Tutu ucho
> Your child is dying of hunger o
> Tutu ucho
> Rope, rope o
> Tutu ucho

The mother threw down the rope and they climbed up, ate to their satisfaction and came down.

Tortoise got back and told the animals that Squirrel was really the cunning animal. He told them that while they all planned and killed their mothers, Squirrel hid his own in heaven. He told them that Squirrel had deceived all of them into believing that he also killed his mother. He told them that Squirrel went often to the mother in heaven to eat delicious meals while they all suffered. Nobody could believe Tortoise's story. He told them to get ready to follow him to where Squirrel's mother was hidden. They all followed Tortoise to the place. Tortoise sang (in his crooked voice):

> Mother throw down the rope o
> Tutu ucho
> Mother throw down the rope o
> Tutu ucho
> Your child is dying of hunger o
> Tutu ucho
> Your child is dying of hunger o
> Tutu ucho
> Rope, rope o
> Tutu ucho.

The woman said, "This is not my child's voice, it is not Squirrel." Tortoise sang again and again. She eventually threw down the rope, though she was still not convinced that it was her child. All the animals were climbing up when a bird told Squirrel that the animals were on their way to kill his mother. "Look, they must be killing your mother now," said the bird.

Squirrel ran to the place and sang to the mother. The chorus should be saying 'Chiba ucho'"

> Mother take back the rope o
> Chiba ucho
> Mother take back the rope o
> Chiba ucho
> The animals want to kill you o
> Chiba ucho
> Mother take back the rope o
> Chiba ucho

The mother took a knife quickly and cut the rope. All the animals fell down making a heavy noise "Ikpokotom." Tortoise fell terribly and his shell broke into pieces. Even though the Black Ant has helped him to join his shell together, Tortoise's shell still remains rough and cracked 'till today.

COMMENT: This Ibo tale teaches us that we should always ensure that we are not part of bad decisions—and whenever one is made, we should always maintain what we believe is right, even if it means sacrificing our personal comfort. Squirrel, who refused to kill his mother, became the better for it. However old our parents are, they remain jewels to us. Their love and care for us can never be equaled. A Yorùbá adage says, "Mother is gold, father is mirror." We also learn in this tale that it is bad to be ungrateful. Mr. Tortoise was ungrateful and he ended up battered.

CONCLUSION

We have been able to examine some tales in this chapter. We have seen that every one of them aims at developing in us humane and true African values. Unlike myths and legends which operate at high levels and which are usually about mythical, metaphysical and mysterious elements, folktales are about simple matters and objects of life. They address day-to-day socio-political and moral issues of our society. One area in which myths, legends and folktales are similar is on the fact that some of their characters possess good qualities that are expected to be emulated in the society. Another area is that myths and legends are most of the times, like the folktales, stories that also contain songs.

EXERCISES AND FIELDWORK

1. What are the major differences you can observe between myths, legends and folktales in the various definitions given in this book and from various examples you have come across?
2. Can you remember the major functions of folktales? Which one(s) among them do you think is (are) relevant to the building of a peaceful, self-reliant and progressive society?
3. What similarities can you observe among the various tales you have read in this book? Are there characters you think share the same qualities? How?
4. Collect as many folktales as you can from your locality, write out both their original and translated forms and compare them with what you have read in this book. Which tale from your locality shares similarity with the ones in this volume? In which way?
5. Why do you think folktales are described as products or creative imagination? Use relevant textual materials to illustrate your answer.

Further Reading and Work
Visual Material (view and analyze):

Akinlana, Obakunle. *Storyteller Obakunle Akinlana presents African folktales, stories, songs and music*. Tampa, FL.: Common Touch Studio, 2004.

Notes and References
1. See Al-Amin Abu-Manga, "The Concept of Women in Fulani Narratives," *Nigeria Magazine*, Lagos: 1984 pp. 52-58.

Chapter Seven

 **Proverbs**

DEFINITIONS

Proverbs are oral compositions and their various thematic and stylistic constituents are derived from all the layers we described as the hierarchy of African values. Proverbs embrace the philosophical and socio-cultural value systems of the people. They point to the individual, domestic and collective life patterns of the society from which they are derived. In other words, proverbs adopt materials from people's cosmological and social environment. Emile Durkheim and E.N. Obiechina perceive proverbs as collective representations of people's ways of life.[1]

Proverbs actually come from the womb of tradition, reflecting the intellect and wisdom of the people. Chinua Achebe says that a proverb is the palm oil with which words are eaten.[2] This shows that proverbs are essential ingredients to harmonize the life rhythm of any community. Proverbs in Africa are, however, a special prerogative of the elders. The elders are always exalted as the custodians of wisdom in Africa. The Yorùbá talking drum always reminds us that "the words of our elders are the words of wisdom." It is therefore expected that the elders display their wisdom and intellect through a profuse use of proverbs in their speeches. Any African elder who lacks this power of the mind and words may lose his respect, no matter his importance in the society.

A Yoruba adage says "L'énu àgbà l'obì n gbó sí"—"It is in the mouth of an elder that kolanut attains its relevance." This proverb always marks the commencement of any ritual or communal performance. The elder normally starts by breaking the kolanut, tasting it and passing it around. A young child never rushes to use a proverb when an elderly person is there. He pays homage and seeks permission from the elders.

A famous Dadakúàdà poet, Omoékeé Àmàó, sings thus, "Proverb is a horse of speech, speech is a horse of proverb, when a word is lost, proverb is employed to search for it."[3] All the gamut of human existence is compounded in this artistic medium, proverb.

Some proverbs may even develop into anecdotes. This will be explained later in this chapter. In this regard, proverbs may provide a forum for poetic and dramatic expression of the power of the intellect. We can say that some proverbs may even house all the genres of literature; prose, poetry and drama.

FUNCTIONS

In our attempt to define proverbs, we have been able to establish the fact that proverbs play very important functions in traditional speech modes, and of course day-to-day activities of an African. We shall state briefly some of these functions.

Proverbs:

a) Give substance to speeches, since ideas are put in concrete terms through this medium.
b) Show the depth of knowledge and wisdom in African heritage.
c) Entertain, enlighten and educate the listeners.
d) Command respect for the speaker and show his level of maturity.
e) Expose and explore the socio-cultural realities and literary culture of Africa.
f) Demonstrate the tradition of rhetorics and eloquence in the articulation of ideas by Africans.
g) Help in settling disputes, explaining and pressing issues.
h) Provide warning, rebuke, praises, suggestions and advice.
i) Present the cosmological views and interests of the speaker.
j) Teach logic and science.

If we may ask, how many of us are really familiar with this mode of communication and expression? If you like, ask your classmates or your friends to say at least two proverbs and explain their meanings and relevance. It is either that proverbs are not said or when they are said that they are mutilated. What then are the factors responsible for this? If you ask your friend this question, his answers may likely include the following:

i) The informal education in the traditional African setting has been overtaken by formal education.
ii) The communal and collective pattern of existence in the traditional settings such as the extended family system and compound culture—"agbo-ile" are no more there.

This implies that communalism or the sense of being one's brother's keeper is exchanged for the European individualism. Favorable socio-cultural settings are therefore not provided for rearing the young ones in the use of proverbs.

Many of us were born and bred in urban centers, which means we are remote from the setting where this power of intellect can be learned. The dominance of foreign languages over traditional ones makes it impossible for the budding generation to acquire potentials in the rich rhetorical components of their indigenous languages. How then do we develop a culture of reclaiming this wisdom of the old age?

Probably the answer is to fashion a sensibility of going back to the roots. This can be developed even within the framework of our indulgence in the urban culture. This work is calculated in that direction. We must collect, learn and introduce proverbs into our daily speeches in both the indigenous and English languages. We should observe elders when speaking and learn more of such proverbs.

TEXTUAL EXPLANATION OF FUNCTIONS

Proverbs perform so many functions that we cannot itemize here. It will not even make our students practically involved if all the functions are listed. We have, however, worked such functions into some broad categories. Students are free to add more to such a classification and penetrate more purposefully into the uses of proverbs. Whatever the functions of proverbs are, we believe that proverbs in most cases are inherently philosophical and educational. We can then examine the functions of proverbs under these major categories:

I) Cosmological Reflections
II) Socio-Cultural and Domestic
III) Morality and Ethics of Behavior
IV) Science and Logic

I) Cosmological Reflections

We have already mentioned under functions, that proverbs reveal the cosmological beliefs and views of the people. They explain issues concerning the existence of man, display the harmonious link between the world of man and the supernatural and they explain the general crisis of creation. Let us consider these examples:

A) Whether you perform a ritual or employ medicine, it is what you had chosen during the time of creation that you will be.
B) We only find marks in our palm; we do not know the creator.
C) The masquerade says it will dance, the rain says it will fall and the "bata" drummer says he will drum, we shall see who will carry the day.
D) Do not deride my going to heaven, all of us are going there.
E) The witch cried yesterday and the child died today, who does not know that it was the witch of yesterday that killed the child.

The first proverb deals with the issue of creation and destiny. The issue of predestination has been a controversial one among people of strong minds all over the ages, but this proverb expresses the Yorùbá belief that there is nothing you can do to change the course of destiny. It is believed that every human being had already chosen his mission on earth during the period of creation. Therefore, it is not possible for him to change it. The second proverb also explains some of the dilemma associated with the myth of creation. Look at your palms, there are some marks there. Can you tell your mates the person who created them? This is impossible. This shows that there are certain things that cannot be explained.

The proverb on the controversy among the masquerade, rain and the "bata" drummer is very interesting. First, it shows the interaction and fluidity of action in all the realms of the African Universe. We can regard it as a dilemma proverb, which resembles a riddle that needs a solution, but it is somehow rhetorical. It is a way of testing the most powerful in the cosmic realm. If the masquerade (who represents the ancestor) has power over man (the "bata" drummer), can the masquerade have power over rain, which is almost cosmic phenomenon? With the power of African magic, such a phenomenon can be averted. Students may wish to debate this issue among themselves to get more and more into the core of African philosophy and culture.

The fourth proverb again relates to the issue of predestination. Death is a universal phenomenon, a fate every man must embrace. This explains that man's life is a philosophical irony, since all our efforts in the world will one day end up in our being buried in a six-foot pit.

II) Socio-Cultural and Domestic

Let us consider the following examples:

A) It is the biggest of the masquerades that leaves the grove last.
B) When there are no elders in a town, the town will be disorganized, when the head of the family dies, the house is deserted.
C) It is with the entire hand (fingers) that we beat the chest.
D) The entire value of the kitchen knife is never known until one wants to use it and the knife is nowhere to be found.
E) A nursing mother does not hear the cries of her child and continue to sleep.
F) No matter how a child has clothes, he can never have rags as an adult.

Apart from expressing the belief of Africans about the ancestors represented by masquerades, the first proverb shows the respect accorded elders in the traditional society. This is further explained by the second proverb illustrating that without an elderly person as the pilot of a community or a house, there will be chaos. This respect for the wisdom of old age is further ascertained by the sixth proverb. The proverb implies that the father has seen more days than his child and that he has a wealth of experience.

The third proverb explains the theory of collectivity, which is always the practice in the traditional society. This proverb is derived from communalism as a mode of existence. The fifth proverb indicates the inherent maternal affection between a mother and her child.

III) Morality and Ethics of Behavior

Proverbs perform educative functions by providing guidelines, codes of conduct and patterns of behavior with which people can make the society function without problems. In other words, proverbs inform and educate the people on the norms, mores and ethics of the socio-culture. We can locate such functions in the following proverbs:

A) A person who wants to eat the honey beneath the rock should not look at the mouth of the axe.
B) The marshy land distances itself from the river as if they are not related.
C) The termites are eating the pot, so strong calabashes should beware.
D) The dog that would get lost would not listen to the whistle of the hunter.
E) They say, "do not do it" and you do not do it. This means you will still be living. But if you do it, it means you are going to heaven (death). That is the divination for "Aremo Alaseju," i.e. the Stubborn Aremo.

The first proverb teaches the lesson of patience and endurance. If you have a lofty goal to achieve, you should not be deterred by the obstacles on your way. You should not even mind to endure pain and agony. It teaches a lesson in sacrifice.

The second proverb exposes the norm of collective will in the traditional setting. Separation from the social totality is not profitable. It also warns those who abandon their associates in the time of trouble. The third proverb teaches a lesson of perception and exercise of will at a critical moment. The fourth proverb is always a warning to avert crisis.

We are interested in the fifth proverb because it is an example of the anecdotal qualities of some African proverbs. Anecdotes are brief and pungent stories used to illustrate a particular issue or position. This again is a common practice among the elders. "Aremo Alaseju" is simply a stubborn character. The story goes thus. He is warned not to farm in "igbo-igbale," the abode of the masquerades. Like the dog that wants to miss the road, Aremo Alaseju does not listen to the warnings given to him. He goes to the abode of the spirits to farm. In his first attempt to set his hoe on the farm, he cuts he head of a child-masquerade "Omo egúngún."

Suddenly from an unknown destination, a crowd of masquerades surround him and they are all singing:

> Ìwo mò ó se sé?
> You knew, why did you do it?
> Ìwo mò ó se sé?
> You knew, why did you do it?
> Kékeré mo wà mo ti n sawo

I have been in the cult since I was young.

And the storyteller finishes with, "and Àrèmo Aláseju, the stubborn man, was killed by the masquerades."

This proverb effectively warns a person of the consequence of his planned action and the repercussion of not listening. On a cosmological level, it shows that the ancestors are very powerful and man must not underestimate their importance. While the ancestors who make the masquerade cult are benevolent, they may also discipline a stubborn and troublesome human being.

As already mentioned, this proverb forms a budding ground for a short story. And from the narrative form, the proverb assumes a poetic form, all of which may be dramatized by the performer and the audience.

IV) Logic and Science

African modes of thought, high level of perception and reasoning, which may be conscious or unconscious, negate what Eurocentric critics regard as the "unscientific world order" in non-literature societies. The following proverbs can be used to authenticate our assertion:

A) A person who blocks one's view of the fire cannot block one from seeing the sun.
B) A person roasting maize does not turn his back to the fire.
C) A child who says his mother would not sleep, he himself will never know sleep.
D) If a man walks alone, his footprints become traceable by his enemies.
E) When the fire dies out, it covers its face with ashes. When banana dies, it is the offsprings. When the adder dies, it is the offsprings that inherit its position.

Some African proverbs delve into science and logic to pass their messages. Logic and science are an integral part of the intellect, wisdom and strong psychic vision inherent in African proverbs and other oral forms. The traditional African man, a compendium of knowledge and master of his natural environment, does not need to go to the laboratory before making authoritative statements about the theories of reproduction, regeneration and cyclical methods in biology as seen in the fifth proverb. The first proverb shows that he is inherently conversant with the theory of vision in physics. His strong sense of logic is reflected in the third proverb. The equivalent of this is "a drier of the locust-bean seeds will be dried together with the locust-bean seeds."

This is the end of our story about the meaning, relevance and utility of African proverbs. And we can then conclude that "it is in proverbs that we beat the agidigbo drums. It is the wise one who hears it. It is an intelligent one that knows it." Let us endeavor to beat our speech drums in proverbs.

EXERCISES AND FIELDWORK

1. Find out from your parents or elderly ones around you other uses of proverbs.
2. Listen to as many traditional singers as you can and try to locate proverbs in their poetry.
3. Try to write out fifteen proverbs from different African languages and probably dialects. Also translate them into English without being assisted.
4. Create stories around five of the proverbs you have collected.
5. Do you remember our contention that some proverbs are anecdotal? Find out some of such proverbs in your locality and write three of them with their stories.

Further Reading and Work

Bryan, Ahsley. *The Night Has Eears: African Proverbs*. New York, NY: Antheneum Books for Young Readers, 1999.

Adéèkó, Adéléke. *Proverbs, Textuality, and nativism in African literature*. Gainesville: University Press of Florida, 1998.

Owomoyela, Oyekan. *Yoruba Proerbs*. Lincoln: University of Nebraska Press, 2005.

Prahlad, Sw. Anand. *African-American Proverbs in context*. Jackson: University Press of Mississippi, 1996.

Notes and References

1. E.N. Obiechina: *Culture, tradition and Society in the West African Novel* (Cambridge University Press, 1975) p. 156.
2. Chinua Achebe uses this proverb to explain the uses of proverbs in the Igbo society and African in general. The importance of this is reflected in his novels where he makes a profuse use of proverbs.

Proverbs

3. Omoekee Amao was a traditional Dadakuada poet in Ilorin. His compositions are typically loaded with proverbs, using them to illuminate his ideas and depict general relevance of proverbs in the African Society. Omoekee Amao died in 1988.

Chapter Nine

 **Stylistics and the Performance of Oral Narratives**

INTRODUCTION

It must have occurred to us by now that oral narratives enjoy styles and performance techniques that are very unique to oral literatures. This is not to say that the general elements of plot, setting, characterization and language we often come across in written narratives are not present in oral narratives. The uniqueness here, however, is that life and real performance are in oral narratives and these features are virtually realized through ourselves, who constitute what Ropo Sekoni calls narrative – performer and audience. We have what we may describe as the living tale.

Our intention in this chapter is to discuss the stylistics and performance techniques in the various types of oral narratives, which is our concern in this volume. We shall identify the introduction is adequately exploited for a successful narrative session. In other words, it is believed that if the introduction is bad, the story or tale proper may suffer passive reception, so introduction techniques in traditional African oral narratives are aimed at achieving the following:

i) Calling the audience's attention.
ii) Arousing the interest of the audience.
iii) Making a formal declaration of the beginning of a story session.
iv) Making some language exercise or display.

The mode of introduction is similar in myths, legends and folktales. Proverbs, riddles and jokes also employ very interesting introduction techniques. In every introduction, there are conscious efforts at creating beauty of the oral narrative. Some artistic elements employed here are repetition, questions, voice modulation, hissing and musical sounds like beating of drums, gong, calabash or any musical instrument.

We shall go into our previous lessons in myths, legends, folktales, proverbs and riddles and jokes to examine the style and performance techniques employed at the introduction. We must remember that we have discussed the rudiments of style and performances in oral narrative in Chapter One. Our intention at this stage is to see how they are used in our lessons.

Our first myth in this book is the Bayagida myth about the origin of Hausa race. The narrator-performer starts:

> Ga Labari!
> Ku zo ga labari!
> Ku saurara, ga labari
> Yara, Kusan Bayagida?
> Anyi wani sunna sa Bayagida.
> This is a story!
> Come this is a story!
> Listen, this is a story!
> Children, have you heard the story of Bayagida?

The myths of Awon Shao and Basaori in Sakí would normally be introduced like this:

> Ní ayé láéláé!
> Ní ayé ìgbà kan!
> Ní ayé àtijó!
> Ní ayé láéláé nígbà tí Elédàá ò tíì dá omi,
> Igi, oòrùn, òsùpá, òkè, ilè àti èèyàn.
> In the olden days!
> Once upon a time!
> In the years of the old!
> In the world of the old when the creator had not created water, tree, sky, moon, ground and man.

Normally, once the narrator so declares the beginning of the story, everybody looks towards him and listens attentively with enthusiasm. Let us find out on our own how the Igbo start story sessions. We should report our findings to our teacher. Yes, we may need to consult elders around us who are Igbo indigenes.

Stylistics and the Performance of Oral Narratives

Legends also start with some introductory declaration. Much as narrators of myths and legends want to use hyperbolic statements at the beginning of the stories, they are always careful, because the stories they are about to tell are regarded in the community as true and sacred. They are stories that touch the life and sensitivity of the people. They would not want to give any impression that may make the audience think that such myths and legends are pure works of imagination, like of course, folktales are.

In folktale performance sessions, the narrator uses every talent at his disposal and employs every linguistic method, including hyperbole and repetition to introduce his tale. Now, he is operating in an imaginative world and right from this stage, he puts his imagination into use. He wants the listeners, usually children, to be impressed. He wants to keep their attention with him 'till the end. Remember some of the introductory remarks of the folktales we discussed in Chapter One? Let us remind ourselves. The narrator starts:

Narrator:	Ààló o
Audience:	Ààlòò
Narrator:	Nígbàa láéláé, nígbàtí ojú wà ní orúkún, tí orí wà ní ibàdí
Narrator:	Here is a tale!
Audience:	Let us hear it.
Narrator:	In those days when the eyes were on the knees and the head was on the waist.

Hear that! "...when the eyes were on the knees and the head was on the waist!!" The listeners would definitely be intrigued. Unlike in myth and legend stories where the narrator just says "Once upon a time," he has extended it here to a total strangeness, a strangeness the children never knew and which they will be eager to hear about. Their attention is therefore totally attracted. In the myth story, we are told, "it is a time when God had not created water, sky and man." This cannot be as striking as the introduction "when the eyes were on the knees..." used in folktales.

We have explained in Chapter Eight that riddles are usually linked with folktales. They occasionally serve as the introduction to folktales and they create a question and answer session to put the children at alert for the tales to follow. At the beginning of a riddle, the narrator may start:

> Who know this?
> Listen and explain this.

Students should recall some of the riddles in Chapter Eight to be able to see their relevance as introductory aspects to a storytelling session.

Proverbs are not like myths, legends, folktales and riddles and jokes. Proverbs are part of the language of narration. There is no formal way of introducing proverbs. The speaker just goes ahead and utters proverbs when he feels they are appropriate, during folktale or story sessions and when he is having a real day-to-day discussion.

FICTIONAL ELEMENTS OF ORAL NARRATIVES

Plot

Plot is the gradual unveiling of events narrated. Like the classical western plot, there may always be a beginning, a middle and an end. The narrator, however, reserves the artistic right to twist his story or tale and bring the end to the middle and the middle to the end, for whatever effects he wishes to achieve. He may describe how mercilessly a greedy man was killed before asking the audience to listen to what led to his tragic end. The African tradition of oral performance does not impose any strick rule of progressional narration.

The plot of Bayagida myth as it is narrated in this text starts from his arrival in Borno, after wandering about for years. The story depicts the growing jealousy between him and his host, his father-in-law, the King of Borno.

The climax of Bayagida's bravery is killing the dreaded snake in Kusugu well and the popularity he consequently enjoys among the people of Daura. The story ends with his marriage to the Queen Sarauniya and the seven children born to him by the queen.

We are told these children founded the seven Hausa States. We can see that one event actually graduated to another. The Bayagida story thus moves progressively to the end. Let us make personal efforts to identify the story lines as they unveil from beginning to the end in other myths narrated in this book. We should discuss them with our colleagues.

Legends and even folktales are wedded together in similar ways. The legend of Moremi starts from the point at which we are told the entire Ife people are in perpetual fear and torture from the regular raid by the Igbos. Morèmi therefore consults Èsìnmìrìn, a river goddess. The story unveils gradually until Morèmi is captured by the Igbos and becomes the wife of their king, who reveals the secret behind the Igbo power to her. We are also told that when the Igbos raid the Ife people again, the Ifè, putting fire on grasses and other tools, set the fire on the bodies of the Igbos. They burn many of them and take a large number into captivity. The reader will undoubtedly be emotionally involved in the plot. The suspense about what to sacrifice to Èsìnmìrìn and the final offering of Olúorogbo, Morèmi's only daughter to the goddess is the termination of the plot.

The tale of "A Duel Between Rain and Fire" as narrated in this book also has a very similar sequential and progressional plot. It starts from the misunderstanding that ensued between Fire and Water over a beautiful lady. It gradually moves to the point where the two engaged in what can be described as physical combat. At the end of the combat, Fire died and Rain married the woman, thus bringing the conflict to a resolution. Yet, we cannot over emphasize the freedom of the African performer to twist the plot according to his artistic desire for spontaneous effect.

We should make efforts to identify the plot structure of all the myths, legends and folk narratives discussed in this book. In particular, we should always identify points of conflicts and how such conflicts are finally resolved.

Setting

We discussed setting briefly in Chapter One. There are two types of setting: place setting and time setting. Place setting is the physical environment where actions take place. Time setting, on the other hand, refers to the exact moment the actions take place. For example, a village market square, Oba or Obi's palace and the riverside would stand for place setting. In the morning, at the sun rise, in the rainy or dry season would stand for the time setting. All these are represented in our prose narratives. Let us examine some of the stories, proverbs and riddles and jokes discussed in this book.

The first one we shall take on here is the 'Igbo myth of creation.' This myth has two place settings. The first one is certainly the abode of man, the world of the Igbos. We should realize that no village or town is mentioned here. The entire Igbo universe, the whole world as the Igbos perceived it then, is the setting. The second place setting is God's abode, where Dog and Toad are expected to go to deliver man's message. Then we have the way where they are expected to follow to reach God. We should remember that it is on this way that the toad passed his excreta.

The time setting may be a little difficult for us to identify here. No particular time is categorically mentioned, except that we are told that it was at a time "when death continued to plague man on earth." We may, however, deduce that it must not be too long from the time of creation, so it must be at the earliest time in man's history.

Let us also take on the Morèmi legend. The place setting is Ife, the cradle of Yorùbá civilization and another Igbo community that is not named in the story. Other place settings within these two communities are the river Èsìnmìrìn and the Igbo King's palace. The time-setting here, too, is not easy to identify, for they are not as explicit in the legend as the place settings are. However, we can understand through the legend that it was in "those olden days." It was in the days of our great ancestors. None of us had been born then. We are also not told when the Igbo raids were always made. Was it in the morning, afternoon or evening?

Let us now consider the Fulani folktale, "Banjankaro and His Dija." The place settings of the tale include a town and several surrounding villages. We also have the ruler's palace. Another important setting within the surrounding villages is the isolated huts, where Banjankaro and his wife live. The time setting here is not explicit. The storyteller says, "Once upon a time." It is certainly one of the times in the old days, though it can also be a not too distant time. Folktales generally are set in man and animal worlds. The Hausa tale of "The Spider and other animals" is, for example, set in an animal world. Some tales are set in the river, forest and mountains. Fairy tales are set in the abode of spirits. It is very easy to identify the setting of a tale when we listen to or read it.

Even proverbs and riddles and jokes have their settings. Let us consider the following proverbs we have discussed before:

i) It is the biggest of the masquerades that leaves the grove last.
ii) A nursing mother does not hear the cry of her child and continues to sleep.
iii) The dog that would get lost would not listen to the whistle of the hunter.

The first proverb above is set in the masquerade's cult's grove 'Igbo-Igbale.' The only sense of time we have in this proverb is the various times that the masquerades leave the grove. We do not know whether it is in the morning, afternoon or evening, but we know that the biggest masquerade leaves last. This proverb is an indication of the timing of an elder's action in a gathering where there are younger people. The third proverb above is set in the forest. We know that both the dog and the hunter are in the forest on a hunting expedition.

We shall also consider some riddles to see their settings:

i) What passes through the King's palace that does not greet the King?
   Ans: Erosion.
ii) I went to the farm and the farm laughs to me
   Ans: A field of cotton when the ripe capsules are opening.
iii) The small god of my father whom we kneel down to worship.
   Ans: Grinding stone.

The first riddle here is set in front of the king's palace. There is no time setting. The second one is set in the farm, the cotton farm. Setting in the third riddle is not directly stated. We can understand one's personal god, here referred to as "small god of my father," is usually at a corner or a hut in a compound. Every morning, the god is worshipped before members of the family leave for the day's job, so we may say that the place setting here is the home and the time setting is morning.

Characterization

African oral narratives have characters that reflect the nature of the inhabitants of the African universe. As we have discussed thoroughly in Chapter One, the characters that occupy the African universe range from supernatural beings to spirits and ancestors, to man, animals, plants and even insects.

The major characters around which stories are told in myths and legends are usually the heroes. In folktales, like in the conventional prose, we have what we often describe as flat and round characters. Round characters are usually the heroes. They are everywhere and tend to do everything. The flat characters, sometimes, can be regarded as "follow-follow" characters. All these characters perform less important actions. We shall identify the characters in some of the prose narratives we have cited.

In the Hausa myth of Bayagida, the characters include Bayagida, King of Borno, Bayagida's wife in Borno, an old woman, the snake, the Srauniya-Queen, the people of Borno and Daura and Bayagida's seven children. Bayagida is the central character. He is the hero of the story. In the myth of Awon in Shao, the characters include Ajakibobo, the founder of Shao. He is called Awonhin. Other characters are barren women, children, Moro and Asa spirits and the people of Shao. Awonhin is the central character.

The character in our legends are sometimes all human beings. Sometimes they even include animals and inanimate objects with heroic qualities. In the legend of Olófin, the characters include the Olófin himself, Odùduwà, Olófin's people and Olófin's sister. In the legend of Morèmi, the characters are Morèmi (the central character), the Ifè people, the Igbo people (including the raiders), the goddess Èsìnmìrìn, Olúorogbo and Morèmi's daughter. In the Crocodile legend in Yenagoa, we have such characters as two brothers, the crocodile, women, Chief and other members of the village. The Crocodile is the hero here.

The folktales we have come across in this book have quite interesting characters. In "A Duel Between Rain and Water," characters include Rain, Water, a beautiful lady, her parents and the spectators. In "Banjankaro and His Dija," the characters include the ruler, Banjakaro, his wife, the ruler's messenger and soldiers. Bajankaro is the hero.

Proverbs, riddles and jokes discussed in this book revolve around different characters. We shall identify some of these characters in some examples.

i) No matter how a child has clothes, he can never have rags as an adult.
ii) Any person who wants to eat the honey beneath the rock should not look at the mouth of the axe.
iii) The dog that would get lost would not listen to the whistle of the hunter.

The characters in the first proverb above are a child and an adult. In the second proverb, the main character is any person; the axe is also important. In the third proverb, the characters are the dog and the hunter. We should also consider some of the riddles and jokes:

i) I went to the farm and the farm laughed at me
   Ans: A field of cotton when the ripe capsules are opening.
ii) There is the stick that lies in the road, and beats everybody. It beats the father, his wife and their children.
   Ans: Hunger
iii) Òrúkú Tindí Tindí, Òrúkú Tindì Tindì, Òrúkú gave birth to two hundred children, all decorated with antimony in their eyelids.
   Ans: Beans.

The characters in the first riddle above are 'I' and the farm. 'I' here is the narrator. In the second riddle, the characters include the stick, the father, his wife and their children. In the third riddle, characters include Òrúkú and two hundred children.

We can see that the characters identified in myths, legends, folktales, proverbs and riddles and jokes are very similar. It is evidence of the type of interaction we have among the various elements of the African universe. It is this interaction that results in harmonious and peaceful living African universe.

EXERCISES I

1. What are the major differences you observe in the introductory parts of myths, legends and folktales? What reasons can you give for some differences? Cite your own examples.
2. What are the conflicts in the 'Myth of How Emedike Has No Stream?' At what point do these conflicts surface and how are they resolved?
3. Which character would you qualify as flat and round characters in all the folktales narrated in this book?
4. What setting would you say is common to myths, legends and folktales? What are your reasons for that conclusion? Give examples from the stories in this book and the ones you gather from your fieldwork.
5. Why do myths, legends, folktales, proverbs and riddles and jokes have common characters? Make your answer comprehensive.

LANGUAGE

Language is the vehicle through which myths, legends, folktales, proverbs and riddles and jokes are passed to the individuals. Benjamin Whorf cannot be more right when he asserts that language is an expression of a people's culture and philosophy of life. This popular contention, regardless of any modern proof to the contrary, is here well demonstrated through African oral narratives. African myths, legends, folktales, proverbs and riddles and jokes are expressions of African customs and philosophy of life through language.

The language of African oral prose is rich, fresh and highly cultural. As discussed in different sections of this book, language is a very important tool of the narrator. He twists it to suit his purpose at any given time. For example, apart from modulating his voice, he is aware of the type of language to use at the introductory stage of the tale. This is a stage where he wants to sensitize the children, to attract their attention and to remove the children from their own world to fascinate them. In other words, language use in oral prose has some psychological relevance.

The African narrator is well aware of the children's psychology and appeals to it duly to attract and involve them right from the beginning of the story. He attracts children's attention with (as we already said in Chapter One):

| Narrator: | Ga ta nan ga ta nan kun (Inffarse) |
| Audience: | Ta zo mu ji ta |

| Narrator: | Here it is you my people |
| Audience: | Let it come, we're ready to hear |

Introduction II

Narrator: Nígbàa láéláé, nígbà tí ojú wà ní orúkún, tí orí wà ní ìbàdí tí enu sì wà ní àtélesè...

In those days when the eyes were on the knees and the head was on the waist and the mouth was beneath the foot...

A question-answer language exercise, riddle and joke, may also be introduced after introduction I to stimulate the children's interest (in that situation introduction II above becomes introduction III) and to get them ready for the main body or middle of the narrative session. This traditional practice in African narrative is today a principal modern introductory method of teaching in our schools.

Proverbs, adages and wise sayings are introduced at this stage. The narrator actually employs his power of rhetorics here. He is faced with the challenge of retaining the children's attention throughout and therefore employs his language deliberately for that purpose. Often times repetitions, metaphors, personifications, similes, ironies, analogies and allusions are used. Let us examine the following Yoruba tale in its middle:

> Lójijì tó bá ti ní 'aburakaka' orùn rè yó sì gùn, orí rè yó tóbi bí òkè Sóbí. Bósè féè dé ègbé ilé oba ló bá gbé gìgísè rè nlè, ó n yó rìn, ó n yó rìn, ó n yó rìn, ó n yó rìn, gbàrà tí ó dé enu ònò rè ni ó bá olójúu pépéye ti rí i kía ló kégbe: 'aburakaka!'

> Immediately he utters 'aburakaka' his neck would grow long, his head would become big like the Sobi hill, so just when he almost got to the oba's palace, he lifted his heel from the ground and was tip-toeing, tip-toeing, tip-toeing. As soon as he reached the gate of the oba's palace, Oba with his duck's eyes, saw him and he quickly exclaimed 'aburakaka!'

We can see the various figures of speech employed in the above:

i) "his head would become big like the Sobi hill" (use of simile)
ii) "and was tip-toeing, tip-toeing, tip-toeing, tip-toeing" (use of repetition)
iii) "Oba with his duck's eyes, saw him" (use of metaphor).

The major intention of language use as demonstrated above is to give a vivid picture of the characters and their activities in the tale. The middle stage is really always very interesting. Children clap and hail the narrator and his performance. Often times songs are also introduced. Song language is important and effective in arousing the interest of the audience.

Language at the concluding or ending stage is usually aimed at rounding up or bringing out the lessons taught by the story. The following is a good example:

> Láti ìgbà náà ni èyìn alábahun ti rí kúrukùru.
> Tani ó mo èkó tí àló mi yìí kó wa?

> Since then, the back-shell of the tortoise has remained rough.

> Who among you, knows the lesson taught us by the tale?

Generally speaking, the language of oral narratives is simple and is usually in past tense form. Since children are usually the audience, the narrator, through uses of various figures of speech, proverbs and adages, ensures that his sentences are not too complex and his analogies are not complicated. The narrator is also conscious of the fact that through his stories he is also teaching the children language. A typical traditional African child therefore grows up with very rich and solid indigenous language background through oral narratives.

Our various narratives in this book are in translation. This has definitely done away with the kind of beauty and riches we described in our indigenous stories. All the same, we shall examine the language of a few of them. We must, however, bear in mind that the completeness of language, both in form and beauty, are in the original indigenous realization.

Let us start to exemplify our discussion with the language of the "Igbo creation Myth." First and foremost, the language here is in the past tense. This is because the narrative is about what happened sometime not too long after creation. Also, Dog and Toad. which ordinarily we would call animals, are personified here. Their names start with capital letters. There is also use of quotations: "Let man continue to die" and "Let man die no more." Even God's reply to the belated Dog is quoted: "God listens to the first word and not the second." This is normally realized in the tale session through voice modulation. In other words, the narrator will try to imitate voices easily likened to those of the Dog, Toad and God. He will probably employ a huge, heavy voice for God to give the impression of His might.

There is regular reference to time: "when death continued to plague man, "when Toad and Dog set off for God's abode, " and "when Dog finished eating the stool." We have also seen the use of irony. Dog by nature is a fast animal. However, he got to God late. Toad by nature very slow, but he got to God first. The myth however, tells us what led to this irony.

Also, 'a heap of stool' is very important in the story. It is what turns the table round against the Dog. 'Heap' is used to describe the extent of stool Toad passed on the way, but let us ask, isn't this a hyperbole? Can the Toad really pass a 'heap' of stool which dog can eat and eat? All the same, the language of narration here is very simple.

Folktales normally have a more hyperbolic and dramatic introduction. The narrator has a license to take the audience to any extent without actually bothering whether they would suspect that he is telling lies or formulating or adding his own piece to the tale. That is why he can say, "In those days when the eyes were on the knees, and the head was on the waist" or "Once upon a time when there was serious famine and there was no food at all for anyone in the animal world."

In the second type of introduction, almost every noun is qualified or given extensive meaning. The narrator talks of 'serious drought' and says it is one 'never experienced before.' He adds that there was no food 'at all.' A picture of an extreme situation is created. This definitely arouses the interest of the audience who want to know how the animals were able to survive in such a situation. In 'Spider and other animals,' we are told 'there was a serious famine in the entire community.'

The middle of the narration in folktales is very similar to what we have in both myth and legend. We must note that the characters are themselves usually allowed to talk. That is why the narrator has to often mimic their voices. In Spider's tale we are told that the spider "approached the doll and demanded 'Why are you disturbing us? What do you want here? Why should you terrify my children? Will you answer or will you not so that I slap you?'" The narrator modulates his voice to imitate the Spider's voice. The ending of a folktale is also similar to those of myths and legends, except that the narrator will always ask the audience what the lesson of the tale is. In the spider's tale, we are told at the end "he was also to remain naked throughout his life."

We have established the fact that proverbs and even riddles and jokes are employed in the folktale narrative. Proverbs are among important artistic elements adopted at the middle stage of the folk narration. These proverbs are always rich in artistic composition, for example:

i) The termites are eating the pot, so strong calabashes should beware.
ii) The marshy land distances itself from the river as if they are not related.
iii) When the fire dies out it covers its face with ashes, when banana dies, it substitutes itself with its offspring, when the aged dies, it is the offspring that inherit the person.

The language employed in the first proverb, for example, makes it very powerful and effective: "The termites are eating the pot." It is declarative. The use of the termites here further helps to make the proverb richer. Termites are by nature aggressive eaters. We also know that pot is very strong and hard, so if termites have acquired the capability of eating pots, what can strong calabashes do to survive the termites? The analogy here is superb.

In the second proverb, our sense of reading is touched through the use of language. In reality, we all know that the bank of the river is always marshy and so the subordinate clause 'as if they are not related' is the real mocking statement here. Sometimes, proverbs are humorous. The incantatory language of narration is indicated in "When the fire dies out, it covers its face with ashes."

We must also note that as much as proverbs are generally in close or contracted poems in that they are in very short lines, we have situations when they are relatively long. The third proverb above is a good example. The narrator tries to establish his ground before making the categorical proverbial statement. He sometimes even plays and displays his wit and language ability. He explores African cultural, natural and domestic items in his analogical displays. After establishing that the fire covers its face with ashes at death and the banana, with its offspring, the narrator states his categorical statement: "When the aged dies, it is the offspring that inherit the person." It is also quite rhetorical. It can go for a kind of argument that establishes both major and minor premises and thereafter brings forth its logical conclusion. It is saying that the fire dies and its ashes cover its face, banana dies and its offspring substitute it. Therefore, when the aged dies, it is his offspring that will inherit him (a kind of covering of his face or substituting him).

Like proverbs, riddles and jokes are also brief but employ rich metaphors, similes and other artistic elements. Like proverbs, riddles and jokes employ its properties from the African cultural setting. Unlike proverbs, however, riddles and jokes are hard knots that the audience must untie. They are often times in question form starting with question tags. When? What? Who? Why? Even if such tags do not begin a riddle, it may end it. If neither of these happen still, the audience is expected to provide an answer. Let us examine some examples here:

i) People run away from her when she is pregnant, but they rejoice when she has delivered.

Ans: Gun
ii) What is it that knocks the King's head?
   Ans: Shaving Knife
iii) When he is going, he faces Òyó, when he is returning, he faces Òyó.
   Ans: A drum with two faces.

The first and third riddles above are not in question form. The narrator normally asks a separate question or, like we have said, the audience assumes the question and goes straight to answer it. For example, in the first one, the question "Who is she?" would be asked. At the end of the third riddle, the narrator may ask "Who is he?" These are like the second riddle which itself is a single question form. Like proverbs, myths, legends and folktales we have considered, we should note the frequent use of personification in riddles. For example, both gun and drum are personified in riddles one and three above. Another point we should note is the humorous nature of the riddles. This includes both a language and a meaning effect. Imagine something knocking the head of such a respected African institution? We should also note the play on words and repetition we sometimes have in riddles. The following is a good example:

Òrúkú Tindí Tindí, Òrúkú Tindì Tindì, Òrúkú gave birth to two hundred children all decorated with antimony on their eyelids.
Ans: Beans.

We can observe the repetition of 'Tindí Tindí' in the above riddle. In fact, the above riddle starts with onomatopoeia, imitating the sound of the drums. It is like announcing the riddle and calling on people (children) to come and hear and attempt to untie the knot.

Performance

It has been emphasized that oral literature is performance-oriented. This feature is very important in oral narratives. The various narrative forms are performed. Ropo Sekoni refers to the narrator as 'performer.' In the course of storytelling, the narrator sits, stands, jumps, bends, crawls, closes his or her eyes, shouts, whispers and frequently changes his or her voice in an effort to present the true actions in the story. He also sings and claps. Sometimes he dances. The listeners also participate in the performance. They sit around the narrator, listening attentively. They chorus, sing and clap along with the narrator.

Performance is at the heart of storytelling. It is the performance that actually constitutes the real aesthetics of oral narratives. Let us identify a few narratives from the ones already produced in this book and see how they can be performed.

The first one we shall consider here is "the myth of how Emedike has no stream." The narrator may sit on a mat with the children listeners sitting around him. He may also sit on a higher stool while the children sit on the mat. If this will be performed in the class, the teacher/lecturer or one of the students would play the narrator while others sit around him or her. The narrator should normally start with the major thesis or title of the myth since the intention of the myth is to unravel the mystery behind the identified people's problem. The song "Mighty Imo give us stream" is sung by the narrator along with the children who clap along. As the narrator continues to narrate, he demonstrates. For example, one will expect that on reaching the spot:

> On one bright Eke afternoon water surged out from an area of land called Ogwugwu Nnabe between the boundary town Mbutu.

The narrator raises a finger to signify one and quickly folds his fingers and throws his fist downward as he emphasizes "one bright Eke afternoon." The narrator must make an effort to demonstrate every part of the myth clearly. His eyes should brighten up when the people of Emedike are happy, when they had the important visitor, and he should mourn when the visitor disappears.

In the legend of Olófin Àgbàlagbà Ogun, the narrator normally starts with "Once upon a time, there was a man called Olófin. He lived in Idanre..." The narrator emphasizes or stresses words such as 'mysterious' and 'fierce.' He should demonstrate the act of beheading the Olófin by suddenty throwing his own head downwards. He should as well demonstrate "Olófin conjured a big maintain..." He should as well demonstrate how his sister came to his corpse and how Olófin rises from where he was laid. The narrator and the other students should sing the various songs together. For example, the narrator should give the solo while others chorus. Everyone of them is expected to clap and dance.

The tale of "Tortoise and Squirrel" actually, like others, makes a very interesting tale if well performed. The narrator, like in other cases, has the actions mostly on him. He either makes or mars them. He must demonstrate every part. For example, as he starts and tells us that Squirrel, unlike others, secretly hides his mother to the heaven. He should demonstrate all points at which Squirrel climbs up to his mother. The narrator must modulate his voice to represent the voice of Tortoise where it is said that the Tortoise said to Squirrel: "Squirrel, you look so fresh, you don't look like others who are dying of hunger." The song sung by Squirrel must be performed by the narrator and (other) students. The students should chorus 'Tutu Ucho.' Also the way Tortoise walked to report the other animals must be imagined and acted. Tortoise's coarse voice must also be represented when he was trying to sing Squirrel's songs to Squirrel's mother and we must see the difference when Squirrel himself runs there to sing that his mother should take back the rope. The sound "Ikpokotum" must be imitated by the narrator to correctly represent the heavy noise made when all the animals fell down from heaven.

Proverbs, riddles and jokes are also rendered with some performances. Usually, hands are thrown here and there and heads are shaken. In riddles and jokes, the narrator expects the children to raise their hands while he calls on one of them to provide the answer. Others clap for the successful child. If none of them knows the answer, the narrator gives the answer and others clap for him. We should attempt to perform the riddles provided in this book in the same way.

AUDIENCE

The audience is very important part of oral performance. In oral narratives, there cannot be any performance without the audience. The audience actually consists of co-performers. The main objective of the narrator is to educate, impress, amuse and entertain members of the audience. In other words, the audience is directly at the receiving end of the narrative. However, they are not passive receivers. They are also performers, creators.

The audience responds each time the narrator and audience are really deeply interested and very involved in the narrative. Also, the audience attempts to give answers to riddles narrated by the performer (narrator). They are always happy each time they get the answers right. The audience also forms a chorus group to the song changed by the narrator. At the end of every narration, the audience is expected to identify the moral lessons contained therein. By implication, the audience also forms the critics of the oral prose. They pass their judgment through their attitude towards the tale. They show boredom, lack of interest towards an uninteresting narration. However, they listen, sing and clap during an interesting session.

EXERCISES II

1. What do we mean by the assertion that an African prose narrator knows the psychology of the children? Give examples of instances.
2. Would you say that the language of oral narratives is complex? Exemplify your answer.
3. What are unique things you observe in the names of the characters in oral prose? Exemplify.
4. Identify the similarities that exist in the language of proverbs, riddles and jokes.
5. Explain the roles of the narrator and the audience in the performance of oral narratives.

Further Reading and Work

(read and compare several chapters on different performances)

Okpewho, Isidore (Ed.) *Oral Performance in Africa*. Ibadan. Spectrum Books Ltd., 1990.

Notes and References

1. See Maud Bodkin; *Archetypal Patterns in Poetry: Psychology Studies of Imagination* (London, New York & Toronto: Oxford University Press, 1934).
2. See *Princeton Encyclopedia of Poetry and Poetics* (London & Basing-broke, Macmillan Press Ltd., 1975).
3. See *Aristotle, Horace, Longinus: Classical Literary Criticism* trans & intro T.S. Dorsch (Harmondworth: Penguin Books Ltd., 1965).
4. The Existentialist philosophers question the existence of God and raise universal problems related to creation. They believe that there is no God and if there is, he has only created man to neglect him on earth and eventually destroy him.

Chapter Eight

 **Riddles and Jokes**

DEFINITIONS

In every traditional African setting, there are various ways by which the strength of human perception, intellect, knowledge and potentials for logical reasoning are tested. Riddles are essential aspects of oral literary forms through which such tests are conducted. Riddles are obscure descriptions of certain cultural elements that the audience is asked to name or identify. Like other aspects of other oral prose narratives, riddles draw their motifs, themes, characters and settings from the whole gamut of the African Universe.

Riddles afford the audience a proper understanding of the totality of their environments in terms of philosophy, religion, politics, economics, culture and science. Riddles are stylistically constructed on the use of analogies, similar images or motifs. What probably distinguishes riddles from the other elements of prose narratives is that they demand spontaneous thinking and response from the audience.

Riddles coming at the introductory stage of a folktale arouse the interest of the children and make them take part fully in the action. A child who provides a wrong answer is made to try again. Other children are also encouraged to try again and again until the answer is found. Answers to riddles are already fixed and people are expected to know the operating formula. It is for this reason that answers do not generate conflict.

Riddles, like folktales, legends and myths, are products of the African Universe. The African traditional setting creates such cultural actions so as to enhance regular communal participation and performances.

Jokes are part of riddles. Normally, most riddles are full of humor. They do not give pleasantry to the story soon to follow. The humor component of the riddle alerts the children and arouses their interest. It has been contended that riddles and jokes also help to relieve the high tension to be created or that has been created by some fearful stories.

FUNCTIONS

Riddles and Jokes perform the follwing functions:

a) Provide a forum for increasing the vocabulary of the young ones.
b) Teach the intricacies in traditional dialects and languages.
c) Teach important lessons about life. In other words, riddles and jokes are didactic.
d) Project culture and ensure its continuity.
e) Prepare the children's minds for the folktales to follow.
f) Entertain the participants.
g) Test one's sound memory and ability to think fast.
h) Brush power of intellect, knowledge and wisdom in the budding generation.

TEXTUAL EXPLANATION OF FUNCTIONS

Riddles and jokes, like proverbs, deal with various subjects and issues of life. Therefore, we shall categorize such functions into socio-political, cultural, nature, domestic, science and logic. We shall provide at least five relevant riddles and jokes for illustration in each case.

I) Socio-Political

What passes through the King's Palace that does not greet the King?
Ans: Erosion.

Who eats with the King without clearing the plates?
Ans: Flies.

People run away from her when she is pregnant, but they rejoice when she has delivered.
Ans: Gun.

What is it that knocks the King's head?

Ans: Shaving Knife.

COMMENT: Three of the above riddles present the position of the King in any African setting. He must be respected, adored and obeyed. He is the 'Kabiyesi,' 'Ekeji orisa,' Kabiyesi the second in command to gods. In each of the above three cases, the King is disrespected, but the humorous nature of the riddles actually solves the riddles. Those who disrespect the King are negligible creatures who could not have done otherwise.

For example, how can Erosion branch to greet the King or Flies clear plates at end of a meal with the King? Also, can the knife used in shaving the King's hair actually knock his head? Let us come to think of it, what can the King do to these elements for such grievous offences of disrespect. Also, the riddle about the gun clearly shows the fear of dangerous elements or moments like war and other social conflicts and love for peace.

II) Cultural

A thing that cries in the bush without bowels.
Ans: A drum.

What is it that smiles at you as you take it to a place, but is gloomy when you are returning it?
Ans: A gourd full of palm-wine.

Everyday in the evening at home, before the girls go out, they give us kolanuts. What are they?
Ans: Goats before going for rearing.

What follows you to a person's house and insists on sitting down before you?
Ans: A walking stick.

When he is going, he faces Òyó, when he is returning, he faces Òyó.
Ans: A drum with a double face.

COMMENT: The riddles here address topics on culture. A drum is a very important element of culture. Apart from being used for communication in the local community, a drum is also at the center of almost all religious activities. We remember the role of the drum in Soyinka's *Death and the King's Horseman*. Also, palm-wine, goats for rearing and walking sticks are all cultural elements in Africa. Our people wake and sleep with them.

III) Nature

I went to the farm and the farm laughed to me.
Answer: A field of cotton when the ripe capsules are opening.

There is a stick that lies in the road, and beats everybody. It beats the father, his wife and their children.
Answer: Hunger.

What followed you to person's house and first ate the kolanuts presented to you?
Answer: Fingernails.

What is it that you cut but it refuses to be cut?
Answer: Shadow.

Tell me what followed you to the bush but did not come back with you.
Answer: Excreta.

COMMENT: The first three riddles are Hausa in origin. The first one, for example, is an admiration of the beauty of nature. The opening ripe cotton capsules, like flowers at a point of brining forth their seeds, are usually very attractive. Imagine yourself in a farm then. Hunger is also intelligently presented in the next riddle. This natural want is definitely a master of everyone, young and old. The next one is Shadow. The riddle actually describes one element that all children always try to unravel. Some hide and see what happens to their shadow. Some cut and cut their shadows; as they grow up, they realize that one's shadow is a representation of oneself.

The other two riddles here are Igbo riddles. Natural elements fingernails and excreta are their thematic focus. Generally speaking, most of the African riddles actually reflect the African natural environment.

The riddles describe every aspect of nature.

IV) Domestic

The small god of my father whom we kneel down to worship.
Answer: Grinding stone.

Immediately a child is born he comes out of a house and immediately moves towards another house.
Answer: Womb/Tomb.

COMMENT: The riddles here are from African tradition. The Grinding stone, through small in size, is very useful to every traditional African home. It is metaphorically called a 'small god' here to signify its importance. Every now and then, women kneel in front of it to grind pepper. The grinding stone is indeed one of the most important domestic implements.

The second riddle is rather philosophical. It talks of two houses in contrast: you come out of one and move towards another. The Womb and the Tomb, otherwise birth and death, are compulsory acts every living thing must go through. This riddle reflects the African strong belief in fate. It is said in African cosmology that every person's fate is determined and the man's fate is unalterable. That is exactly what the riddle projects.

V) Science and Logic

What was cut into pieces and buried but came out in a complete and bigger form.
Answer: Yam.

Òrúkú Tindí Tindí, Orúkú Tindì Tindì, Òrúkú gave birth to two hundred children, all decorated with antimony in their eyelids.
Answer: Beans.

Òrúkú Tindí Tindí, Orúkú Tindì Tindì, Òrúkú gave birth to two hundred children, all with clubs in their hands.
Answer: Baobab fruit.

A small stick that touches the ground from the sky.
Answer: Rain.

We drum in Gboji and we do not hear in Gboji.
Answer: Eyelid.

COMMENT: Like the African proverbs, riddles are also good for scientific explorations. The first relates to Biology. It discusses reproduction in plants, especially in yams. Crops such as beans and the Baobab tree are other such crops that the riddles above personify, describing their vivid forms. Also, both Rain and Eyelid are described using metaphoric elements like stick, drum, ground and sky. Nature appears in the riddles in various forms showing the links between the African cosmology.

It is therefore highly recommended that African riddles be adopted for verbal communication. This will not only make them very rich in African literary culture, it will also be a very valid forum of entertainment and expansion of one's power of wit.

EXERCISES AND FIELDWORK

1. Collect as many riddles and jokes as you can from your locality.
2. Identify the answers to these riddles and try to adduce reasons for such answers.
3. What major differences can you observe between riddles and proverbs? Are there areas of similarities? Illustrate your answers with textual examples.
4. Categorize riddles and jokes you collected to the various themes you believe they address and pass your comments on them.
5. How would you say these riddles operate within the African cosmology?

Section 2

ORAL POETRY

 *Introduction*

We want to re-emphasize our submission in Section 1 that our lessons in all the chapters of this book "are not intended to be mere memory works as has been traditional of language and literature learning in contemporary schools" especially in Africa. Our methodology remains learner and situation based. What we have done in this section is to give some samples. We emphasize the appreciative, critical and explorative skills of the learners and scholars of African oral literature and performance.

The fieldwork culture is central to oral literature and we encourage learners to go to the field. We realize that an African oral literature and performance course must emphasize the process of a return to the source. We cannot stress enough the essence of performance. We have therefore attempted a process of perfecting fieldwork strategies and methodology to make the discipline of oral literature more viable and interesting to our students.

RECOMMENDED FRAMEWORK FOR TEACHING-LEARNING PROCESS-POETRY

In this section, we also recommend guidelines for the classroom teaching of this genre. The teacher, in the context of the teaching-learning methodology of this course, is merely a guide, an adviser and a supporter. He could adopt as a sample, the following teaching processes in the lesson. Its framework should apply to all lessons.

LESSON: THE LULLABY

Objective of the Lesson

The objective is to guide the students through the appreciation and performance of lullaby. At the end of this course, students should be capable of discussing a lullaby from various traditional African communities and also understand lullaby's performance

Class Activities

I) Teacher's Role

A) Teacher asks the students to cast their minds back to when they were young. He may ask a question such as "each time you were crying, what did your mother or nurse do?

B) Teacher tells the students that the day's lesson is on lullaby.

C) Teacher writes the topic of the lesson on the board.

D) Teacher asks the pupils to open the relevant passage in their *Introduction to African Oral Literature and Performance* and read silently.

E) Teacher makes sure the students pay particular situation to the use of words and cultural references in the lullaby cited in the text.

F) Teacher asks students to do the following:

1) Explain what they understand by lullaby.

2) Discuss the examples they read in the text

3) Think if they have heard similar examples in their different traditional cultures before.

G) Teacher creates a situational atmosphere relevant to the thematic and aesthetic experiences presented in the text.

H) Teacher asks students to come out to perform the lullaby acting like the mother or elder sister. At times, carrying the baby on the back, standing or sitting with the crying baby and performing the lullaby.

II) Learner's Roles

A) Students read the text in silence and aloud, as directed by the teacher.

B) Students examine the use of language and other stylistic elements in the text.

C) Students discuss the text in the class, bringing out its theme(s) and explaining its lessons and effects.

D) Students come out to perform the text.

III) Exercises

Students should be asked to attempt the questions and carry out activities contained in the exercises at the end of the lesson.

Introduction to Section II

We are still consistent in our attempt to create viable scholarly sources as well as scholarly materials for the teaching of the Syllabi on African Oral Literature and Performance. The approach adopted in our study is relevant to the teaching of oral literature and performance at elementary, high school and university classrooms. Working guidelines are provided to encourage the understanding of the disciplines at all educational levels.

Chapter Ten

 **Religious Poetry**

INTRODUCTION

In our discussion of religious poetry, it will be essential for us to have some reflections on Chapter One in Section 1 of this book. We, therefore, refer our students to the section on "The Nature of the African Universe." The relevant linkage is the importance of African cosmology to the people's perception of the universe. The existence of the supernatural layers in the gradation of values implies that man. who is at the center of the Universe, must take care of his existence and beingness by worshipping those forces above him.

This involves rituals and sacrifices that are accompanied on many occasions by chants, songs, incantations, musical elements and dramatic oral performances. These are necessary for properly locating the importance of these supernatural forces. We must mention that the liturgical system or mode of worship in traditional societies is organized around the survival of man.

What constitutes religious poetry is fundamentally philosophical and socio-cultural. Traditional religious poetry in its various forms is related to the African belief system. Therefore, the various components of the African Universe have poetic renditions with which are associated with myths, legends and archetypal forms.

In the renditions of this genre, cultural artifacts are very important. It has been argued that cultural artifacts are essential apparatus in the poetic descriptions of the supernatural forces. Each of the gods and goddesses being praised in poetry has images and other extra verbal apparatus. These embellish the performance of the poetry and make for the actualization of the poetics of the object of description.

Religious poetry also embraces other structures of the belief system such as taboos. Religious poetry guides certain values and ethics of the social system. For example, it is believed that worshippers of certain gods and goddesses should not eat certain types of animals, hence sacrilege will be committed. It may even be specified that certain categories of people must not be involved in the ritual process as in the case of the Oro Festival in Yoruba, where women should not participate.

There is the belief that when the rain clouds are formed, people must not smoke cigarettes to avoid the wrath of Sàngó associated with thunder and lightning. This is formulated into a poetic chant

> B'ójò bá sú
> E má mà mu sìga o
> Olúkòso kò gbodò rí i

> When it threatens to rain
> Do not smoke cigarette
> Olúkòso must not see it

Olúkòso is another name for Sàngó. The contents of traditional religious poetry regulate the norms and behavior in traditional and modern societies.

However, our readers should bear in mind that we are not merely discussing the philosophy and sociology of religion, we are arguing that most of these belief systems are contained or integrated in the poetic imagination of the traditional artist.

The position of Plato may be tenable in appreciating the creative milieu and psyche of the custodians of traditional religious poetry. Plato asserts that the poet must be inspired by gods and goddesses through divine frenzy. This frenzy is translated into poetic verbalizations of the artist. In this case, it is possible that there is a reciprocal link between supernatural forces and human beings. Man is not the only dramatic personae in the performance of traditional religious poetry. The muses are at times responsible for the spiritual energies of the anointed, which may result in creative spiritual outpourings.

In our discussion of myths in volume 1, we observe that the relationship between the supernatural forces and Man can be explained by myths. "Myths therefore recreate experience of Man's interaction with the forces above him." Traditional religious poets anchor most of their compositions on myths and archetypal formations. Such myths or archetypal formations may not be explicit in the poetic composition and rendition, but there are allusions that the critic of the poetry can fall back on for his appreciation.

CATEGORIES OF RELIGIOUS POETRY

It may be very difficult for us to make a clear-cut classification of types of religious poetry. The nature of rendition and performance may not warrant this. However, it is possible to make classifications based on the occasions in which a specific type of poetry is rendered. Let us base our classification on the following examples:

1) Religious poetry dedicated to gods, goddesses, spirits and deified ancestors such as Obàtálá, Sàngó, Ògún, Wovengi, Ani, etc.
2) Religious poetry in the context of communal activities and symbiotic relationships noticeably observed in festivals. Life rhythm and spiritual strength are provoked by such communal festivals.
3) Oracular poetry.

FUNCTIONS

We shall in the course of our analysis discuss these types of religious poetry, but meanwhile, let us examine and consider the functions of religious poetry, which is a concrete verbalization of inner and spiritual yearnings of the mind. Religious poetry:

a) Expresses inner feelings that have bearing on transcendental forces and values.
b) Plays an important role in human process of appeal, supplication and invocation of the forces above him.
c) Provides a form of psychological therapy for human passions, solves their problems and resolves conflicts and desires. Solace is reposed in the forces above man; hence, man's accretions are purged for spiritual catharsis.
d) Makes philosophical statements about human existence.
e) Provides guidelines for socio-cultural survival as embedded in norms, ethics, mores and institutions.
f) Serves as a way of articulating, dramatizing and practicing communal injunctions and beliefs.
g) Provides insight into the cosmic and social origin of human problems and solutions through communal deliberations.

h) Provides pedagogical values in terms of enlightening and educating the budding generation about the codes of survival and related issues like creation.
i) Plays vital roles in cultural affairs, such as marriage, naming, and funeral.
j) Plays crucial roles in the modes of worship of modern religions in Africa as reflected in songs, chants, incantations.

ANALYSIS OF SAMPLES

Our aim in this section is to discuss the classifications of religious poetry already itemized. It may be necessary to ask our students, in how many of these classifications they have participated. What is the nature of performance? Can they recall the characteristics of the types of religious poetry identified? Along with our students, we can respond to these questions.

1) Religious poetry dedicated to the cosmic forces makes a category. In this case, gods, goddesses, spirits and ancestors are adored, praised and admired. The spiritual motivation behind this is the attempt to recall the role of such gods during creation or in protecting man. In most cases, the poet is a specialist, who is familiar with the myth and activities of the gods at the primordial state of affairs. In fact, the poet is a part of the ritual process, he/she has some intimacy with the priest or priestess. At times, the priest/priestess in the ritual process renders the poetry as in the case of the priestess of Òsun in Osogbo. This does not mean that other poets do not chant or sing during the occasion.

The settings for such poetic performance vary. It may be in the shrine of the god/goddess, an open or a secret rendezvous. There may be cultural artifacts in the shrine, representative or emblematic of the power of god/goddess. For instance, there are "Òpá Osoko" (an instrument which is made like a sword) in the shrine of the goddess of the earth and farming called Osoko. Osoko is synonymous with Ani — the goddess of the earth in Igbo society.

The typical shrine of Ògún is decorated with "màrìwò" — palm fronds, surrounded with guns, cutlasses and his other habiliments of war. A dog may be used for sacrifice depending on what has prompted the ritual. All these have mythical and cultural values. These are some of the materials that the field researcher seeks explanation about from his informants. In the ritual process, the poet who may be an ijala chanter or even the priest starts to perform:

Ò-ògún oo
Ògún Onírè okoò mi
Ògún d'ágbède o
Ògún d'ágbède
Ògún aládàá méjì
Ó fi kan sánko
Ó fi kan yènà
Ojó Ògún n torókèé bò
Aso kín lée bora?
Aso iná lée bora
Èwù èjé ló wò

Ò-ò-gún oo
Ògún Oníre my husband
Ògún created àgbède o
Ògún created the smithy
Ògún the owner of two cutlasses
He used one to clear the forest
He used one to pave the path
The day Ògún was coming from heaven
What type of clothes did he wear
He covered himself with a wrapper of fire
He wore a garment of blood.

The poet sings the praise of Ògún. In the process, references are made to professions associated with Ògún such as warring, blacksmithing, farming and hunting. But what is strategic in this excerpt is the involvement of Ogun in the myth of creation? It is believed that Obàtálá and Ògún were with "Elédàá," the Creator, during creation. After creation, every place was a jungle. It was Ògún with his two cutlasses that paved way for the other gods in their journey through the abyss to the abode of man. Wole Soyinka develops this element of traditional myth into a theory of modern literature in his book, *Myth, Literature and the African World*.

The limited space will not permit us to present a whole body of the materials collected during fieldwork. Excerpts would be cited to promoteour discussion and analysis. At a point in the ritual process, Ogun is admonished in a form of prayer not to stir confusion:

Òmgún má k'áráa 'le pò m'árá oko
Òmgún má k'árá oko pò m'árá ilé
Òmgún ló n'igbá
Òmgún ló làwo
Òmgún ló nílé
Òmgún ló l'oko
Ojó èrù Òmgún ti n bà mí ò se
Ó p'oko sórí iná
Ó p'aya s'éhìn ààrà
Ó tún wá p'alárinà s'ta gbangba
Adarin: Enií p'Ógùún ò tó l'órìsà kó wí o
Egbe: Òmgún tó l'órìsà

Òmgún, do not cause confusion between those in the
   house and on the farm
Òmgún do not cause confusion between those on
   the farm and in the house
Òmgún is the owner of calabash
Òmgún is the owner of plate
Òmgún is the owner of the farm
I have been afraid of Òmgún for long
He killed the husband on the fire
He killed the wife behind the hearth
And he still killed the intermediary at the open
   place
Solo: Let anybody who says Òmgú is indeed not a
              god pronounce
Chorus: Òmgún is indeed a god.

The poet identifies the mannerism of Òmgún. Òmgún is capable of provoking chaos anywhere. His destructive tendency is noted in the killing of the husband, the wife and the intermediary. This destructive tendency in Òmgún is quite antithetical to his creative role in the creation myth. The fear of the poet is more confirmed in the solo/chorus appraisal of Òmgún.

Ijala chant identified with Òmgún, the god of war and iron, is not only sung during religious ceremonies. It is also the professional poetic genre of hunters. As discussed by S.A. Babalola in his book, *The Content and Form of Ijala*, it is used on different other occasions such as communal festivals, funeral ceremony, naming and other social activities.

Religious Poetry

Another god highly adored in Yorùbá tradition is Sàngó. Among the Igbos, he is called Amadioha, the god of thunder and lightning. Sango is believed to have power over climate. This time, we did not record our materials in a shrine setting. The researchers were on an outing with the Sango priest and adherents for some days. Here, not the Priest but some of his adherents made up of men and women, were involved in the poetic rendition. Examples of some poetic renditions collected in the process of fieldwork would be cited. The poetic renditions depict the belief of Sango worshippers that their god can protect them and make them prosper and comfortable. Hence, he is praised and at the same time invoked for support:

> Olúkòso, èrùjèjè
> Olúbámbí, Oko oya
> Elénpe Àjobo
> Eké níí gbówó arólé
> Àwon àláàmù a máa f'owó t'ògiri
> Aburú má kùú
> Ó d'owó ìwo Sàngó
> Bóo ti b'Ólúgbón s'ayé è t'ó dùn
> Bémi náà se tèmi
> Bóo ti b'Árèsà s'ayé è
> A ló'kú lówó gborí
> Bámi se tèmi
> Bóo ti b'Árèsà s'ayé è
> A ló'kú lówó gborí
> Bá mi se tèmi
> Nkò leè dáa se

> Olúkòso, one regarded with great fear
> Olúmbámbí, the husband of Oya
> Elénpe Àjobo
> It is the rafters that support the house
> The lizards support the wall
> The stubborn one who would not die
> It is left in your hand Sango
> As you helped Olúgbón to make his life comfortable
> Assist me to do my own
> As you have helped Arèsà to make his life easy
> He who wrestled with Death and took the head
> Assist me to do my own
> I cannot do it alone

Sàngó is not usually acceptable to many people. He is sometimes considered with contempt and bias, but to his worshippers, he is regarded as a great god who can assist in moments of adversity.

Religious poetry embraces some qualities of the objects of praise as seen in the excerpt below:

>Ajala Onnaso
>Ìjì a b'oko l'órí
>Já lu'mo bi àfòn
>Alára ní yàngbe
>Oko Oya
>A ló'kú l'ówó gborí
>Okoò mi Ogin-ni ko-nko-wì
>Ajala Onnaso

>Hurricane with grass on his head
>He who falls on a person like a baobab tree
>The owner-of-thunder-in dryness
>The husband of Oya
>He who wrestled with Death and took the head
>My husband, Ogin-ni-ko-nko-wì

There are indications in the above poetic composition that Sango is another tough and troublesome god. We have referred in Volume I to the mythic legend that discusses his status as a former Alafin of the Old Oyo Empire, then deified as god. The imagery of the hurricane provokes the violence associated with Sango's personality.

We also noted in the course of our fieldwork that religious poetry in this category is even rendered along with musical accompaniments. At some moment, the tempo of action is heightened by the tempo of drumbeats. A large body of religious poetry may even be produced by drummers. The following religious praise of Sango is produced by "Bàtá" drum:

>Sàngó, Sàngó, ako Sàngó
>Eni tó bá f'ojú di Sàngó
>Sàngó á pa á
>Sàngó, abojú k'oro
>A boro o koju
>A bìwà pèlé bí ako sèbé
>À f'eni tí Sàngó ó pa

> A f'eni tí Sàngó tí kogílá kolù
> À f'eni tí Sàngó ó pa
>
> Sàngó, Sàngó, brave Sàngó
> He who despises Sàngó
> Sàngó will kill him
> Sango with bitter eyes
> Of bitter eyes
> With a gentle character like a male adder
> He who Sàngó will kill
> He who Sàngó will waylay aggressively
> Except he who Sango will kill.

It implies that the critic or researcher of African traditional poetry must understand some language of musical accompaniments. The qualities of Sàngó, such as bravery, aggressiveness and violent anger, are properly documented by the traditional drummer-poet. After the poetic production by the drummer poet, the traditional poet resumes praising Sàngó.

We have decided to discuss Obàtálá or Òrìsàálá last in this type of religious poetry because he is the supreme divinity of Yorùbáland and he is regarded as the god of creation. It can be likened to Murungu, the Agikuyu god of creation. In the beginning, there was absolute purity, because it was believed that the "evil-one" had not polluted the earth. This is the reason why Obàtálá, who was present during creation, is praised for his qualities of purity both in appearance and attitude. Hence, he is described as:

> Obàtálá
> Apàgbínje léhìn ìkarahun
> Olúfón Adé
> Omo Aládée sésé efun
> Òrìsà tó rí'yò tó jòfún
> Ò r'épo, ó je 'láa rè ní funfun
> Olúfón lólá Òròlú
> Olúfon lólá ohun gbogbo ní funfun ní funfun
> Kúkúmoo baba funfun ni
> Sòkòtòo rè funfun ni
>
> Obàtálá
> Who kills and eats snail from the back of the shell
> Olúfón Adé

> Son of the owner of the crown of white chalk
> The god who sees salt but eats tasteless food
> He sees palm-oil but eats okro soup plain
> Olúfón lólá Òròlú
> Olúfón lolá, everything is in white, is in white
> The jumper of father is white
> His knickers is white

It was observed during fieldwork that all the worshippers of Obàtálá dressed in white costumes. Òrìsààlá is an embodiment of the Yorùbá ideals of ethical purity. Consequently, he demands a high sense of morality from his disciples. The rituals and worship are performed with immaculateness. Worshippers and the shrine must be arrayed in white.

In Yoruba mythology, it is ardently believed that Obàtálá was present with "Elédàá," the Creator, during creation. He was the arch-sculptor responsible for shaping various human parts and determining their existence. As the god of creation, he is endowed with the power to make his worshippers wealthy and productive. The poet praises him thus:

> Àdìmúlà
> Ikú tíí báni d'ìgbé'lé k'ólá ranni
> Ó so enìkan soso d'igba-a-a
> So mí dirún
> So mí d'igba
> So mí d'òtà-lé-'lé gbè-je-ènìyàn

> Àdìmúlà
> Death who lives with somebody and enriches him
> He turns only a person to two hundred persons
> Let me multiply
> Make me to two hundred
> Make me one thousand four hundred and three persons.

It is therefore not surprising that the religious poetry reaches a crescendo in terms of the tempo of rendition and that of the rhythms of the drum production. In a solo/chorus poetic production, which eventually links the performer to the audience, worshippers are advised about the need to make rituals and sacrifices to Obàtálá:

Religious Poetry

> Adarin: Obàtálá ni e rúbo sí
> Orìsàálá ni e sìn
> Obàtálá ni e rúbo sí
> Elegbe: Obàtálá ni e rúbo sí
> Orìsàálá ni e sìn
> Obàtálá ni e rúbo sí
>
> Solo: We say you should sacrifice to Obàtálá
> Orisala should be worshipped
> We say you should sacrifice to Obàtálá
> Chorus: We say you should sacrifice to Obàtálá
> Òrìsàálá should be worshipped
> We say you should sacrifice to Obàtálá

Religious poetry forms a substantial part of modes of worship in many parts of Africa. Mazisi Kunene discusses the various gods and goddesses among the Zulu and how they are adored through poetry. His Epic, titled *Anthem of the Decade* is celebration of the roles of goddesses in the traditional African setting.

2) Religious poetry in the context of communal activities and relationships are related to festivals and ceremonies that have collective communal importance. Such festivals may assume religious dimension because they emanate from creation myths and the survival of a lineage or clan. The New Yam Festival among the Igbos is a commonplace in African societies. The Òsun Festival in Òsogbo also falls into this category.

Religious-oriented communal festivals are at times concerned with deification of ancestors. This is the case with the Òsun Festival. It is meant to celebrate the ancestor that rescued the people and provided shelter for them. During such festivals, there are poetic compositions that reflect the myths behind the deification of some human beings as we see in the case of Sàngó.

The ritual setting at the Òsun shrine happens to be the area where the founder of the town first sojourned. This is more or less an historic and mythical fortress. The river goddess is symbolic of the spiritual essence, existence and survival of the people of the community. Apart from the teeming population of worshippers, the Priestess and the virgin lady "Arugba" are singled out as the most prominent and revered dramatis personae. The Priestess herself dresses in gorgeous traditional costumes. She renders utterances in form of prayers and warnings that are poetic:

> Eni tó bá f'ojú d'oba
> Àwówó á wó o
>
> He who despises the King
> Destruction will befall him.

The Egúngún Eléwe Festival and the Okura Festival have their respective poetic contents. Masquerade festivals, elaborate traditional rituals in many parts of Africa, have the contents of what we regard as communal religious poetry. It is important for our students to dig out a category of poetry in their various communities.

3) Oracular poetry is fast rooted in metaphysics and associated with the Ifá oracle. This aspect of religious poetry based on occultic forces validates Plato's theory of divine poetic imagination. The Ifá Priest is spiritually anointed and his activities are highly inspired and controlled by the cultic hemisphere occupied by the Oracle itself. The Oracle is a divine force, but it assumes poetic force in the manner of articulation and rendition of divine blessings, warnings and prophecies.

Oracular poetry is organized on complex magical and formulaic contents and stylistic patterns. The language of rendition is mythopoetic, since all the forces of the cosmic abode are put together into the divine creative potentials. Oracular poetry assumes a power source for tracing the crises and problems of mankind.

Individuals, groups, communities and larger societies rely on the Ifa Oracle for the conduct of their affairs. We can recognize this from the literature emerging from the cultural womb of tradition, such as Ola Rotimi's *Kurunmi* and *The Gods Are Not to Blame*. It is also necessary to remark that Oracular poetry is constructed on occultic, cabalistic, incantatory and magical formats.

We want to locate the structural process of oracular poetry. The oracular poet is highly specialized and it is difficult for a freelance to perform this function. We can identify three stages in oracular poetry:

A) Invocation
B) Supplication
C) Admonition/Divination

A) Invocation

This is the dramatic beginning during which the Ifa priest, the voice of the oracle and the poet, spiritually and solemnly invokes the supernatural forces. As a stylistic device, it is the juncture at which he calls the attention of the force associated with the divinity to listen to him. This conscious poetic attempt of recognizing their presence is to solicit their divine support. The poet praises their potentials. Here, we want to cite a case study of a woman, who is barren and who consults an Ífá Priest. It is from our fieldwork experience. The poet goes into invocation by chanting:

> B'álàrà bà jì,
> Àwon Alárá a máa p'olúwo rè nílé Irá
> B'Ájerò bá jí
> Àwon Ajerò a máa p'Ajerò lóde Ìjerò
> Ifá Àgbonmìrègún
> Ìwo ni mo jí rí lóníí
> Ìbà Akódá, Ìbà Asèdá
> Ìbà Òrúnmìlà Ìbà re

> When the Alaras wake up
> The Alárás invoke cultic head at Ará
> When the Ajeròs wake up
> The ijero invoke Ajerò in Ìjerò
> Ifá Àgbonmìrègún
> It is you I wake up to see this morning
> Homage to the creator
> Homage to you Òrúnmìlà, homage to you.

B) Supplication

Having paid homage to the forces of the Ífá Oracle, the priest-poet goes on to make a plea of knowledge and wisdom that will enable him to discern and diagnose effectively the woman's problem. At this juncture, he invokes the source of the origin and fountain of knowledge and wisdom:

> Alárá ló l'ogbón
> Alákòtún ló nìmòràn
> Oba Òràngún ilé Ìlá ló l'omi iláwúsere
> Nbá r'éni tí n r'Òrángún ilé Ìlá
> Nbá fún un L'ágbè yere

Kó ponmi Ìláwúsere fún mi wá
Òun ló d'Ífá fún Òbàràkòsì
L'ójó tí n lo Ogun kóyèkóyè
Mo ní Ifá,
Tóo bá ti jí máa jí mi
Ifá wá ní tó bá se bíi t'omo òun ni
Isu kìí p'eyin kó gbàgbé ongo
Àgbàdo kìí pon'mo kó gbàgbé irùkèrè
Ojú mérìndínlógún l'Oníyèmúyè ní
Gbogbo won ní fíí mu mi
Òrúnmìlà, Àgbonmìrègún fún mi lóye tèmi
Òyè là kí n rína
Òyè là.

Alárá is the owner of wisdom
Alákòtún is the owner of advice
Oba Òràngún of Ìlá is the owner of water of Ìláwúsere
If I can get a person going to orangun in Ìlá
I would have given him the gourd of yeere
To fetch for me the water of Ìláwúsere
He makes a divination for Òbàràkòsì
On the day he was going to the battle of memory drain
I say Ifá
Wake me up as soon as you wake up
Ifa says if it is for his own child
The germinating yam does not forget the bud
The maize does not carry its without tassel
The Oníyèmúyè plants has sixteen openings
All are used for drinking water
Òrúnmìlà Àgbonmìrègún, give me my own intellect
Cloud disappear and let me see clearly
Cloud disappear

This is a concrete demand verbalized in strong poetic terms. It is evident that supplication has a strong verbal construction, depicting the strength of the creative consciousness and vision of the artist, the protégé of the Ifá Oracle. Supplication is made up of historico-magical contents, which the solo audience, the barren woman, cannot unravel. Some clear vision emerges towards the end of the plea. This is the stage that paves the way for knowledge and knowing.

C) Admonition/Divination

Supplication logically produces counseling from the oracle to the priest-poet. Admonition opens the way for knowledge through which the priest in turn can counsel or advise his own client, the barren woman. There is no strict demarcation between admonition and divination. The difference is in the logic of sequence. Now that the priest-poet has been counseled, he is now imbued with the knowledge of knowing. It is through this knowledge that he diagnoses the woman's problem and profers solution. But the divination may still be robed in mystery, since the poet is still operating in a mythical and magical world. The crisis of the woman is still mystified in the mythopoetic language.

However, admonition implies that the priest-poet intercedes on behalf of his client, appealing to the oracle to open up fortune to solve her problem. A mythical unraveling is thus provoked by this admonition. For example, the Yoruba Ifa Priest chants thus:

> The voice force of males and females
> The voice force of t he initiated and the uninitiated
> Ogwugwu force!
> Urasi force
> Twenty spirits forces!
> Four hundred spirits forces
> Ofo which is part of tree,
> Ofo which is hung
> Ofo which is in the bag
> Arise all of you
> God ask the Father ask Mother Earth force,
> Ask medicinal leaves
> Ask God the Father
> Who created the helpless
> You ask the habitable Earth who spoils
> Agwu the white ash.

Characteristically, the divination beckons to and invokes the cosmic forces at the morning setting. The invocation touches on the creation motif, since the poet reflects on both males and females, initiated and uninitiated. The poet invokes many cosmic forces in their different abodes. These forces have to work in unison to protect the mortal world. The healing force of the divine power is indicated when the poet invokes the "medicinal leaves." This is a symbol of the healing power of the cosmic forces. The poet solicits for those who are "created helpless." The emphasis on the "habitable earth" towards the end of the divination is to seek the protective and productive power of the "mother earth." The nature of this Igbo divination is of a general appeal to the cosmic forces for the survival and existence of men.

No matter the name given to the oracular poetry in different parts of Africa, its total philosophical relevance to the socio-cultural values and norms cannot be overemphasized. In an interview with Yemi Eleburubon, a renowned Yoruba oracular poet and diviner, he exalts the power of the Ifa oracle:

> We can say that Ifá functions,
> It acts as a doctor,
> Philosopher, it prophesies about
> the future. It also has generic
> link with Yorùbá language, origin
> of towns and everything around us.
> Ifa is involved in everything.[2]

It is also necessary to emphasize the fundamental essence of the Ifá oracle in Yorùbá tradition to the genre of poetry. Other gods and goddesses have links with poetry because of their mythical role in the creation process and the potentials of their worshippers in composing adulatory poems for them. Ifa assumes the role of the original Yorùbá god of craftsmanship to which poetry is germane, but the Ifa oracle is the fountainhead of creative poetic impulse. The craftsmanship of Ògún is more acknowledged in occupational creativity. It is logical to argue that while "Ìjálá" is not necessarily the creative production of Ògún himself; oracular poetry is a philosophical construction of Ifá.

STYLISTICS AND NATURE OF PERFORMANCE

It is essential to recall our view that the language of religious poetry is condensed, specialized and inherently loaded with metaphysical elements. This implies that the creative imagination too is a product of some spiritual motivation and impulse. Besides, the nature of performance again differs in types of religious poetry. We shall be able to briefly explore the stylistic contents and nature of performance in religious poetry. It will then be necessary for us to consider the form and method of delivery, musical instruments, the audience, the stylistic and linguistic components of this type of poetry.

Religious Poetry

The Ìjálá chanter who is the poet associated with Ògún, the god of war and iron, is a specialist in his own field. The nature of delivery will be determined by the occasion when the god is being respected and praised. If it is in the shrine, the composition of the artist may vary. It may even be an individual chanter. Where they are many, there may be the leader, who moderates the poetic rendition at various stages. What is noted in the course of fieldwork is that the leader is highly experienced and vast in the poetry. Others may consist of those about to graduate and those still fresh in the pupilage stage.

Though there is no concrete adherent to rules, usually, a religious priest of Ògún wears smart costumes called "Gbérí Ode." On the dyed black costumes are hung charms and remains of animals killed during expeditions. The hunters who constitute the body of the artist may even carry their guns. Occasionally, they shoot into the sky; the echo corresponds with that of their godfather. During the Ògún Festival, a dog is usally sacrificed.

It is observed that oral performances may be at times complex. A stage is set. The chanters may stand or sit around the shrine depending on the needs of a particular moment. As already pointed out, the group may be led by one or more specialists, who dictate the tempo of action. At times, they constitute the main singers and the others chorus. Those who are still in the pupilage stage try to follow their master's chants.

A spectacular element of this type of poetry is the use of musical accompaniments. Any type of drum can be used to produce the specialized dance rhythm associated with this category of poetry. "Bàtá," "Dùndún" and "Emele" can be adjusted to suit or produce special rhythm. Again, the Ìjálá artist engaged in this type of poetry and other worshippers must have to know the special dance step.

The application of musical accompaniments must also be well scheduled. At times, the chanters engage in their art without any drumming. At the culmination of a rendition the chanter(s) logically invite the drummers to add the accompaniments. This may lead to some period of dancing not only of the chanter but also by worshippers. When the chanters produce their art without any musical accompaniment, the team leader of the drummers occasionally praises the chanter, reminding him of some historical or mythical events.

Indirectly or directly, we have indicated the importance of the audience in the oral performance of this type of religious poetry. If the setting is in the shrine, as many worshippers as the shrine can contain will be inside. Others may be outside. If it is an open place, the scope of the audience is not limited to the worshippers alone. At this juncture, it is transformed into a communal fiesta. After all, everybody patronizes Ògún. This encourages the dramatic scenario of performer-audience rapport.

The delivery of religious poetry of Sàngó or Oya assumes a dimension slightly different from that of Ògún. As earlier mentioned, the worshippers after an elaborate service, including sacrifices and rituals in the shrine or Sàngó Priest's house, move out into the community. Apart from the immediate audience constituted by the worshippers, the community constitutes another level of audience. The worshippers have to follow the Chief Priest who is out on performance visit for seven days.

In the poetic rendition, the chanter may be a female or a male, the sonorous voice of whom we hear throughout the outing. It is occasionally that the audience participates in chanting, with the exception of when the drummers sensitize the audience into dance.

In terms of costumes, a Sàngó Priest wears specialized habiliments decorated with cowries and charms. He carries "Osé," an object made of a special type of wood, with the structure of an axe but highly charmed. At times, the priest, throughout the seven days, chews a magical chewing stick and orogbo and murmurs relevant incantations.

The system of delivery of oracular poetry seems to be far different from what obtains in the worship of Ògún and Sàngó. Whether during a meeting of the Ifá Priests of the visit of a patient to an Ifa Priest, the audience is always selective and the performance conducted in a kind of seclusion and secrecy.

This has been illustrated in the course of our discussion of the case of the barren women. On this type of occasion, musical accompaniments are not involved. The Ifá priest uses his "Opón-Ifá," "Òpèlè" and cowries with which he conjures and consults from time to time. These constitute artifacts in religious poetry. When the Ifá Priests or Babaláwos are out on a special occasion, which is rare, the only predominant musical accompaniment is the sonorous "agogo," which produces a highly metaphysically loaded poetic form. In the traditional practice, one may not be able to locate any standing audience with the oracular poetry, except individuals or groups or representatives of a community who go to consult the oracle. However, with the attempt to modernize the Ifá worship, the worshiper-audience rapport assumes a new dimension. Ifá assumes

Religious Poetry

the liturgical pattern or mode of worship, which provides room for a large congregation, which now makes the audience.

The stylistic composition of religious poetry is highly influenced by what Biodun Jeyifo describes as "the pantheon of gods, deities, and supernatural beings and archetypal characters."[3] The nature of diction, the complex nature of the language and the use of classical allusions are produced by this cosmic hemisphere.

Religious poetry is therefore noted for its mythical exposition and the use of mythopoetic language. This is the type of language and poetic force that has its fountain in the cosmic abode. In the sample used on Ògún, there is a trend of the Yorùbá myth of creation, which must be properly understood before any meaningful appreciation can be made. Mythic legend is also embedded in the religious poetry dedicated to Sàngó.

The essence of such mythic poetic force is reflected in the use of language and the choice of words. At times words used are a complex formation of a highly mytho-magical origin. At times, the poetry has an incantatory force as in the one dedicated to Sàngó.

> It is rafters that support the house
> The lizards support the wall

A more condensed use of mythopoetic language is found in oracular poetry. This is not surprising since oracular poetry is the direct voice of the Ifá Oracle itself. The mythopoetic language has its functional rigour in the dramatic nature of oracular poetry. The Ifá priest, who is at the same time the poet, consults with the invisible forces. He in turn consults with the human world. Classical allusions are also common in religious poetry. It is advisable for our students to work on samples in this text and materials collected from the field to appreciate critically the language situation in religious poetry.

The poet of religious poetry also draws complex images constructed from the materials of the metaphysical and physical realms. For instance, Sàngó is described as:

> Hurricane with grass on his head
> He who falls on a person like a baobab tree

These lines illustrate the characteristic violent temper and disposition of Sàngó. Such images are further invoked through the use of studded epithets or word pictures such as "the owner of –thunder-in dryness/The husband of Oya." Obàtálá is lauded with epithets such as "the son of the owner of the crown of White chalk," a symbolic representation of Obàtálá's puristic essence.

What is probably more invigorating in this type of poetry is the arrangement of lines whether in the form of repetition, contrasts and antithetical balancing of ideas. We give our students the task of locating these in the samples.

CONCLUSION

The essence of existence is survival and survival is linked to the spiritual and social forces that support man. Poetry is a practical effort through which man invokes, consolidates and re-affirms his source of being. Depending on beliefs, religious poetic forms vary and the approaches of rendition, performance and practice vary. We have abundantly provided study samples in this chapter to encourage our students to be able to do some more elaborate work. One thing is clear. The divine will of man does not create his creative potentials and aesthetic strength as revealed in our discussion of religious poetry.

EXERCISES AND FIELDWORK

1. Explain the link between African cosmology and religious poetry.
2. Identify the classification of religious poetry through explanatory and illustrative examples.
3. Explain how the spiritual functions of religious poetry can be transformed into social relevance.
4. Discuss the various performance and stylistic contents of oracular poetry. Illustrations must be from your own traditional setting.
5. Is it possible to draw any relationship between traditional religious poetry in terms of composition and performance and songs in modern religions?
6. Conduct a fieldwork in your community and collect and compare different types of religious poetry.

Further Reading and Work

Abimbola, Wande. "Continuity and change in the verbal, artistic, ritualistic, and Performance traditions of Ifa divination."

---. *Ifa divinatory Poetry*. New York: NOK Publishers, 1977.

---. *Ifa: an Exposition of Ifa Literary Corpus*. Ibadan: Oxford University Press, 1976.

Ilesanmi T. M. "Language of African Traditional Religions" Research in Yoruba Language and Literature. Burbank: Technicians of the Secred. No. 4, May 1993: 63-7.

Murphy Joseph M. and Mei-Mei Sanford. *Osun Across the Waters: a Yoruba Goddess in Africa and the Americas*. Bloomington: Indiana University Press, 2001.

Notes and References

1. See Ezike Ojiaku, I.P.A. "Igbo Divination Poetry." *Abu afa: An Introduction*. No. 150, 1984, p. 37.
2. An excerpt from an interview with Chief Yemi Eleburubon, collected during a fieldwork exercise.
3. See Biodun Jevifo 'Soyinka Demythologized: Notes on a Materialist Reading of a *A Dance of the Forest, The Road* and *Kongi's Harvest*. Quoted in Niyi Osundare's "Words of Iron, Sentences of Thunder: Soyinka's Prose Style" in *African Literature Today* Vol. 13, p. 24.

Chapter Eleven

 **Incantatory Poetry**

INTRODUCTION

It is necessary to call the attention of our readers or students to the connection between the last chapter and this one. It is very important for them to note the relationship between the two chapters. As we continue our discussion, we shall get a clear clarification about this connection.

Incantatory poetry can be discussed in relation to the metaphysical deposits of the African Universe. Every stratum of the hierarchy of values of the African Universe has potentials of magical elements that interweave the cosmological and social components. Incantatory poetry is therefore associated with this magical world, identified through its magical formulaic codes. Charms, armlets and other magical apparatus referred to as "juju," have bearings with incantations. Incantations constitute another category of poetic expression in oral literary tradition.

We can therefore describe incantations as magic-oriented formulaic expressions, saturated with mystical power of emotions and loaded with word images and contents that are highly mythopoetic. The origin and nature of this type of poetry seems to limit the audience and those who participate in it. It is also reasonable to argue that the belief of Africans in the power of magic and charms makes the audience of incantatory poetry almost unlimited. This is not to say that we do not have the traditional custodians of these magical and formulaic expressions. Albert Mosley[1] gives the catalogue of those that we can regard as the real poets of the incantatory poetry.

LOCATING INCANTATIONS

It will be necessary for us to clarify the placement and location of incantatory poetry in terms of usage. First, incantatory poetry is employed or applied in conjunction with charms and other magical materials. Such materials must be accompanied by incantatory poetry to make them functional and meaningful. For instance, a form of charm called "Ase" among the Yorubas may not have effect without rendering the relevant incantations. The supplicant holds a small horn containing medicinal soap, touching the soap with the tip of his tongue and saying:

> Igi tí Sàngó bá pa kìí r'ójú rúwé
> Òkú tó bá kú kìí r'ójú s'òrò
> Àsìse ló bájá tó fi dó 'yàá rè
> Eni odò bá n gbé lo
> Kìí r'ójú bèrè aso è mó
> Èyí a wí f'ógbó l'ogbó gbó
> Èyí a wí f'ógbà l'ogbàá gbà
> Ohun tí mo bá l'ágbájá so lánìí
> Ni kó gbà o.

> The tree struck by Sàngó becomes barren
> A dead person does not talk
> It is a mistake that makes the dog to copulate his mother
> A person being carried away by the river
> Cannot ask for his clothes
> It is what one tells 'ogbó' that 'ogbó' accepts
> Whatever I tell this person today
> He must accept.

In terms of usage, certain conditions must be met. The user may be asked not to eat anything before usage. He may even be told not to talk to anybody after usage, before confronting his target or enemy. These prescriptions create dramatic actions that are highly magical and ritualistic. A priest who has taken sacrifice to "Orita," or crossroads, in the middle of the night is instructed not to look back once the incantations are made. A violation may produce an archetype of the biblical wife of Lot. But if we may ask, how many of our readers are familiar with the application of incantations? A practical involvement will give a full import and essence of usage.

Incantatory poetry may be used without any magical material. Such incantations have inherent magical potentials.

FUNCTIONS

In their philosophical and psychological state, human beings are bundles of contradictions. The problems of the society may even compound the unstable conditions. As in the case of religion, people look for forces that can rescue them and make their existence possible and peaceful. Incantatory poetry associated with magical apparatus serve the same purpose. We can then recall what J.S. Mbiti refers to as the "vital force" in the survival of human beings. There are many ways in which incantations provide this safety valve for human existence. Incantatory poetry:

A) Initiates or boosts luck and fortunes in human endeavours as in the case of incantations associated with 'Awure' among the Yorubas.
B) Stabilizes human psychology by its philosophical power of protection as in the case of Yoruba incantation used for "Isora," "Modarikan" and "Agbelepota."
C) Affords man the opportunity of looking into the future and predicting the motion or direction of human existence.
D) Assists in negating the destructive power of other cosmic or supernatural forces and even dangers posed by other elements in the cosmic and human environment.
E) Explores the relevance of metaphysics in language development.
F) Suggests the scientific force emanating from the cosmological predilection of Africans about their universe.
G) Revitalizes the physique, intellect and memory as in the case of "ajidewe" and "isoye" in Yoruba tradition.
H) Affords the artists the opportunity of recalling, composing philosophical, cultural, genealogical or historical records. This can be easily located in incantations used in oracular poetry.
I) However, incantatory poetry may be used for negative effects, comprising a negation of all the positive enumerated Evils, bad amen and malignity can be invoked on people through incantations. People's memory can be sealed. People can be turned lunatic, etc.

ANALYSIS OF SAMPLES

We can now discuss the relevance and importance of incantatory poetry by analyzing some samples. We may not attach a particular function to a particular specimen, but we shall attempt a general explanation to really bring out the functions.

The first sample to be discussed is concerned with protection, but such an incantatory poem may be or may not be used in conjunction with magic or charms. "Modarikan," among the Yorubas, is to neutralize the conspiracies of enemies. This can be regarded as an extreme form of protection, which may have a dastardly effect on the opponent or enemy. The incantatory poetry goes thus:

>Wón ní orí igi ni igi gbé rúwé
>Orí òpè ni òpè yo ògómò
>Bí àgbònrín bá làwo gàgàrà
>Orí ara rè ni fií rù ú
>Bí Ségisóòrùn bá ségi nígbó
>Orí ara rè ni fií rù ú
>Eni tó bá dárí kan apá.
>Apá a pa á
>Ipá omodé kò ká igi osè
>Torí pé òjiji nigií dá
>Òjiji ni Sàngó í fa igi tu
>Òsán gangan làá túfò ejò
>Okùnrin ni, obìnrin ni
>Ló bá ro tèmi níbi
>Òsángangan ni kí n gbó ikú rè

>They say it is on the tree that the tree produces leaves
>It is on top of the palm tree that the bud emerges
>If the antelope produces huge horns
>It carries them with its own head
>If Ségisóòrùn gathers firewood in the forest
>It carries them with its own head
>Any person who conspires against 'apá'
>"Apá" kills the person
>It is unexpectedly that Sàngó kills a tree
>Because the tree breaks unexpectedly
>It is in the afternoon that the news of the death of snake is broken

> Whether it is a man or a woman
> That wishes me evil
> Let the news of his death be broken in the afternoon.

This specimen is highly philosophical, dealing with the protection of the poet. The poet may not necessarily be an herbalist or a dibia. He may just be an individual who feels that he is being threatened by some people around. That poetic force may be conferred on him by an herbalist, the traditional custodian of the poetry.

The pattern of operation in the poem is worked out through the logic of thesis and antithesis. The poet accumulates various characteristics of natural phenomena, such as trees, animals and thunder, to set a premise for the destruction of the enemy who wishes him evil. The ability of the poet to draw these powerful analogical inferences is built from his cosmic and mythic intellect. The power of creativity and aesthetic formula in this case are produced from the generic wisdom and intellect of the cosmic worlds.

The reference point in the first six lines is the backfiring effects on the enemy wishing the poet evil. The central physiological segment is "Orí," or head, which traditionally is believed to be the strategic location in human body responsible for success or failure. Leaves are only produced on the top of a tree and the budding palm frond "Ògómò" surges on the top of the palm tree. The general implication carried by all these parallel structures is that of a "boomerang." It is the evil invoked by the enemy, that he himself will reap.

The movement towards the seeking of total collapse of the evil-doer is gradual. In the second segment of the poem, the invocation of the ultimate wrath of death on the enemy is more brutal. The piling up of the images and word pictures for invoking death authenticates this observation. If a tree breaks unexpectedly, and if Sàngó can uproot a tree unexpectedly, the total implication is that the enemy will die in such a sudden manner. As one of the Alafins of the Old Oyo Empire, Sàngó, was noted for his magical power, symbolized in thunder, his powerful arsenal of destruction.

The last two lines that summarize the poem negate the concept of death wished for the enemy. The poet who is the one seeking protection is sure that the enemy can only be making attempts. He cannot succeed. One strategic issue emanating from the use of this type of incantation is that confidence of safety instilled in the poet-user.

We may wish to consider another example of this type of incantatory poetry:

> Bí Aláró bá dáró
> Owó ara rè ni kó fi pa
> Bí Ònlosùn bá losùn
> Owó ara rè ni kó fi pa
> Èlulùú tó bá p'òjò
> Orí ara rè ló pè é lé
> B'ókùnrin, b'óbìnrin ló bá robi sí mi
> Orí won ni kó dà sí.

> When the dryer prepares the dye
> Her hands first get dyed
> When the camwood owner prepares camwood
> The camwood first dresses her hand
> "Èlulùú" that invites the rain
> It invites it on its own head
> Whether it is men or women who think evil against
>   me
> Let the evil fall on them.

The same structure of analysis emerges as in the first example. The poet-versus-the-enemy-syndrome is again signaled, but the key emphasis by the poet is that of the enemy himself, embracing the evil he proposes for another person. The enemy first embraces the evil as indicated in the poem. The bird "Èlulùú" is noted for calling the rain, but the rain eventually falls on "Èlulùú" since it has no abode for protection. Again, this carries the motif of "boomerang." This motif is also reflected in the proverb: "it is the stone thrown to the palm tree that the palm tree sends back to the thrower".

This evil-aversion poetic device is also illustrated by an incantatory poem used to ward of evil among the Nupe people. The rendition goes thus:

> Eba do zhigi, zhigi
> Eba do zhigi, zhigi
> A lisa book a lisa ko kpato
> Ekagi a duwa; da bodin lo mi
> Lo kun kpata da cin a mile
> La kpangi; ace za wongi ka
> Ce na cice soko ca ce a
> Gomichi gaga ago dabo
> Eza ga mi nga za

Incantatory Poetry

Ta pati o le y a ndozhi ye
Ki fino le fin o
Tsaku tsaku bante
U ge ye dzu eni a ye da
Eni ma ga ye do
Edun a ye fe a
Efogi fo lo fo zhin

Eba is shaking
You the most powerful
Thorn of adoa tree, you can enter into a home
    through any part
Go to the stream and look at their house
La kpangi; a man can be dodged
But no one can dodge god
Sitting at home to boast, what about the forest
If you think you are powerful,
Someone else is more powerful than you,
You stand on the hill and see the future
You can stand while sleeping
Bante made of wood cannot be worn
If you wear it, you can't tuck in its tail
If you can tuck in its tail
You can't sit down
La 'kpangi-pierces through any thickness and
    returns safe.

The mythical and spiritual relevance of this incantation cannot be over emphasized. The incantatory poetry takes the form of an invocation of the spiritual force "Eba" to assist in finding the cause of evil omen in the life of an individual or the society in general. The incantation is a powerful force to expose the cause of any evil occurrence or sickness before the healing. The poetic form praises the qualities of the spirits, "Eba" and "La kpangi." The latter has an omniscient strength and knowledge. The healing power of the incantation is metaphorically embedded in the line that portrays these spirits as more powerful than any source of evil. This is portrayed in the imagery of the "bànté" made of wood that cannot be worn and if worn, its tail cannot be tucked in. "Bànté" is a form of traditional knicker usually made of cloth. Also, La kpangi has the efficacy to pierce through any thickness: he has the supernatural force to neutralize any evil force.

"Àwúre," as it is commonly called among the Yorùbás, is a kind of power charm with which incantatory poetry is associated. It is generally used for invoking positive effects of love, kindness and harmonious world order by the user. Let us consider the following lines:

>Bí òrí bá f'ojú kanná
>Yíyó níí yó
>Bí epo bá f'ojú kanná
>Yíyó níí yó
>Bí àdí bá f'ojú kanná
>Yíyó níí yó
>Ibi tí mo n lo lónìí
>K'ómodé y'ónú sí mi
>Kí àgbà yónú sí mi
>Agbe ní gb'ére pàdé Olókun
>Àlùkò ní gb'ére pàdé Olósà
>Odíderé ní gb'ére pàdé Oníwòó
>Oníwòó omo odò Obà
>Omo Odò Obà Atólúmere
>Èlà Ìwòrì
>Wá gb'ére pàdé mi lónìí

>If the sheabutter is exposed to fire
>It melts
>If the palm oil is exposed to fire
>It melts
>If the palm kernel oil is exposed to fire
>It melts
>Where I am going today
>Let the children love me
>Let the old love me
>It is 'Agbe' that bring fortune to Olókun
>It is 'Àlùkò' that brings fortune to Olósà
>It is Odidere that brings fortune to Oníwòó
>Oníwòó, the son of Odò Obà
>Odò oba, the son of Atólúmere
>Èlà Ìwòrì
>Bring fortune for me today

This is an incantatory poetry in which the poet-user seeks people's love towards him. If he is loved, luck and fortunes can easily attend his way. Certain objects are situated against a position of hope. Palm oil, palm kernel oil and sheabutter when situated against fire make for a positive motion, which the poet-user is actually looking for.

The poet creates an interlude, interjecting his incantatory mind and thought with what he actually wants. He then resumes in his conjuring some powerful images and archetypal mythic values. "Agbe," "Àlùkò" and "Odíderé" are all birds of fortune influencing the success of Olókun, Olósà, and Oníwòó respectively. Behind the poet's incantatory exposition is the historical and mythical value that reinforces not only the aesthetic effect of the rendition, but its utilitarian essence. Our students need to do some investigation to be able to know the philosophical relevance of those birds mentioned in the incantation. They also need to probe why "Iwo" as a town is referred to as "Omo odò obà Atólúmere." It is these probings that can enhance the students' knowledge of some names, expressions and values that go deep into tradition. We can take another example on the use of "Àwúre":

> Sìnkínnímìnì, Sìnkínnímìnì, Sìnkínnímìnì
> Sìnkínnímìnì a fi àìmoni kóni móra
> Àse iná niná fíí m'óko
> Àse òòrùn ni òòrun fi n là
> Ìwà ata ò dáa
> Ìwà ata ò sunwòn
> Gbogbo ayé níí b'áta re
>
> Sìnkínnímìnì, Sìnkínnímìnì, Sìnkínnímìnì
> Sìnkínnímìnì embraces one without any previous intimacy
> The fire raps the bush with its power
> The sun shines with its power
> Though pepper is hostile
> Though pepper is tough
> Everybody makes friendship with pepper

One pattern is discernible in the examples given thus far. The poet-user of incantatory poetry invokes elements from all the strata of the African Universe. The general linkage in the archetypal process of creation suggests the Great Chain of Being. All forces in the African Universe are interrelated, such relationships may affect positively or negatively. For instance, "Sìnkínnímìnì" invoked is a type of creeping plant that readily sticks to somebody's clothes or body, when one moves near it. For the traditional mind, this is a gesture of love and good companionship. The blending of the black and red colours of "elérèjeje," the seed of "sìnkínnímìnì" complements this tendency of affection.

But in the characterization of "pepper," the poet provokes the negative to effect the positive as reflected in the lines: "Though pepper is hostile/Though pepper is tough." The implication is that even if the attitude of the incantator is not good, the lines are magically imbued to transform his image. Associated with "Awure" incantations is the idea of personality boosting. The respect, glory, love and honour for people can boost their personality. Cosmic invocations that are incantatory in nature are used to seek for honor and respect. This is the relationship between the incantatory poetry dealing with "Awure" and "Owo." The following example is to boost respect for the incantator:

> Tólá tólá ni ekun í s'íjú
> Tíyín tíyín l'ekun í rìn
> Òkú "efòn", a buyì fúnni
> Ààyè "efòn"; a buyì fúnni
> Àti òkú àti ààyè, òhun ni ekùn fíí níyì
> Njé gbogbo ará ayé, panu pò e gbé mi ga
> Bí ewìrì bá p'anu pò won a féná

> The tiger opens its eyes with majesty
> The tiger walks with dignity
> A dead "efon" has dignity
> A living "efon" has dignity
> Dead or alive the tiger had dignity
> Everybody, come together and raise me
> If 'Ewiri' come together they fan the embera in the smithy.

There is an intriguing scenario in the relationship among the forces of nature. Despite the fact that the tiger and "efòn" are dangerous animals, they represent symbolic values in boosting dignity, respect and honor for the user.

Among traditional hunters and warriors in different parts of Africa, incantatory poetry is a common affair. When confronted with hazards of wars or dangers of hunting expedition, they tap their small gourd containing charm. They blow some black powder from inside to the four corners of the world and incantate:

Incantatory Poetry

> Dàmbírí, Dàmbírí, Dàmbírí
> Ojú olóko ni Dàmbírí fo go l'éhìn igi
> Fírífírí l'ojú rímú
> Bòòbo l'àgùtàn wò aláso dúdú
> Ségisóòrùn kìí kú sílé oníle
> Atàkàrà kìí kú s'álè ojà

> Dàmbírí, Dàmbírí, Dàmbírí
> It is in the presence of the farmer that
> Dàmbírí hides behind the tree
> The eyes faintly see the nose
> The sheep hardly recognizes a person in black cloth
> Segisorun does not die in another person's house
> The cakeseller does not die in the market

Unlike in some other incantatory poetry, where the incantator expresses his wishes, action is spontaneous in the types of incantatory poetry associated with "àféèrí" and "egbé." The effect of the incantation above is spontaneous. The resultant effect is that the hunter will be elusive and the threatening dangerous animal will not see him again.

At times, incantatory poetry assumes a narrative dimension, but the plot of such a narrative is always incomplete. It is complementary to the incantatory design itself:

> Akíntònà dá
> Akíntònà so
> Funfun ni eye àfòn
> Tí n je nígbó òrun
> Ló d'ífá fún Òrúnmìlà
> Ní ojó tí ó n rin ìrìn àjò
> Ó pàdé Ògòngò baba eye l'ónà l'ójú òrun
> Ó ní ìwo Òrúnmìlà
> Ó lóun ò jáde nínú igbó
> Ó ní toríi kí ni?
> Ó ní nítorí àwon Àjé
> Mo ní kí ni wón ó fi èmi omo Èsúlékè se?
> Ó ní wón ní àwon ó pa mí je ni
> Mo ní won ò ní lè pa mí je
> Mo ní ohun tí kò jé kí won lè pa ìyá mi
> Mo ní ohun tí kò jé kí won lè pa a je
> Kò ní jé kí won lè pa omoò mi je

Akíntònà who breaks
Akíntònà who joins
White is the 'afon' bird
That feeds at the forest of heaven
That divines for Òrúnmìlà
On the day he was going on a journey
He met Ògòngò, the father of bird on the road of Òrun
He said, You Òrúnmìlà
He said he would leave the forest
He said because of what
He said because of witches
I said, what will they do to me, the son of Èsúlékè
He said they said they would kill me
I said, they would not be able to kill me
I said, what made them unable to kill my mother
What made them unable to kill her
Would not allow them to kill the child.

In a situation of conflict, rivalry and antagonism, incantatory poetry provides a succour of protection and strong will for the incantator. The incantator conjures series of images, symbolizing power of victory over the rival or assailant. The example below can be used to discuss this functional relevance:

Olúborí, Olúborí, Olúborí
Esinsin ní s'orí imí woin woin
Ló d'ífá fún esè méjì
Tí njìjàdù ònà.
Ló bá júbà àwon ìyá mi Òsòròngà pé
Ológbònsésé Ológbònsésé, Ológbònsésé
Tí Ológbònsésé ní se l'áàrin igi
T'akese ní se l'áàrin òwú
Enìkan kìí bá yínmíyínmí dumí
Enìkan kìí bá oyin du afárá rè
Enìkan kìí bá òòrè du ìpé rè
Gbogbo igi tí Elégbède bá f'owó kàn
Dídún níí dún

Olúborí, Olúborí, Olúborí
It is the flies that swarm around excreta
That divines for two legs

Competing for a road
He then pays homage to my mother, Òsòròngà
That Ológbònsésé, Ológbònsésé, Ológbònsésé
It is Ológbònsésé that excels among trees
It is 'akese' that excels among cottons
Nobody contests the excreta with the beetle
Nobody contests the honeycomb with the bee
Nobody contests the spines with the porcupine
Whatever tree Elegbede touches
Sounds.

The incantation starts with the conjuration of a mythical figure whose name implies "the owner of victory." It is obvious that there is a situation of rivalry, since two legs are competing for a road, but the victory of the incantator is ascertained by the fact that flies swarm the excreta. The rendition enters the cosmic realm. The incantator invokes the strength of the witchcraft of his mother Òsòròngà to assist in the battle at hand. Our students may wish to investigate the supernatural essence of witchcraft in African cosmology. Witches are powerful forces respected and feared in the cosmic social realms.

"Ológbònsésé," which appears in the incantation, is a tree with flowery brilliance that can be recognized from far away. This accounts for its importance among other trees. The authority of the beetle over the excreta, the bee over the honeycomb and the porcupine over the spines reinforces the victory for the incantator. We have applied some relevant samples to discuss and illustrate the relevance of incantatory poetry in the socio-psychological existence of man. To ascertain this type of poetry as a literary document, we shall discuss its stylistics and nature of performance.

STYLISTICS AND NATURE OF PERFORMANCE

There are some intriguing issues that should be considered in our discussion of incantatory poetry. There is the volatile argument as to how incantatory poetry can be assessed in terms of setting and time. There may not be a fixed setting or time for the performance of this form of poetry. This is determined by the prescription of the herbalist or the nature of the usage of the incantation. Incantations may be recited on the bed of a sick man or it may be chanted for easy delivery of a woman in a state of labor.

At times, there are prescriptions in terms of time. Incantatory poetry may be recited in the thick and dark night, when forces of evil can be properly confronted. The time prescription may be very early in the morning, before the incantator tastes anything or talks to anybody. In the traditional ritual drama for a gallant hunter, called "ipa-ode" among the Yorubas, the ritual carrier recites the incantations in the quiet of the night on his way to "Orίta," or crossroads, at the outskirts of the town.

It is, however, essentaial to note that incantatory poetry and magic defy the impression of Eurocentric scholars whose perceptions in non-literate societies are primitive and non-scientific. Once the incantator misapplies the instructions in terms of setting, time and usage, the desired effect will not be achieved. Accuracy, precision, measurement and calculations are yardsticks to guide the user of incantatory poetry. These are the essential yardsticks of any scientific method.

It is necessary to stress the fact that incantatory poetry is somehow different from others, such as praise, religious and funeral poetry. We cannot rule out occasional instances of overlapping. Incantations are more the preserve of elderly ones, but not just every elder knows incantations as in the case of proverbs. There are also professionals who provide the poetry for the users. While we are almost tempted to say that the audience of incantatory poetry is limited, we recognize occasions when an incantator may confront a large audience, as in the case of a traditional ruler addressing his rebellious subjects. In Duro Ladipo's *Oba Koso*, Gbonka directs his incantations for support to all the citizens of Ede.[2] Also, the usage of incantatory poetry is open to many people, since all human beings seek for cosmic protection for survival.

It is also necessary to argue that incantations cannot be subjected to arbitrary creative prunings and refurbishing as other forms of poetry. Its metaphysical nature seems to make it immuned against constant embellishment through improvisations.

The beauty of art in Africa implies both the functional and the aesthetic. All along, our discussion has contained this interplay. This suggests that both the functional and aesthetic components are generally interwoven. Beauty is always visible in the dramatic and dialogical rendition of incantatory poetry. It is also necessary to point out that the diction of incantatory poetry is more esoteric because it is a product of a metaphysical construct. This is responsible for our inability to translate some words in this discussion to avoid contermination of meaning and effect. Such words include "Ológbònsésé," "Òsòròngà," "Akese," "Sìnkínnìmìnì," etc. This is to emphasize the magical strength of the diction of incantatory poetry.

Incantatory Poetry

Like other forms of traditional poetry, incantatory poetry makes use of abundant repetitions, images and antitheses. For instance, words like "Ológbònsésé," "Dàmbírí" and "Olúborí" are repeated in odd numbers of three. Odd numbers are symbolic of mystial forces and magical structures. At times, lines are repeated. When they are not repeated, there are parallel structuring of lines to make for rhythmical effect as in:

> Nobody contests the excreta with the beetle
> Nobody contests the honeycomb with the bee
> Nobody contests the spines with the porcupine

The underlined words in the three lines show consistency of rhythm through repetition. As in some samples used, the essence of repetition and rhythm can be captured in the arrangements of words in the vernacular version.

The poetic cadence and thematic logic in incantatory poetry are realized through the use of antithetical juxtapositions that balance forces as in:

> Though pepper is hostile
> Though pepper is touch
> Everybody makes friendship with pepper

Such use of antithetical juxtapositions appears when hostile phenomena are symbolically conjured to seek that which is positive. For instance, we know that the tiger and "efon" are ferocious animals, but the poetic formation in which they appear moves man towards the realization of the positive, like dignity and honor.

The mythic value of incantatory poetry comes out more forcefully in the use of archetypal patterns. Such archetypal formations are realized through the use of words that go deep down into the womb of traditions. There are also mythical figures that emerge in the case of poetic rendition as in the case of "Akíntònà," "Sàngó," "Olúborí," "Òrúnmìlà," etc. Besides, what Isidore Okpewho says about historical myths emerges as revealed in the genealogical ancestory of "Oníwòó, Omo Odò Obà Atólúmere." The semi-narrative construct in incantatory poetry is a necessary feature of archetypal patterns.

Generally, incantatory poetry taps from the wealth of the natural and culture envirnonment, images and rhythm with mythopoetic strength. All these added to the nature of performance make incantatory poetry a beauty of aesthetic construct. Through our consistent critical analysis of the cognitive-aesthetic contents of incantatory poetry, we have succeeded in correcting the erroneious impression of Ruth Finnegan, who asserts that incantations cannot be classified as poetry.[3] The nature of traditional incantatory poetry as discussed in imbued with aesthetic candor.

CONCLUSION

Incantatory like religious poetry digs more into the spiritual and magico-mythical springboard of human existence. Metaphysics is visible in its composition, rendition and performance. Incantatory poetry is one of the ways by which man seeks solutions to the spiritual, socio-cultural, political and economic problems that confront him. Incantatory poetry is not a thing of the past, neither is it only relevant for the traditional man, the modern man also seeks refuge in this spiritual aesthetics. A deeper study into incantatory poetry will show a true manifestation of its scientific nature. The functionalism of incantatory poetry is in its aesthetic essence.

EXERCISES AND FIELDWORK

1. Discuss the relationship between religious and incantatory poetry.
2. Compare the performer and the audience of proverbs studied in Section I, with those of incantatory poetry in this section.
3. Collect samples from your own fieldwork, identify the various components of African Univese in incantatory poetry.
4. Discuss the various issues involved in the performance of incantatory poetry.
5. Do you agree with Ruth Finnegan that incantations cannot be classified as poetry? Make a reasonable and properly illustrated discussion to support your opinion.
6. Appreciate the nature of diction, images and other stylistic methods in incantatory poetry.

Further Reading and Work

Fadahunsi, Ayo. "The Logic of Incantation." *Journal of African philosophy and studies*. Lagos 1 (1 & 2), 1988, pp. 39-48.

Ogede, Ode. "The Power of Word in Igede Incantatory Poetry." *Africana Marburgensia*. 27.1-2. 1994, 13-20.

Notes and References

1. See Albert Mosley. "The Metaphysics of Magic: Practical and Philosophical Implications" in *Second Order: An African Journal of Philosophy*. Vol. Nos. 1 & 2 (Ile-Ife: University of Ile-Ife Press: 1979).
2. Duro Ladipo. *Oba Koso* (Ibadan: Institute of African Studies, 1972).
3. Ruth Finnegan: *Oral Literature in Africa*. (Nairobi: Oxford University Press: 1970) pp. 182-4.

Chapter Twelve

Salutation or Praise Poetry

INTRODUCTION

The subject of discussion in this chapter is not totally new to our readers. We have mentioned the issues of praise, adoration and invocation during our discussion of religious poetry earlier on in this Section. Therefore, praise or salutation poetry is a form of oral composition that deals with invocation, adoration or criticism of the objects of praise. These objects of praise, as will be enumerated later, cover all the gamut of African reality from the metaphysical, socio-cultural and political to natural elements. Also, animate and inanimate objects are praised. All these objects have their relationship to the African cosmological setting.

Praise poetry is common in African communities. When a child prostrates, kneels or bends to greet his parents in the morning, he or she is greeted with praises. The elder who wants to appreciate the kindness or assistance rendered by a child, chants some praises. The traditional poet who wants patronage and material rewards from members of the community chants the praise poetry of those involved. Today, a greater percentage of what public poets sing during performances and recordings is praise poetry.

CATEGORIES

A greater percentage of Afrian performanec involves praise poetry. To guide our readers, we shall attempt a classification of types of praise poetry. These categories include:

A) Praise poetry for supernatural forces, including the Supreme Being, lesser gods and goddesses, spirits and ancestors.

B) Praise poetry for individuals, towns, lineages and at times groups and communities.
C) Praise poetry for animate and inanimate things such as animals, plants, rocks, etc.
D) Praise poetry for philosophical concepts such as death, the world, etc.

These categories will be discussed later during our critical study and analysis of samples. Meanwhile, let us examine the relevance and roles of praise poetry in Africa.

FUNCTIONS

Fundamentally, praise poetry brings into focus the objects of praise. For instance, an individual is appreciated, encouraged and commended for his/her social, physical, moral, spiritual and economic achievements and contributions. Sometimes, these qualities are condemned depending on how well they meet the values of the society. Generally, the functions of praise poetry can be identified as follows:

A) It boosts the morale of individuals who are adjudged good, patriotic and nationalistic in the society. At the same time, it indicts individuals that violate and contradict the ethics and values of the society.
B) It serves as records for the historical life, and experiences of the people for improvement on the social, cultural, economic and political life of communities. This is the great relevance of oral tradition to the study of history.
C) It helps to unveil and propagate the medicinal potentials and general utilities of inanimate objects such as plants, rocks, etc.
D) It affords Africans a very effective medium for praising, consulting, invoking and requesting for favors from the supernatural forces.
E) It affords the elderly members of the community opportunities to display their knowledge of the history and culture of the people, for educating the young generation.
F) It enables the members of the community to exhibit their artistic talents in oral composition, performance and language of expression.
G) The budding generation is able to imitate good qualities demonstrated by some objects of praise and shun those that are inimical to their growth and that of the society.

Salutation or Praise Poetry

ANALYSIS OF SAMPLES

Our discussion here will be based on the categories of praise poetry we have itemized. It will be necessary for readers to quickly recall these categories to enable them to follow the discussion properly. The first category is praise poetry to supernatural forces, including the Supreme Being, lesser gods and goddesses, spirits and ancestors. To be able to understand fully the contents of this category, we want to refer readers once again to the first chapter of this book. Let us now work together with our teacher to be able to practically grasp the definitions, meanings, functions and contents of praise poetry dedicated to the cosmic forces.

In our categorization, we have also identified praise poetry for individuals, lineages, towns, groups and even communities. Praise poetry to individuals such as traditional rulers, warriors, influential and non-influential alike has its origin in praise names, which among the Yorùbá is called "Oríkì." Such praise names may be in form of nicknames, titles, family praises and epithets compiled together to make a poetic whole for the objects of praise. These varieties effectively capture physical, cultural and social qualities of those who bear them. Among the Yorùbás, there are names like "Arówólò" (one-who-has-money to spend), "Awòlúmátèé" (one-who-enters-the-city-without-disgrace), and "Àjànàkú" (Elephant). There are Hausa nicknames such as "Ba ka son Karya" (You hate lies), "Kura" (Tiger), "Dan tsofo" (child of an aged person). Students should compile a list of such names among their various ethnic groups. As we go further in our discussion, readers will be able to see how these nicknames, titles and epithets are synthesized to make for an organic poetic rendition.

In praise poetry dealing with lineages, genealogical expositions of ancestral origin, social, moral, political, economic and spiritual life of the family are common. Among the Yorùbás, we have lineages such as Òpómúlérò, Oníkòyí, Olójèé, Àfònjá, Èsó and Arèsà. The compilation of such poetry may not be static. The poet adds new items and information according to the demands of each epoch. Praise poetry to lineages is always rich in terms of issues and poetic diction and classical materials. Let us consider this example from the Soke Family in Òwu in Abéòkúta. It is one of the five ruling houses that produce the Olówu of Òwu:

> O se é, pèlé oko mi
> Ìlòkó omo Àrélù

Omo Òtilèta bí isu
Eru masa, omo ajóba lele
Tétù wón joba lóhùn èrò
Omo pàna jàre àna
Òpá nà tàn ó tún tì í mólé
Amú'dà mímú fi bé àna lórí
Wón l'éni bá seni lóore làá lù pa
Omo Aketa l'ona osi eta
Se we se we o lo ko, e ma mo se sìgo
Eni tó se sìgo lòdàlè
Eni tó se sìgo lèké
Òtún ìlòkó ti múdà òde le
Òsì ìlòkó ti múdà òde rò
Àrin gbungbun ìlòkó ti múdà
Ò dí bérí...
Kábíyèsí ò

Thank you my husband
Ìlòkó, the child of Àrélù
The descendant of he who springs up like a yam tuber from the soil
Eru masa, the child who becomes king by force
They must be king at all cost
He who kills his in-law and justifies it
He kills his in-law and imprisons him
He who uses a sharp sword to behead his in-law
They say it is he that helps them that they must kill
The descendants of Aketa along the road of Osieta
Oloko, do not attend Sìgo
He who attends Sìgo is a traitor
He who attends Sìgo is a liar
The Ìlòkó on the right side employs sword to fight
The Ìlòkó on the left side employs sword for peace
Ìlòkó walks, sword-in-hand to behead
No one dares query you
Kábíyèsí.

The praise poetry depicts the qualities of bravery, gallantry and fearlessness of those that make the lineage.

Salutation or Praise Poetry

Genealogical tracings are evident in the mentioning of the word "child." The Soke Family had great warriors. The poetry portrays Soke as a royal lineage and how they ascended the throne of Òwu. In terms of morality, they detest cheating. This is why, for example, the King beheads his in-law. Whether or not the child of Soke ascends the throne of Òwu, he is praised as "No one dares query you, Kábíyèsí." In other words, he is always accorded respect as a king.

We have another similar example from Omuahia in the Igboland. It is addressed directly at the king. It must be emphasized that the Igbo King does not enjoy the same authority as the Yoruba, Hausa or Nupe King. The Igbo community is traditionally clannish and the King's power is highly decentralized. Nevertheless, he is always accorded great honor, respect and dignity. The poet sings to extol his qualities and he encourages him to display love and steadfastness in his leadership role. The poetry shows his linkage with the royal lineage:

> Eze di ndu rue mgbe ebighi-ebi
> Eze ozuru oha, Eze Chimere ga gaa riogwu
> Anu kporo nku n'eju onu
> Ome ka nna, Nwadiala, Eze ndi eze
> Ome puru onye odiri, ozuru Umu
> Ogbenye Nna muru oha
> Udo dikwava gi
> Odi mkpumkpu na-eme iri Ntakiri
> Ose na fu ufo n'owu, ogbu agu
> Anu ana-agba egbe ya ana-atanri
> Out mkpuru nkwu na-agbaju ome ka nna
> Birikwa o
> Ihe anyi chaso bu ndu, oga ni nhu aku na uba,
> Udo a omumu
> Ndu miri, ndu azu, Egbe bere
> Ugo beta, nke sikwanu ibe ya ebela, nku
> Kwapukwaya n'ike
> Onye ariala, Ma onye anwiila
> Eze Ohanyere Ugol
> Aka aja aja butere omu Mmanu Mmanu
> Ihe anyi na-ekwubuka
> Nwa Muo emegbula, nwa madu ka
> Nwa madu emegbukwala nwa muo
> Eze Ohanuyere Ugo! Oha ekelee gio
> Eze! Gadi ndu rue mgbe ebighi ebi

King, live forever
King who cares for all, who is ordained by God
Powerful king, dry meat that fills the mouth
Like father, like son
Son of the sol, king of Kings
The king who cares for the needy
Husband of the poor
Father of us all
Peace unto you
The shortman that does wonders
The small pepper that is hot in the mouth
Lion killer
The animal that is being shot and he is still chewing curds
A palmnut that fills the pot
Like father, like son
Live forever o.
What we are asking for is life, progress
and prosperity, peace and plenty
The life of the stream, the life of the fishes
Let the Hawk perch and the Eagles, too
But the one that says the others should not
May his wings break with force
Let no one fall sick and let no one die
King who is crowned as Eagle by all
The sandy hands that oil the lips.
We implore
The spirit should not maltreat man
And man should not maltreat the spirit
King, encrowned as Eagle by all
The Community greets you
King, you will live forever.

This Igbo praise poetry discusses the attitudes and qualities of the traditional ruler being praised. He is a true and genuine leader who is generous and loving to his subjects. He "cares for the needy/ Husband of the poor/Father of us all." But at the same time, he is tough man, courageous to kill a lion. His smallness matches high toughness, for he is "a small pepper that is hot in the mouth."

The idea of democratic governance and existence is raised in the poetry. The poet presents the vision of an egalitarian, peaceful and prosperous society they want from the king. The democratic

Salutation or Praise Poetry

principle if depicted in the lines: "Let the hawk perch, and the Eagle too/But the one that says the others should not/May his wings break with force." This is the political philosophy, ideal and humanism that many contemporary African leaders lack.

Student may wish to collect praise poetry of traditional rulers in their society. They should study their qualities and how they can be compared to contemporary leadership politics in Africa. Literature, our students should understand, is a reflection of the experiences and ideas of many ages, for a dynamic development of the socio-culture.

A Nupe praise poetry dedicated to King Idirisu Gana, Etsu of Patigi, throws more light on our discussion. The poetry is rendered thus:

> Yiko mya Etsu
> Kana gbe ye tu k'ana gbe yeshi
> Ezu ye ga ta lu ezu sunma ga ta ba u
> Za na ke na wun nya na ke na o
> Etsu na soko gi na
> Kagbu nya makiri banza
> Soko a ya o U ma aya wo a ni
> Za na ga a ga na a higwa u ga
> Wun e gaga banza
> A ma e la 'wunki gba ye a
> Ka ga u fe wawa, makiri ede tetengi a
> A ga ga a rogo de wo
> Rogo de wo a ma tu de de wo fa a
> A kiwa be rogo e
> Rogo ma ga a lawa be manza e
> Soko a higwa e fo a Gila de
> Lukangi be a u won ma
> A ga za gi gbekini wun tsua tiu ye ugi
> Etsu na soko gi na
> Talaka ma e sagitsu a
> Etsu na soko gi na

> The Fate of an Etsu
> When something moves, something else follows
> If the man in the front moves,
> the next man follows
> The living inherits what is left behind
> You are a king installed by God

> The power of an enemy is in vain
> Since God has given you,
> who else can challenge
> Whoever will rumble, let him grumble
> He is grumbling in vain
> But then you cannot belittle an enemy
> Only a fool will say an enemy is small
> It is true that a lazyman is rich
> He who is rich but has not cloth to wear
> To hell with his riches
> He too says to hell with the hardworker
> The hawk will never
> Be harmed by the dove
> One appointed a leader must reappoint
> himself a leader
> You are a king installed by God
> Poor man never initiates kings
> You are a king installed by God.

The above Nupe praise song presents a picture of their king as insurmountable. Even though he is warned not to belittle an enemy, it is quickly asserted that he can never be threatened by anybody, because he is enthroned by God. The concept of the divine rights of king, in whatever form, is after all not exclusive of the English tradition. Probably the concept of the divine rights of king may be archetypal to many traditional political cultures. The Etsu has the strength and qualities that cannot make his enemies victorious over him, as revealed in the antithetical juxtaposition of the imagery of the hawk and dove; strength and weakness.

It must be mentioned that almost everybody in the traditional setting, whether ruler or subject, rich or poor, strong or weak is praised by traditional poets. This gives everybody his proper place in the society in philosophical, socio-cultural and political terms. Contemporary poets, on the other hand, mostly praise those who can enrich their pockets.

What can be regarded as community poetry has ethnic groups, villages, towns and nations as its subjects of praise. Probably the philosophy behind the "national anthem" has its origin in praise poetry. Unfortunately, the cognitive and philosophical relevance of such a poetic innovation is underscored by the immoral, unethical and uncultured nature of modern communities. In traditional set-

Salutation or Praise Poetry

tings, this type of poetry is an illumination of the philosophy and cultural attitude of the community.

The Hausa, Fulani, Yoruba, Igbo, Bantu, Masai, Zulu and Nupe all have praise poetry for their language groups or towns. For the community, such praise poetry may trace the history and pre-occupations of the group and tell us the persons and groups involved in their origin. A comprehensive understanding of this type of praise poetry may mean digging into the roots of myths and legends that explain the background and genesis of such settlements. Let us examine the praise poetry of Sakí, a Yorùbá town located in the Oyo North of Oyo State:

> Sakí Ògún kò ro'kin
> Àgbède kò ro bàbà
> Asabari kìí kòjà
> Ológùún kìí kòre
> Bí ó bá di ojó ìjà kí e ránni s'Asabari
> Bí ó bá di ojó eré, ki e ránni s'Ológùún
> Sakí a r'ógun yò
> Omo a f'ogun s'òwò se
> Eni tí kò bá lè jà
> Kó má d'ásà a n gbé Sakí
> Nítorí ogun nisé won
> Bèèrè kí o tó wò ó
> Kí o má baà sá gíjogíjo b'óbá d'ojó ogun
> Alaluwon Alabalakubolo!
> Ekùn bí'mo síbi ti ajá kò gbodò tè
> Ekùn bí'mo síbi tí ajá kè gbodò gbó
> Bí ó bá gbó a di jíjí f'éni tí n w'óúnje kiri

> Sakí, Ògún cannot manufacture ivory
> A blacksmith cannot manufacture brass
> Asabari does not hate fighting
> Ológùún does not hate playing
> On the day of fighting, send for Asabari
> On the day of playing send for Ológùún
> Sakí who is happy when it sees war
> The son of one who makes war into business
> He who cannot fight
> Should not attempt living in Sakí
> Because war is their occupation
> Ask before you enter it

So that you will not be in panic on the day of war
Alaluwon Alabalakulobo!
The leopard gives birth where the dog must not step
The leopard gives birth where the dog must not bark
If it barks, it becomes food for the person
searching for food.

Sakí is presented as a community of warriors. The praise poetry emphasizes the habitual interest of the town in fighting wars. Asabari, the mythical hill that provided protection in the early days of the settlement of the people, has become a scene of annual rituals and sacrifices. Such rituals and sacrifices are archetypal in providing security, peace, order and abundant means of existence for the people. Paradoxically, Olóògùn linked with playing is equally fierce in war. Ìgbóológùún is a settlement where the worship of Ògún is greatly practiced. It is thus symbolic that the god of war and Ilon will perform its duty and profession if provoked.

Myths have it that Sakí was never conquered in any war. No wonder, warnings are given that people should be careful or else they may be gripped by panic during wars. The gallantry and fierceness of the people of the area is emphasized by the threatening image of the leopard. Community praise poetry as we have earlier emphasized recalls the idiosyncrasies, mythical and historical explanation surrounding the origin of this town and its bellicosity. Chief S.O. Ojo, the Bada of Saki, an acknowledged traditional historian, makes a comprehensive and critical study of the fundamentals of this town.[1]

Ìlorin, a community founded by Yorùbá hunters, has grown a multilingual setting through trade, migration and wars. The praise poetry, quite popular among the people of the area, is a representation of the present position of the city:

> Ìlorin Àfònjá
> Ìlorin enú dùn jú iyò
> Ìlú tóbi tó yií ò l'éégún rárá
> Esin l'eégún ilée won
> Okò loròo be
> Arík'éwú s'olá
> A fi wàláà tore...
>
> Ìlorin Àfònjá
> Ìlorin, mouth sweeter than salt

Salutation or Praise Poetry

> A town this big without masquerades
> Horses are their house-hold masquerades
> Swords are their custom
> People who perceive honour in Kèwú
> People who use Wàláà as gifts...

The praise poetry educates us about the history of Ìlorin. Àfònjá is very significant to the historical development of the city. Àfònjá was the Àare-ònà-kakanfò, the generalissimo of the Yorùbá army in the 17th century Oyo Empire. He led the Oyo army. He later settled in Ìlorin and actually first brought the community to the limelight. The poetry testifies to the power of oration of the inhabitants of the city. Egúngún worship is today a very important religious affairs among the Yorùbás. Ironically, Ìlorin, a Yorùbá cultural settlement, today has no masquerade due to the introduction of Islam in the 19th century. The "horse" which replaces "the masquerade," is a result of the influence of Hausa/Fulani culture in the area.

Both "kéwú" and "wàláà" are products of the influence of Islamic religion and Quranic education. "Wàláà" represents the spiritualism and intellectualism inherited from the influence of Islam. It is essential to mention that "Wákà" music which influences some modern musical types in Nigeria is a product of Islamic culture. The Fuji music of Ayinde Barrister, Ayinla Kollington, Wasiu Ayinde and others has its origin in the Islamic poetic forms.

Animals, plants, rivers, rocks and other gifts of nature are praised in Africa. We can briefly discuss the praise poetry dedicated to "Òbo" (Ape):

> Edúnjobí, lánré Òròkí – Opomu
> Omo edun kóróbótó orí igi
> Irinwó láti lo, egbèfà láti bò
> Egbèjìlá nbá wògbé
> Lágídò nítorí ó se oko àna òun ni
> Kò sí ní'lé ó pín 'pákò dè wón
> Eni èwà npa bí otí
> A bi 'yan ti ko
> Ó ní won kò jé k'óun d'Óyòó
> Láti lo f'ojú kan oba
> Iwajú gbagba, ní àgbásínú
> Ìpàkó tìtì láti èyìn.
> Edúnjobí, lánré Òròkí -Opomu

> The fat son of Edun on the top of a tree
> Four hundred to go, twelve thousand to come
> Lágídò says it is because it is his in-law's farm
> He is not in the house, he shares occupit for them
> He who is intoxicated by beauty
> With majestic walk
> He says that he is begin disallowed to go to Oyo
> To visit the King
> Firm forehead, pressed inside
> Big occupit, pressed to the back.

Elements of pride and respect for the in-law show the communal format of existence among the animal kingdom. The majestic walk of the ape and its appearance are emphasized by the poet.

We can also cite the example of the praise poetry dedicated to "Ehoro" (Hare), among the Yorubas:

> Ikú, Onítiro
> Eni tí wón tì'bàdàn
> Wá bè lówè eré sísá
> Nítorí ó mo eré sá ju gbogbo eran lo
> Eni tí wón kì, kì, tí won kò lè kì mó
> Ni wón fi n s'orin ko pé:
> Ehoro n lo, Ojeje-moko
> Ehoro n lo, Ojeje-moko
> A rétí bora bí aso
> Irúnmolè a t'ààlà là
> Òbèjé a r'ítò gbígbóná gbara rè sílè

> Death, that leaps
> The person hired at Ìbàdàn
> To come and run
> Because it can run faster than any other animal
> One who they try to catch but they could no longer catch
> Praise
> And they turn it into a song:
> Ehoro is going-Ojeje-moko
> Ehoro is going-Ojeje-moko
> He possesses ears like a covering cloth
> Irúnmolè that rescues itself at the farm's border
> Òbèjé who rescues itself with hot urine.

The hare is a very athletic animal and this attribute has been properly captured in this praise poetry. An animal that can run fast, hunters and herbalists use its toes for charms that will make for running fast. Hence, it is referred to as "Death that leaps." It is this athletic nature that gives the animal prominence even among human beings. The song-within-a-song "Ehoro is going, Òbèjé-Moko/ Ehoro is going/Òbèjé-Moko" reflects its expertise in running. The poet also recognizes the large ears of the hare.

As depicted in the poem, the hare has defence mechanism such as "hot urine," with which it scares away his assailants. The border of a "farm" is the appropriate lane for the hare. Once it links the farm's border, it becomes difficult for the assailant to catch it. The traditional poet is a typical scientist, x-raying the physiognomy or body structure of the object of praise. He also identifies the characteristics of animals, one of the preoccupations of the discipline of zoology. It is necessary to investigate the role played by hunters in this type of poetic composition.

Farmers at times compose poetry for their products. Such composition may also aid the advertising of the products as we see in the case of "gyad'a." The Hausa traditional poet intimates us with the mathematical structure of gyada-groundnut, and its food nutrients:

> Gyad'a mai sihiri,
> A bara a gan biyu
> A murza agan hudu
> A tauna a ji gardi
> Ga kirarin Gyad'a,
> Ba don K'in yawa ba
> Sai 'yan Sarki!

> Groundnuts with seeds
> Break the cell and see two (seeds)
> Rub the seeds and see four (segments)
> Grind them in your mouth and enjoy the flavor
> That is the chant for groundnut
> If only it is more than this
> Oh! What a royal crop!

Abstract and metaphysical issues also attract the attention of traditional praise singers. Such philosophical objects include death and the world. The poem titled "Aiye" (World) among the Yoruba can be used for illustrations:

> Ayé Àkámarà o-o-o
> Ayé tótó fùn-ún-ùn
> Ayé tó bèrù o-o-o-o
> Eni tí kò bá b'èrù ayé
> Ara rè ní n tàn je
> Eni tí kò bá sóra f'áyé
> Ebora a bó o l'áso
> Ayé níí gúnyán eérú
> Ayé níí rokà eèpè
> Ayé níí s'oyin di májèlé
> Ayé níí so aségità d'olówó
> Ayé níí s'olówó d'aségità
> Ayé níí s'ogbá d'ògbún
> Ògbún kò dédé gbun kónbú-wórókó
> Ayé níí s'ogi tútù di gbígbe
> Ayé má se mí
> Ibòmíràn ni kóo d'oríko
>
> The world, Àkámarà
> The world, I pay homage to you
> The world should be feared
> Whoever does not fear the world
> Deceives himself
> Whoever does not beware of the world
> He will be stripped naked by the Devil
> It is the world that prepares pounded yam of ashes
> It is the world that prepares yam flower of mud
> It is the world that turns honey into poison
> It is the world that turns the woodseller to a rich man
> It is the world that turns the rich man to a woodseller
> It is the world that turns good calabash to a crooked one
> A crooked calabash is not without cause crooked
> It is the world that turns fresh tree to dry tree
> The world, do not punish me
> Go to another place.

This is a philosophical exposition of human nature and his existence in general. The poet with a comprehensive and profound

Salutation or Praise Poetry

creative force describes the anti-aesthetic crisis of human life "Àkámarà." Àkámarà, an epithet by which the world is described, means that the world is unpredictable, impossible and dangerous. Equivocations and ambiguities are predominant in the poem. The poet emphasizes the need to fear and pay homage to the world.

The predominant antithetical juxtaposition of "pounded yam of ashes." "Yam flour of mud," honey turned to poison, a woodseller turned to a rich man and vice versa, all illustrate the precarious nature of the setting, where human beings play their drama of existence. Complex images of the good calabash turned crooked and fresh tree turned dry further illustrate the evil in man. Such a poetic rendition affords man the opportunity of making a deeper philosophical reflection on the nature of his existence. It is obvious that the mood and setting for such a poetic rendition are always serious. Such a rendition is always dramatized in a sober and somber mood. Our students are expected to examine their own mind and intellect on the complex philosophical subject matter, which now touches the mind of the poet in the next example. It is a Yoruba poem about death. We present the poetry to our students for experimental study and analysis:

> Ikú Àlùmúntù, Ikú òrónro
> Ògo l'ówó Elédàá
> Ikú Àlùmúntù, alágbo ìbànújé
> Eni tí a kò rí tí n dá yánpanyánrin s'áyé
> Ìdágìrì tíí dó'mo l'óru
> Ìdágìrì tíí dá'mo l'ósàán
> Májèlé ikú tí a je, lójó ìsèdáyé
> Kò sí o, kò sí o, òrun lèròo rè
> Ikú nbe nílé, ikú nbe l'óko
> Òkan soso òòrùn tíí ràn kárí ayé
> Òjò nikú, kò s'éni tí ò níí pa
> Bóyá l'owó, sùgbón túláàsì n'ikú

> Death Àlùmúntù, death the bile
> Club in the hands of the creator
> Death Àlùmúntù, the owner of concoction of grief
> The invisible that causes confusion on earth
> The danger that threatens a child in the thick of night
> The danger that threatens a child in the afternoon
> The poison of Death we eat on the creation day
> No, No, Heaven is the remedy

Death is in the house, Death is in the farm
Death is on the way, Death is on the river
The only sun that shines world-wide
Rain is Death, there is none it will not touch
Money is uncertain, but Death is certain

STYLISTICS AND NATURE OF PERFORMANCE

We must not make a mistake that the performance of these various categories of praise poetry is the same. Every performance is determined by the nature of the songs, the objects of praise and the artist himself. When young ones at home prostrate or kneel down to greet their parents or elders, praise poetry is chanted. The elders may just pat their backs or heads as a symbol of blessing. Traditional rulers such as Etsu Nupe, Aláàfin Òrànmíyàn, Obi of Onitsha and Alhaji Ado Bayero may be praised in their palaces by the court poets and minstrel. This makes for palace praise poetry. They can also be praised during public occasions. The public poets perform on the open fields, village centers, market squares and other designated settings in the community.

In the process of performance, the oral poet identifies his objects of praise in any setting. This is noted with freelance praise poets who scout for gifts. As they sing, they point to their objects of praise. As they sing, their vocabulary of actions are cut according to the poetic performance. They use their hands or any part of their body to add meanings to the poetic rendition. The objects of praise, especially human beings, make corresponding responses, dancing and acknowledging encomiums showered on them. Part of the dramatic responses is showering of gifts on the poet. At times, the audience is consciously or unconsciously dragged into the fiesta of performance by making relevant actions.

Musical accompaniments are important in traditional poetic rendition. Relevant and appropriate musical accompaniments, apart from being inherently a part of the rendition, embellish further the performance. Some of the traditional musical apparatus are also involved in poetic rendition, either making additional poetic comments or re-echoing the poet's production. Flutes and Kàkàkí do this for the Emirs. The Aláàfin of Òyó and Olúbàdàn of Ìbàdàn are daily woken up by the traditional musical apparatus that produce their praise poetry.

As already witnessed, praise poetry is typically stuffed with images to make realistic portrayals of the objects of praise. To conform the rustic nature of his setting, the praise poet taps from the total gamut of his environment. The traditional Igbo rule is described as "the small pepper that is hot in the mouth." He is also described as "dry meat that fills the mouth." This is an acknowledgement of his concern for and sense of responsibility to his people.

In the praise poetry to Etsu of Patigi, Idrissu Gana, the poet gives a portrait of his physical appearance. The imagery of the Eagle, portrays the royal candor of the ruler. Zoological imagery also abounds in the praise poetry of Sakí to depict its bellicose attitude in wars. Oratorical, spiritual and intellectual prowess represented by the metaphors of *Kéwú* and *Wàláà* feature prominently in the praise poetry of Ìlorin.

The rhythm in traditional poetry is achieved through the use of repetitions, antithetical juxtapositions and rhetorical formula. Probably, the depth of the poetic mind in the traditional art is projected through the use of concrete words, for which we may not find equivalent in modern orthography. Such words we refuse to call "archaic." They still retain their traditional flavor, meanings and candor. Only acculturation has eroded their relevance. Take for example "Alaluwon Alabalakubolo" in the praise poetry of Sakí. We expect our students to explore and investigate into the mythical and legendary allusions in praise poetry.

CONCLUSION

Salutation or praise poetry is a very rich oral genre in Africa. We must not forget our contention that this poetry is not intended to pamper the objects of praise. While praise poetry extols good qualities, it also condemns and castigates bad ones. We should emphasize the essence of performance and style in bringing out the contents and functions of this genre. We advise our students to explore more comprehensively the subject matter of praise poetry.

EXERCISES AND FIELDWORK

1. Comment on the basic philosophy behind salutation or praise poetry in Africa.
2. In your own view, what is the basis for the classification of praise poetry in Africa?
3. How relevant are the functions of praise poetry to the dynamics of modern society?
4. Explore the performance structure of each of the categories of praise poetry identified in this study.

5. Can you give some peculiar characteristics of the style of traditional praise poetry? Collect samples of praise or salutations poetry from your community.

Further Reading and Work

Opland, Jeff. "Praise Poetry: Praise Poetry of the Xhosa" in *African Folklore: An Encyclopedia*. New York: Routledge, 2004, pp. 361-62.

Ogede, Ode. *Art, Society and Performance: Igede Praise Poetry*. Gainesville: University Press of Florida, 1997.

Pongweni, Alec J. C. *Shona Praise Poetry as a Role Negotiation: The Battles of the Clans And the Sexes*. Gweru, Zimbabwe: Mambo Press, 1996.

Notes and References

1. Ojo, *Iwe Itan Saki*, Saki

Chapter Thirteen

 **Funeral Poetry**

INTRODUCTION

The issue to be discussed in this chapter is very crucial to every living being. Death is a universal phenomenon, the fate every human must embrace. Funeral poetry therefore deals with a universal theme based on the philosophy of human existence. It is necessary to recall the Zulu myth of creation discussed in Section I[1]. The myth tutors about the origin of man's mortality. There are various versions of it in different societies.

Philosophers compare the sojourn of man on earth to a market session. When you go to the market, at the end of the day you will return home. This is the situation in which human beings find themselves. Every person must go back to the Superme Being, the Creator of the Universe, at the exact time he has chosen during creation. Myths dealing with this subject matter reveal this pathetic and philosophical irony of human existence. Hence, the traditional poet recalls two antithetical moments of human existence:

> Níjó táa wá'lé ayé
> T'èrín t'ayò
> Níjó tá ò rí àlùkìámò
> Ariwo a gba'lé
> Òkiki a gb'àdúgbò

> The day we come to the world
> It is laughter and happiness
> The day we shall go to heaven
> There will be noise in the house
> It will resound in the neighborhood

The last segment is sung on a tragic note:

> Ijó kan n be
> Tá ó sùn tá ò ní jí
> Owó òtún ó ro
> T'òsì ó d'áko òwú
> Enu táa n fi n jobè
> Yó wá d'enu àgbógiri bo

> One day is one day
> When we shall sleep and we will not wake up
> The right hand will be paralyzed
> The left hanging down loosely
> The mouth we use for eating
> Will now be facing the wall.

Funeral poetry recalls occasions of despair, loss and tragedy. It also presents celebratory performance of the passage to the ancestral world. The artist consciously or unconsciously builds his poetic creation around archetypal rites of passage into the mortal world while that of death is the passage to immortality. The celebration of the rites of passage is organized around the cosmological beliefs of the people. While death causes panic, lamentation is minimal if the deceased is aged with many children. The death of a young person or a child is always mourned with a deep sense of grief. It is believed that an elderly person's "death" is actually a transition to the ancestral world from where he takes care of those still living. As an African ancestor, he or she attains a higher level of the ancestral status and power. This is African concept of apotheosis. Therefore, at the moment of burial, traditional rites must be fully and comprehensively observed to settle the deceased peacefully in his new abode. If this is not done, the living stand the risk of being haunted by the roaming spirit of the deceased.

The cult of the ancestors has been perfectly built into the African perception of cosmic and social existence. The living remember and constantly pay homage to the dead through sacrifices, rituals and routine traditional worship and celebrations. This is the link between religious poetry and funeral poetry. The ancestors concretely transform themselves to Egúngún and come to the world occasionally to feel the spiritual pulse of the kindred spirits. Ewì Egúngún poetry for celebrating the ancestors on earth is closely related to religious poetry among the Yoruba.

Other forms of death may throw the community into panic and the mood is more gloomy when a young person dies in the society. On the whole, any occasion of death is always a moment for the people in a community to display the sense of harmonious existence through their emotional consideration and consolation for the family of the deceased. The poet on this occasion recalls the mood of the setting of the occurrence. While his poetry raises emotional tension, outbursts and fears, he at the same time attempts to purge them of tension.

The nature of poetic composition for any funeral occasion may be determined by the age, social and cultural status of the deceased within the communal traditional framework. For a traditional ruler, herbalist or even hunter, the ritual ceremony that may go with the burial may be elaborate. Occasionally, this can be transformed into a communal traditional scenario. Status notwithstanding, the traditional African man is always in a tragic mood of compassion and mourning with the family of the deceased.

We want our readers to express their own feelings about the atmosphere caused by death. Have you lost somebody dear to you? What was your impression about life? What mood were you in? Your answers will be able to provide some basic rudiments that form the content of the creative mind of the funeral poet.

FUNCTIONS

The situation of funeral poetry has been discussed in terms of the metaphysical position of man in relationship to the myth of creation. Also, within the communal and socio-cultural realms, the poetry discusses the position, reactions and rites involved when somebody dies. We want to be more specific by discussing the essence of funeral poetry in the traditional set up. Funeral poetry:

a) Expresses sorrow, condolence and sympathy for the family of the deceased, as a means of displaying the communal solidarity typical of traditional settings.
b) Touches on philosophical and metaphysical components that create the linkage between the cosmic realm and the abode of the generic man. This implies the supernatural correspondence between the world of the dead and that of the living.
c) Contains elements of adoration and praises, which at times necessitate the process of deification of the dead. This happens when the deceased is an heroic individual in his community.

d) Relates the heroic performance of the deceased in terms of social status, traditional influence and political relevance. This may influence the attitude of the present generation, since such heroic feats he had performed whle alive can be emulated to raise the status of the modern man and the society at large.
e) Employs death as a metaphor of existence, which sensitizes people to know about the ephemeral nature of human existence. It thus orientates man towards didactic moral and ethical values for humanistic behavior and modality of good living.
f) Makes available historical documents thus serving as a source of oral tradition for the historians for the purpose of dialectical continuingy.
g) Exposes some anomalies about the deceased, such a poetry serves as a form of checks and balances to human behaviors.
h) Tangential to the study of modern African literature as reflected in Negritude poetry of Senghor and others. Negritude poetry is heavily constructed on the worship of ancestors, which is emphasized in traditional poetry. This dialectical link between traditional and modern African poetry provides a suitable arsenal for cultural renaissance and nationalism as reflected in the Negritude poetry. Thematic and aesthetic features of traditional poetry can be located in Senghor's "In Memorian" and "Night Du Sine." They are modern examples or versions of traditional funeral poetry.
i) Expresses the tragic-comic nature of human life, thereby enabling people to accept loss and the nature of human existence, which is robed in philosophical irony.

ANALYSIS OF SAMPLES

The explanation of textual materials can be broadly based on three premises:

1) Poetry rendered immediately somebody dies.
2) Funeral rites and poetic rendition.
3) Funeral poetry or purpose of immemorial or recollection.

Funeral poetry is a commonplace artistic preoccupation of Africans. Among the Yorubas, "rárà òkú" is a common practice. We can cite the following example to show the expression of sympathy that ensues immediately somebody dies. The "Asunrárà òkú," the person who sings about the death, here is a female. This is even indicated in the poem. In most cases, women are involved in this type of poetry, probably because of motherhood – *abiyamo* – and ability to readily develop a sense of compassion in a tragic situation like this:

> Àtólé Òpó oo, okoò mi
> O relé o, o re le
> O lo gb'ésin wò bíí babaà re
> Ìyako mi sáà gbésin wo bíí baba rè Àkàngbé...
> Omo Ògúnjobí, baba okoò mi ti rí àlejò omo rè se
> Ó n wá èye o, Àtólé Òpó
> Ó n wá èye, ó sì rí i
> Omo Ògúnjobí Bello
> Àtólé Òpó, Ìyako mi lo sí àgbésìn bíí baba rè
> Àtólé Òpó o o , okoò mi
>
> Àtólé Òpó o o, my husband
> She has gone home, gone home
> She has died like her father
> My in-law just died like her father Àkàngbé...
> The son of Ògúnjobí, my in-law plays host to his son
> He is looking for fame, Àtólé Òpó
> He is looking for fame, he has got it
> The son of Ògúnjobí Bello
> Àtólé Òpó, my in-law has died like the father
> Àtólé Òpó o o, my husband.

The opening line of this poem is synonymous with what we regard as opening/introduction in folktales in Section I. The attention of the audience whether afar off or near the place of the occurrence is drawn to the name of the deceased. The audience is immediately provided with the identity of the deceased. For a stylistic effect, the poet employs the use of apostrophe. His ululating call of "Àtólé Òpó" is symbolic as if her poetry can resuscitate the dead. It may be that the poet could not believe that the woman was truly dead. The poet further informs the audience about her relationship to the deceased. She was the mother-in-law. She provides us with some other information that the father of the deceased had died. The deceased is traced back to her ancestors. The poet also signals some communal affection that exists in the world of the living. She informs us that the father of the deceased, who was already dead, would warmly welcome this new visitor to the land of the ancestors. The poet re-affirms the African belief in life after death.

Funeral poetry reveals the human attributes of the deceased in terms of physical complexion, intellectual strength and heroic deeds. In most cases, the informants we met on the field said that these materials are spontaneously built into poetry. According to them, they are the memorable expressions that make the living to occasionally recall the deceased, even many years after his death.

> Òroko roko kápáa fújà l'ébè
> Baba Adénínhún
> A pé lájò má bàjò jé
> Baba Deborah
> Àjàní t'óbìnrin kò l'ónà
> Tó bú púrú s'ékn
> O nií bírú eléyìí ò bá s'oko eni
> A a sì jé àlè ani
> Kuruwe, oko Adédigba.

> He farmed and farmed and claimed victory over the ridge
> The father of Adénínhún
> One who successfully sojourned in a foreign land
> The father of Deborah
> Àjàní, whom a woman greeted on the road
> And burst a-weeping
> Saying that, if this is not one's husband
> He should be one's concubine
> Kuruwe, the husband of Adédigba.

This funeral poetry suggests the occupation of the deceased, which is farming. He was a well-behaved man, who put up a cultured behavior while sojourning in a foreign land. The poet seems to be envious of the handsomeness of the man. A woman will want him to be her husband or concubine. It is necessary to point out that despite the fact that the poet recounts a sad experience, he creates the atmosphere for disburdening the tension and sorrow in the audience.

What is remarkable in the way the Yorùbá chanter ends this poetic rendition with the creation of artist/audience rapport. This part of performance is an intentional or unintentional practice by the artist to release the tension in the sympathizers. She turns her rendition into a solo/chorus performance to make the audience participate. She then proposes the solo/form, while the audience chorus:

Akorin:	Baba oko mí relé,
	Abókèdé relé
Agberin:	Àwa n wá'ye wa
	A ò rí'ye wa mó
Akorin:	Baba tó so'gbó d'ílé
	Abókèdé tó sò'gbé d'ìgboro
Agberin:	Àwa n wá'ye wa
	A ò rí'ye wa mó
Poet:	My father-in-law had gone home,
	Abókèdé went home
Chorus:	We are looking for our beloved
	We cannot find him
Poet:	The father who turned the bush to home
	Abókèdé who turned the bush to town
Chorus:	We are looking for our beloved
	We could not find him.

Among the people of Lálúpon in Ìbàdàn, dirge is an important poetic form, commonly referred to as "òkú pípè," calling the dead. As typical of the funeral poetry from other parts of Nigeria or Africa, the contents of such poetry share the features of panegyrics, rendered with a mournful tone. Specialized form of poetic conduct and tone of lamentation are adopted among different peoples of Africa. Among the people of Lálúpon, this specialized form is referred to as "Ìrèmòjé." According to our informant, this is a typical conduct and poetic manner of distinguishing Ìrèmòjé from other tonal patterns and structures of performance of dirge. As learners and potential researchers who may likely be on the field, we should note these peculiarities. As we have stressed and fully discussed in Chapter Two, physical and gestural aspects of performance cannot be properly captured without going to the field. The effectiveness of the dramatics of the poetry can be fully perceived in the chanter's mournful apparel, modulating wailing sonorous voice, which is occasionally terminated by mild or total outburst of weeping or shedding of tears. Such action also contributes to the painting of sorrow and heavy sense of despair in which people are engulfed. The practical action of poetic rendition, which is intermittently punctuated by outbursts of weeping, wiping away of tears are concretely integral part of the dramatic actions in staging funeral poetry.

There are other actions that complement the oral performance of funeral poetry. While the poetic rendition continues, the poet intermittently stops to acknowledge the entrance of mourners. She reports to them on what death had done to her beloved husband or mother-in-law. The chanter castigates death:

> A-a-a-a Àjoké ògò, o ò rí mi bí?
> Ikú dá mi l'ójú
> O so mí di aláìlárá
> Ikú pa baba oko mi

> A-a-a-a Àjoké ògò, see my plight
> Death has caused disaster for me
> Turning me to a deserted person
> Death killed my father-in-law

The audience's response in this type of tragic setting varies. The audience in this case consists of the other mourners who troop in and out or who are maybe sitting down on mats. Some of them join in the lamentation by weeping. "Uu-uu-uu." The sobbing and the dripping of tears provide occasional dramatic responses to the poet's performance. Some of the mourners who can control their emotional feelings appeal to others not to weep again.

As evident among the people of Lálúpon, dirge goes into protracted philosophical structure. It itemizes the various characteristics and behaviors of the deceased. His achievements are recounted. What probably makes dirges penetrate into the marrow of the hearers is the evocation of concrete and analogical images that paint the gloom of the dreadful action caused by death. Such images also produce the conduct of the deceased in a war, to shock the other mourners out of their grief. Let us consider the elements in the following dirge:

> O lo nílè yí, kò rílé ayé wá mó
> Ikú yìí ò se
> Ikú p'Agbe, ó p'aro
> Ikú p'àlùkò, ó p'olósùn egàn
> Kò s'éniyàn tí ò níí kú

Funeral Poetry

> Kò s'óko baba eni tí ò ní d'egàn
>
> He had left this place, he will not come to the world again
> This death is painful
> Death kills Agbe, killing the dye
> Death kills Àlùkò, the camwood maker of the jungle
> There is nobody who will not die
> There is nobody, whose father's farm will not turn
>   jungle

The images of deprivation and philosophy of existence are visible in this dirge. Birds such as "Agbe" and "Àlùkò" are noted for their colorful and beautiful apparel. Such beauty of existence for which the deceased is noted has been terminated by death. The image of a farm turning into an unkempt setting jungle reinforces the philosophical assertion of the poet and the fallow picture to which death has always subjected people. It also stresses the inevitability of death.

The poet continues emotionally to recall the situation in which the deceased meets his death. As a warrior, he died at the warfront. As characteristics of his family, the arrow could not hit him at the back, but he confronts the bullets of his enemy. This traditional poet has the knowledge and hazards of other professions. To be hit at the back during a battle implies cowardice, but to be hit in the front implies courageous and gallant performance. The poet does not make any statement about the cause of death. She gradually moves her audience to this by drawing analogies from other professional hazards. Hence she sings:

> Ikú ode n be nínú apó rè
> Ikú agbe n be ní bèbè ebè
>
> The death of the hunter is in his scabbard
> The death of the farmer is on the edge of the
>   ridge

The implication is that his death is caused by war, but dirges do not concentrate on the attributes of the deceased alone. Death itself is a focus of attraction, since it is the dreadful enemy around. The poet makes a poetic appeal, which is an afterthought that if death would take money and meat, all these would have been provided. But this Yoruba belief about sacrifices to placate a crisis, is not applicable to death. Besides addressing this enemy, the audience of the mourners is another target of the poet:

> Those of you who are standing, I greet you
> Those of you who are sitting, I greet you
> Thank you for sympathizing with me
> Do you see anybody who names his child Kokumo?

The greeting is still a respect for communal solidarity at this trying period, but then, the poet goes on to a rhetorical question about the inevitability of death. It is a reminder that nobody can escape death. The poet is only confirming the proverbial statement that:

> Òkú n sunkún òkú
> Akáso-lórí n sukún ara won
>
> A dead person is mourning a dead person
> Those with covers on their heads mourn their own
>   death

"Aka so lori" implies mourners who gather to sympathize are actually mourning themselves.

Funeral poetry among the Egbe people of Kogi State seems to be characterized with brevity and precision, but the poems are pregnant with philosophical realities that one may find in long dirges. We shall consider some examples in our discussion.

The inconsequentialness of man's life on earth is contained in a funeral poetry:

> Eda gogogoro sodo, sodo, sodo
> Eda gogogoro s'odo

As laconic as these repeated lines may be, they are pregnant with meanings. The meaning of the song is simple but strong. Since the man is dead, the spirit has left him, and he is only an empty shell. Hence, the poet directs that he should be "committed to the earth." This recalls the biblical reference to the relationship of the dead to the earth. Thy stylistic method of repetition is effective. We should also take note that the words reach far into the root of tradition and they may be difficult to translate. The semantic composition of the words make for natural rhythm.

At times, funeral poetry depicts some of the characteristics of heroic poetry. The valour and gallantry of the deceased is revealed. These two lines from among the Egbe people reveal this:

> Ajíbólú Okun o
> Osobìnrin p'amado

The funeral lines above revisit to the heroic deed and performance of a female figure called "Ajibolu" who single-handedly killed a bush pig. Ajibolu is a woman who lived long ago. She went into the forest unarmed and naked. She only had an "apete," a piece of cloth for covering her navel. She came back in a few days with a dead bush pig. Funeral poetry helps to dig up and reference some legendary heroes and heroines.

But there is another side to the appraisal of funeral poetry. There seems to be an immediate demarcation between he world of the living and the dead. The two-line funeral poetry from Egbe illustrates this:

> Egbé l'a wa ayé la se
> A ò bókùú lo

> We in Egbé, we belong to the world
> We do not follow the dead

This is a philosophical dimension that, even with death of people, life still continues.

STYLISTICS AND NATURE OF PERFORMANCE

Oral performance in traditional literature naturally involves the use of musical accompaniments. We should then ask ourselves whether such embellishments are necessary in this tragic situation? If necessary, what is the appropriate time during which musical accompaniments can complement or even produce dirges? At the initial occurrence of death, everybody is shocked probably because of the sense of loss or because they themselves remember that oneday they will die. The death of a child or youth so provokes a pensive mood that the issue of musical accompaniment is ruled out.

Introduction To African Oral Literature & Performance

However, the death of an aged person involves musical accompaniment at the appropriate time. When a traditional ruler or any cultural head dies, the announcement can be made by a distant sonorous lamenting sound produced by a musical accompaniment designed for the purpose. This may be a part of the inherited palace culture. For members of certain traditional cults, musical signs are produced to inform the other members. But in most cases, musical accompaniments may not be fully employed until after the burial. While the corpse is lying in state at the center of "agbo-ile" (compound) the poet can still continue his practice.

Immediately after the burial, musical accompaniments are fully mobilized as the audience dances around the town to publicize news of the death. In fact, the musical accompaniments at times produce the poetry to be re-echoed by the audience now involved in dancing. "Dundun" (a type of Yoruba drum) produces the poetry thus:

    À f'eni omó sin ló bímo
    Omo ò láyòlé
    À f'eni omó sin ló bímo

    It is only a deceased buried by his children that bore
        children
    Children are sources of happiness
    It is only a deceased buried by his children that bore
        children

This poetic statement depicts a crucial belief in Africa that to beget issues is a matter of philosophical and socio-cultural relevance. A deceased without children or offspring suffers double loss. The tragic note is also signaled when somebody without any issues dies. The process of cultural continuity is therefore noted in the biological metaphor of regeneration by the poet:

    B'áláró bá kú, omo rè ní j'ogún ebu
    B'áládi bá kú, omo rè ní j'Ogun agbádá
    B'óká bá kú omo rè ní j'ogún oró
    B'íná kú a f'eérú b'ojú
    B'ógèdè kú a f'omo rè rópò
    Omo wa ni yó s'elédè l'éhìn wa

    When the dyer dies, her child inherits the ebu

> When the adi worker dies, her child inherits the cauldron
> When the adder dies, its child inherits its poison
> When the fire dies, it covers its face with ashes
> When the plantain tree dies, it substitutes itself with its offsprings
> It is our offspring who will inherit the house after our death.

Through series of analogical inferences, the poet reproduces the regenerational and survival syndrome. The African poets are not only artists, they are combination of disciplines. They bring the natural phenomena of their environment to bear on their creativity. The processes of regeneration and biological continuity are noted in creatures and plants like the "adder," "plantain" and even the elemental force, water.

The repetitions in every line of some words and items make for a structural flow of the poem. Structurally, the first five lines in the poem above are necessarily aimed at achieving the purpose stated in the last line. The last line, which is a form of prayer, is central to the philosophical issue of a deceased getting offspring. The poet prays that it is our offspring that will inherit the house. For a deceased person who has no children, it is a double tragedy. For the mourners, it is a prayer that needs sound acknowledgement with "Àse", let it be.

The nature of performance after burial will be determined by the status, cult membership, profession and general communal beliefs. For a hunter, the Yoruba Ujala chanters would render the funeral poetry recalling the fame and professional skill of their colleague.

Funeral poetry may have some partial narrative format in case the chanters want to recall a heroic hunting expedition where a fierce animal was captured. The hunters may carry guns, which they shoot into the air. For the hunters, funeral poetry is more comprehensively dramatized in a religious ritual called "Ìpà Ode" to celebrate the death of a chief hunter. "Bàtá," a form of conical drum, is amply used. The performance is made sumptuous with the fast-pace dance rhythm of the Ìjálá chanters.

Among the Egbé people, the processes and modalities for burial provide some structural and aesthetic format. Burial arrangements, costumes and nature of musical accompaniments provide this aesthetic format. The dance patterns are also part of this grand aesthetic design. For instance, the "Èkà" dance is the first stage of performance after burial. The Èkà is the dead man's personal dance rhythm, and therefore, no one can dance it properly as the deceased himself. Hence, this dance rhythm is not always performed by any other person at the funeral. The dance rhythm of Èkà will still be determined by the clan to which the deceased belongs. Such clans include: Okua, Ijaku, Isaba, Ahimke and Okedisin.

After the Èkà drumming and dancing comes the "Ogbogunmo." Everyone present can participate in this funeral dramatic performance. The dance is performed in the dead of the night as a sort of wake-keeping for the dead. The last of the dances is "Ìjó kòó." This is special to the "Ijalu" clan. The corpse will then be accompanied to the grave.

Our informant contends that no special costume is used for any funeral dance in Egbé, but the case is different when the deceased is a member of a cult or profession. For example, if the deceased is a hunter his colleagues in the profession dress in full hunting habiliments, called "Edewo", which is adorned with cowries.

Generally, the aesthetics of funeral poetry recasts the usual tragic atmosphere. The diction used by the poet reflects the mood, tone and appearance of the mourners. Musical accompaniments are used according to the dictations of the funeral process. The philosophical nature of the poetry is adequately reflected by the stylistic and performance structures.

CONCLUSION

Funeral poetry is essentially a depiction of the phenomenon of transition, which again recalls archetypal patterns of the rites of passage. Death, as illustrated in the examples studied, is a transformation up the ladder of the cosmic realm. As a strategic aspect of poetry and drama of human life, funeral poetry explains the characteristics of tragedy as a literary phenomenon. Funeral poetry has elements of remorse, pathos, celebration, and at the same time catharsis. Its tragic and celebratory nature shows its communal relevance. The language of rendition, the mood of dramatization of action and use of musical accompaniments provide the scenario for the catharsis.

EXERCISES AND FIELDWORK

1. Look around you and compare the funeral setting and aura in traditional and contemporary societies.
2. Using some of the items you collected from the field, discuss the tone, mood and setting of funeral poetry.

3. Explore critically the functions of funeral poetry and how they related to the destiny of man.
4. Consider the structural and stylistic patterns of the funeral poetry in your own traditional setting.
5. Compare the nature of diction employed in religious, incantatory and funeral poetry.

Further Reading and Work

Ajunwon, Bade. *Funeral Dirges of Yoruba Hunter.* New York: Nok Publishers International, 1982.

Uzochukwu, Sam. *Traditional Funeral Poetry of the Igbo.* Lagos: Lagos University Press, 2001.

Notes and References

1. See Bayo Ogunjimi & Abdul Rasheed Na'Allah, *Introduction to African Oral Literature and Performance (Section I)*

Chapter Fourteen

Occupational and Heroic Poetry

OCCUPATIONAL POETRY INTRODUCTION

As we begin our discussion of Occupational Poetry, we must emphasize the fact that a strong work ethic is extolled in the African tradition. Every African grows to be an occupational man. He is trained from childhood to appreciate his society and explore the very rich physical, cultural and human resources in his environment for his spiritual and material well-being. Every African is trained through traditional culture to be an acceptable and useful member of the community. The first question posed by the African people in judging the acceptability of an individual is about his occupation or nature of work. This work ethic forms the basic philosophy behind occupational poetry. This type of poetry is common to all communities in Africa.

Occupational poetry expatiates on traditional occupations and technology. These include fighting in wars, hunting, farming, fishing and animal-rearing. We can also list blacksmithing, goldsmithing, carving, pottery, dyeing, etc. Some of these may be more pronounced in some areas than others. For example, people who live around hills and thick forests are predominantly hunters. People who live around rivers are fishermen and farmers. Those in savanna grasslands are cattle-rearers.

Of particular importance is traditional technology in Africa. Africans explore the mineral resources in their localities for better creativity and development. Those areas where the womb of the earth is rich in gold, iron, tin and columbite engage in smithing relevant to these minerals. You may wish to inquire further what these traditional occupations entail in terms of actual performance.

Poetry is important in traditional African life. People sing during peace and war. People sing at birth and death. People sing at work and play. The modern idea of music while at work in radio programs is borrowed from this traditional attitude. People sing during worship for spiritual effects and entertainment. Occupational poetic compositions are made at work.

We may wish to ask, who composes these songs? The workers, of course. They are usually the composers and performers of their own songs. There are specialized occasions, as in the case of hunting poetry Yorubas call "Ìjálá," when the audience may expand the performance scheme. Even then, this will be determined by the time, setting and occasion of performance. Again, we may ask, do other members of the society lack freedom to perform a type of poetry simply because they do not belong to a particular occupation? This is certainly not so. Every African has the right to sing, perform and enjoy these songs.

Apart from the rendition of occupational poetry during the actual working session, this genre can also be rendered during relaxation, occasional rituals and festivals involving workers at home, in the market place and at the village square. Occupational poetry is also important in creating communal interaction and links. The poetry provides communal ethics and values. Sometimes it presents and highlights the qualities of members of the community who have been very successful in the various occupations.

FUNCTIONS

The following present a summary of the functions of occupational poetry:

a) Boosts the morale and rekindles the energy of the worker at the performance of his/her job.
b) Brightens the otherwise occasional dull life of the worker and sharpens the creative faculty.
c) Serves as a forum through which workers propagate their involvement in their profession.
d) Helps to advertise their products.
e) The tempo of poetic rendition and performance stimulates the mental and physical fitness of the worker.
f) Serves as a forum through which workers are known, especially their domestic, cultural, political and moral backgrounds.

g) Teaches children strong work ethics. Communal interests, mutual understanding and symbiosis, social ideals and interaction are encouraged by this type of poetry.
h) It is employed in social functions such as marriage, naming, funeral, etc., that involve the members.
i) Entertains and provides a medium for communicating with gods and ancestors that are identified with the particular occupations as in the case of Ogun among the Yoruba hunters and blacksmiths.

ANALYSIS OF SAMPLES

The various occupations in a traditional setting are greased with one form of chant or the other. It is necessary for us to be able to list some of these occupations and find the poetic expressions that accompany the performance. As usual, we shall provide our students some working examples to allow for their practical involvement and appreciation of such poetry.

We have mentioned before that "Ìjálá Ode" among the Yorubas can be performed on different occasions. Specifically here, we shall consider such poetry that is used for hunting as an occupation in the traditional societies. The concern that a hunter has for his profession is expressed in the chant below:

> Ògún l'ode
> Èrò òwúrò o
> Èrò òwúro o
> L'ode n jí pa
> Òwúrò kùtù o
>
> Ògún is the hunter
> The early morning planning
> The early morning planning
> Makes the hunter's success
> It is the early morning

The ideas suggested in these few lines are important. Planning for a hunter means many things. He has to choose the setting for his game. He has to clean his guns and take the quality of gunpowder needed for the expedition. He has to prepare all his magical forces, apply some at home and put some in his hunting bags. All these create a creative process at the root of the poetic rendition and performance. His occupational poetic expressions do not end at this level. There in the forest, he entertains himself, reinforces himself and congratulates his own success. The following is performed right in the jungle by a hunter from Ìkéré-Èkìtì:

> Ode a ta etí Eréke
> Tí wón bá ti dé mògún òde
>
> The hunter changes form
> When he gets to the hunting forest

The performance here is an exposition of the hunter's magical prowess. The hunter changes to some other creatures as part of his defence methods. This encourages him the more to confront dangerous animals and other inimical forces in the forest. If you are from a family noted for this occupation, you should have been told many experiences and encounters of hunters in the forest. Can you relate some of them to your classmates for discussion?

In the forest, the hunter entertains, reinforces and celebrates his catching big game. At times, he is joined by fellow hunters who display their professional and communal solidarity with him. After catching a big game the hunter settles down under some shade to rest and roast the meat. In the forest, hunters communicate with one another through poetry. Their whistles and flutes ar put into effective use on these occasions.

We also recall one of the experiences from our informants from Ilésà, a Yorùbá town. Five hunters named Anaya, Ilaje, Omofe, Tiruni and Aranmora were involved in a dramatic performance in the forest.

Awon Ode	Ìmùlè mi dàbí ìlú Eni mo bá mulè kó má dà mí Eni bá dalè ìjòngbòn ló kò Werewere làá dá 'lù ode
Anaya:	Ó tóó-o-o-o gbogbo elégbé mode L'égbé m'ode, mo kí kékeré Mo sì kágbà ode Mo kí gbogbo Àgbonmìrègún Omo Alésìwodò

Occupational and Heroic Poetry

Hunters:
: My oath is like a town
Whoever has entered to the Oath
with me should not betray me
Whoever betrays me only meets
with trouble
It is with rapidity that the hunter's
drum is beaten

Anaya:
: It is enough now, all you co-hunters
Co-hunters with spectacular
dancing steps
I salute the young, I salute the elder hunters

I salute all the descendants of
Àgbon mìrègún of
Alésìwodò

This collective performance by the hunter demonstrates the strong ties among them. Such mutualism is strengthened by oath-taking. Oath-taking strengthens communal bonds, since it does not allow for betrayal. Betrayal in traditional African communities is a sacrilege. It goes beyond the interpersonal level, since it means provoking the wrath of the cosmic forces. The betrayal of man is the betrayer of gods, the force behind the oath. This is a strategy of unity and solidarity among the Mau Mau in Kenya in their struggle agains the British imperialism. The Agbekoya group of the old Western Region of Nigeria and the Maji Maji of former Tanganyika (now Tanzania) employed "oath-taking" as strong motivator in liberation struggles.

Occupational poetry boosts performance in traditional cooperative called "Òwè" and "Àáró" among the Yoruba. Traditional cooperatiaves are organizes on occupational basis. Farming, building a new hut for example, are occupations for which people gather together to give support to their clansmen. The issue of collective realization of goals is still paramount in traditional cultures. The following occupational poetry is generally chanted and performed to match the rhythm of actions at work:

Àjèjé owó kan kò gbérù dórí o
Àgbajo owó làá n fi n sòyà
Àjèjé owó kan kò gbérù dórí o

Introduction To African Oral Literature & Performance

> A single hand cannot lift a load to the head
> It is in the cooperation of hands that we boast
> A single hand cannot lift a load to the head

Wood-carving is an essential aspect of traditional craftsmanship. Apart from being a manifestation of people's aesthetic faculty, it provides avenues for exploring the philosophical world view of the people. Images and sculptural representations of gods, goddesses and ancestors' spirits are the handiworks of this occupation. In the process of carving the artist sings:

> Mà gb'égi l'ére
> Mà s'ogi d'èèyàn
> Àseyè, àgb'égún
> Fá gb égi l'ére
> Fá s'ogi d'èèyàn

> I will carve wood into an image
> I will turn wood into a human being
> Success, accurate carving
> For him that carves wood into an image
> For him that turns wood into a human being

The woodcarver creates the accurate image of the society, supernatural forces and human beings. The popular Nok Culture in Nigeria has its root in this profession.

The process of creativity in handiworks like carving, pottery, smithing etc. is synonymous with the process of poetic creativity. The rhythm of creative thinking, the rhythm of the aesthetic beauty of the product and their cultural functionalism are all basic to the art of carving and the art of poetry. Niyi Osundare confirms this thesis.

> You...know when I see a Sculptor sitting
> at a block of wood, at a block of stone
> or whatever and chiseling away, it
> reminds me very much of what I do in
> my agonizing period when I hold the
> pen in my hand and I'm chewing the
> upper tip...so, the two really come together[1]

Students are advised to collect poetic samples from fieldwork on indigenous occupations like pottery, fishing, weaving, beadsmaking, blacksmithing, etc. They should examine the songs used by local traders and hawkers to advertise their goods. Osundare[2] calls these songs 'Ipolowo Poetry'. It is also necessary for students to investigate how much of these songs are transformed into modern business advertisements.

HEROIC POETRY INTRODUCTION

Heroic Poetry

Heroic poetry is related to occupational services in African tradition. There is also intimacy between heroic poetry and praise poetry. By now, we should have been able to note the appearance of praise poetry in all forms of poetry already discussed.

Heroic poetry, like any of the other form of traditional poetry, is communally owned and employed to celebrate individuals, towns and lineages that had performed great feats during their lifetime. The human hero or heroine can be a hunter, a warrior, a farmer, a priest, an oracle man, a traditional Chief, King, Queen or any other person of spectacular record of achievements in a community. Also, some towns, and lineages are recognized because of their important positions in the history of their communities. The settlement of peoples in traditional communities always involved some heroic performance.

In heroic poetry compositions, African people keep the memory of their heroes alive. Oral poetry has been able to serve as a more natural custodian of such memory than modern written forms. In oral tradition, such memory is recalled with freshness of rendition and performance. The heroic activities performed by people during their lifetime are gradually stored in the memorybank of the society. The poet translates the residue of the memorybank to poetic compositions. The subjects or objects of the poetry may be praised even while still alive. The cumulative compilations of such heroic praises survive to make historical documents for the society.

Epic Poetry

African epic poetry are compositions about adventures, episodes, challenges and victories of legendary (and sometimes even mythical) individuals and about the community. The epic is a rich tradition in African culture. The oral singer of epic, or oral story teller of epic stories (where the epic is in the oral prose form) have legend memories of community history and can perform a single epic poetry for hours and more. It has been said that an epic poetry can be performed for days. Apart from the traditional oral composition and performance of epic poetry, epic poetry has been written in African languages using the Arabic writing system such as the *Ajami* in Northern Nigeria well before European colonization of Africa.

Jan Knappert, Isidore Okpewho, among others, have done very useful works on African epic including discussions of performance of epic poetry. It is essential to mention here briefly the relationship between heroic and epic poetry. There is much closeness in terms of the gallant performance and towering personality of the hero or heroine. The area where the hero or heroine is distinguished may be in war, perilous expeditions or a remarkable communal task. However, heroic poetry is transformed from the level of individualism to a communal effort in epic. The task that makes the diginity of the hero assumes a communal or national dimension, affecting the general life of the citizens. Historical legend can be classified as having epic contents. The heroism of Morèmi we discussed in Section I is about the destiny of the total community, not the glorious achievement of an individual.

Besides this, epic assumes some mythical force because of the intervention of the cosmic forces in the adventures of the epic hero or heroine. This is also illustrated by the heroic performance of Moremi. The seven hunters in *Ògbójú Ode Nínú Igbo Irúnmolè* by D.O. Fagunwa are involved in epic performance and ventures. The heroic feats of Sol Plaatje's heroine, Mhudi, in a novel of the same name assumes an epic dimension, since it affects national destiny.

In terms of the stylistic patterns of epic, the language is more condensed into narrative mythopoetic format. Classical allusions and mythical influences bear heavily on the stylistic formation. Much more work should be done in the area of data collection as far as epic is concerned. This is the more reason why Eurocentric critics argue that there is not epic in Africa. However, Isidore Okpewho in his celebrated book, *Epic in Africa* has refuted this erroneous conception. As students and scholars of African oral literature and performance, we are thus saddled with the responsibility of digging deep into tradition to be able to have more concrete evidence to illustrate the reality and nature of the African epic. Students and scholars should take the queue for this investigation by being familiar with the existing African epics, such as the Sundiata and Kambili epics in the ancient Mali as well as the Mwindo Epic in the Belgian congo (also the Lianja epic of the Nkundo of the Congo) and the epic of Chaka the Zulu in South Africa.

Functions

As usual, we shall outline the functions of heroic poetry so that it will be very easy for our students to follow the lesson. The moral basis of heroic poetry is the tendency in Africans to show gratitude and appreciation for a service rendered or job well done either to individuals or the community. The moral mind is thus the fertile intuition for a poetic mind in heroic poetry. Heroic poetry performs these functions:

a) It is a medium through which people express their appreciation to a courageous and patriotic member of the community, either for rescuing the people from a monster, an impending disaster or paving the way for the society's progress and development.
b) Helps to keep intact the historic contributions of notable individuals alive or dead. Thus it gives the community historical continuity.
c) Serves as a morale booster to the man or woman of achievement and selfless service propelling him or her to work more for the community.
d) Encourages younger ones to imitate the good qualities of the hero or target of the poetry, thus providing opportunity for people to demonstrate their skills for patriotic purposes.
e) Sensitizes the contemporary social, political and economic establishments to the ardent spirit of nationalism. This is the inherent dialectics in heroic poetry.

ANALYSIS OF SAMPLES

Several people have attained heroic status in Africa and have heroic poetry orally composedand chanted in their honour. In every hamlet, village or town, there are heroes and heroines to whom such poetry is dedicated. We can easily identify Aduloju, Ogedengbe, Sarauniya Amina Zazzau, Alafin Oranmiyan and Chaka the Zulu. Our students need to know some heroic lineages and towns. The poetry for the Offa lineage contains the rigour of heroism.

Let us study some examples of heroic poetry for a proper understanding of the issues we have raised concerning this poetry. The heroic poetry of Sarauniyar Amina Zazzau is taken from the Hausas:

>   Mun gode Daular
>   Ta K'warai!

Kowa da kowa
Lallai
Ya ambace ki
Ba wai!
Zai ko yabonki
Lallai
Kowa
Kudu da Arewa
Duk dai! Suna yabonki
Lallai

Ai sai nishadun
Dad'i
Don babu yunwa
Ko d'ai!
Dun babu kiwo
Lallai!
Fatara abun ki
Ko d'ai!
Sarauniyarmu
Kinji…[3]

We are indeed grateful
Yes indeed (we are)
Everybody
Definitely grateful
Whoever mentions your name
Extols your great qualities
Yes indeed!
East and West
Everybody!
South and North
All the people
Extol your name
Yes indeed!

It is only feeling of enjoyment we have
For there is no hunger
Whatsoever!
For there is no disease
None indeed.
Or that which to detest

Occupational and Heroic Poetry

> Whatsoever
> Oh! Our Queen
> You do hear our praise song

This example extols the leadership qualities of Queen Amina. A historical legend, she was a source of strength and pride for her people. She was a charismatic figure generally accepted by the people. Amina enjoyed the good will of the people from all quarters of the community. A brave warrior, she captured many communities and nation states to expand the territorial scope of her Kingdom. The traditional African community blames the leadership whenever there are hunger, disease and moral morbidity. As indicated in the poem, Queen Amina portrays good qualities of leadership.

The heroic poetry dedicated to Queen Amina raises the issue of feminism, properly articulated in traditional oral performances and African culture generally. The fact that we have the likes of Amina, Moremi and Mhudi as heroines in Africa clearly demonstrates the importance of women. Like their male counterparts, they excel in wars, politics, education, economy and other spheres. This traditional concept of feminism can be applied in the production of a pragmatic and utilitarian feminism in modern Africa.

The heroic song for Adúlójú, an Èkìtì warrior, is also relevant for our study and analysis. Let us recall the composition:

> Adúlójú àlá pàlá
> Ó p'ara ogun bí ení ké pa ilé
> Ó pa ilé bí ení ké p'ara ogun
> Omo ètù, omo ìbon
> Omo ení ká Àkókó
> Bímoó sìn lósè òkè
> Aba eru, e ba omo
> Ó ró gùrò bí ohun múbon tì
> Aba Ologunja ni ge ba
> Okùnrin bebe bí ení ko òjò ba sin
> Aba Ologunja ni ge ba
> Okùnrin bebe bi ení ko ejo ba ku
> Agba Ologunja ni ge ba
> Omí dá kéké bí eni ké yíò gbéni lo
> Aba Ologunja ni ge ba
> Ego wo riri bi eni ko yo ga
> Aba Ologunja ni ge ba
> Ibi ki an pe Ologunsi

Òun ponuda níbè
òun mo pese gbogbo akoni loko Eda
Ke so Lenin ku'ile Edemo

Adúlójú, a dream that kills a dream
He who goes to war like one going to his home
He who goes home as if going to war
Son of gunpowder, son of gun
To worship at the foot of the mountain
Father to slaves, father to children
Father with six marks that stand out clearly
He who stands as if he is resting on the gun
It is the father of Ologunja we are referring to
Man full of face like the threatening rain
It is the father of Ologunja we are referring to
Man with great power like when heavy downpour releases its whistle
It is the father of Ologunja we are referring to
Water keeps silent as if it cannot carry someone away
It is the father of Ologunja we are referring to
Snake crawls on the ground as if it is powerless
It is the father of Ologunja we are referring to
Where we call the braves to
We must not call the cowards
Son of the brave man of the farm of Eda
Which has its cradle at the back of Edemo's house.

The above sample is a celebration of the qualities and behavior of the warlord, Aduloju. The gallant and courageous performance of the warrior is highly praised by the poet and appreciated by the audience. His lineage praise names are evoked by the poet. His steadfastness is illustrated by the fact that he is never caught unawares and he takes fighting war as a common and familiar business. The poet also acknowledges his generosity, love and kindness to all. The poet praises the humaneness of a man who is "a father to slaves, father to children." He does not discriminate among his children, subjects and slaves. As a warrior, he is a great strategist and tactician as illustrated by the line "Snake crawls on the ground as if it is powerless." The whole of the poem is full of praises for Aduloju's bravery. Akinyemi's discussion of the poetry of the Alafin of Oyo is an excellent work on community's use of heroic poetry (see Akinyemi 2004).

STYLISTICS AND NATURE OF PERFORMANCE

For the purpose of organization we have decided to discuss the stylistics and nature of occupational, heroic and epic poetry under this sub-heading. This also will give our students the opportunity of revising the issues at stake in the chapter.

There is nothing really spectacular about the performance of occupational poetry. Usually, the rendition and performance are always made during the working session. Women pounding any materials in mortars keep up the tempo of action by just making the monotonous rhythm "Koya koya," quick quick, or by imitating the sound of the mortar "Pa po, po pa." The same may be true of other occupational poetry rendered and performed at the doomestic setting. It must be emphasized that occupational poetry is typified by brevity and unending repetition.

However, in some other occupations, the poetry may go into some few lines as in the case of the woodcarver's poetry we cited earlier. Brevity and repetition are still noticeable. This is usually sung at the workshop of the carver. What we can observe is that the rhythm of performance at work produces the rhythm of rendition. Since every occupation tasks human physiognomy, almost every part of the body is involved in the process of production and performance. Concrete images are less visible in this type of poetry.

Occupational poetry is not always accompanied by any elaborate musical supports. Musical productions are naturally improvised. Intermittent striking of the pestle against the mortar in tactical and calculated ways produces its own music. The pestle may be thrown up with punctuating claps. This is always done with perfection and accuracy. The occupational poetry produced while hoeing or making ridges on the farm are occasionally started with whistling. In fact, the whole of the poetry can be rendered by whistling. The situation seems to be a bit more elaborate with hunters' occupational poetry. Their flutes and other instruments may produce the musical accompaniments. Also, they can dance without elaborate musical accompaniments.

The heroic poetry, intended for the celebration of notable figures in the community, is performed communally in public. Collective performance is a common attitude of communal or oral literature. Chanting, dancing and corresponding appraisals, re-appraisals and acknowledgement are performed collectively. There is frequent use of gestures to demonstrate the greatness of the hero. At times, performances include imitating or mimicking some of the activities of the hero. The nature of performance in praise poetry and heroic poetry is similar.

CONCLUSION

In contemporary literature, occupational, heroic and epic poetry recur. In poetry, narratives and drama, some of these heroes are made protagonists. This at times produces archetypal patterns in modern African literature. However, it must be observed that traditional poetry has been misused, misplaced and contaminated in an attempt to satisfy the materialist ego of the modern age. These crises not withstanding, some of these songs are moderated or modernized to be dialectically relevant to the present.

EXERCISES AND FIELDWORK

1. Describe what you understand by occupational poetry. Cite examples from your own fieldwork to back up your explanation.
2. What purposes do heroic poetry serve in the traditional African society? Collect some Heroic poetry on your own to explain your ideas.
3. Compare heroic and epic poetry.
4. Collect materials on traditional heroines from your locality. What is the relevance of these materials in discussing the ideology of Black feminism?

Further Reading and Work

Akínyemí, Akíntúndé. *Yorùbá royal poetry: a socio-historical exposition and annotated translation.* Bayreuth: Bayreuth University, 2004.

Johnson, John Williams, et. al. *Oral epics from Africa: vibrant voices from a vast continent.* Bloomington, Indiana University Press, 1997.

Knappert, Jan. *Epic Poetry in Swahili and Other African Languages.* E.J. Brill, 1983.

Okpewho, Isidore. "The Resources or the Oral Epic" *African Intellectual Heritage.* Ed. Molefi Kete Asante and Abu. S. Abarry. Philadelphia: Temple University Press, 1996. 119-130.

Notes and References

1. Bayo Ogunjimi's interview with Niyi Osudare titled "Niyi Osudare: The Literary Evangelist combs the World" in *The Guardian* June 5 & 12, 1993, Lagos, p. 19.
2. See Osundare's *"Poems For Sale:* Stylistic Features of Yoruba Ipolowo Poetry" in *African Notes* Vol. 15, Nos. 1 & 2, 1991, pp. 63-72.
3. B. Ahmed, *Amina: Sarauniyar Zazzau* Zaria: Hudahuda Publishing Company, 1983, p. 13.

Chapter Fifteen

Topical, Lullaby, and Occasional Poetry

TOPICAL POETRY INTRODUCTION

As the name implies, topical poetry addresses issues that cover all the areas of human reality. Usually, they are issues that can be described as matters of the moment. They fall into the category of what the news media regard as "current affairs." Some of the oral poets we identified in Section I of this book pass comments on the day-to-day cultural, social and political life around them. Topical poetry may be addressed to individuals, and groups based on the moral precepts, norms and beliefs of the society.

CATEGORIES

For convenience, it will be necessary to make classification of this poetic form:

A) Domestic Topical Poetry

These are songs that address domestic issues like love, loyalty between husband and wife, rancour in polygamous settings, jealousy and rivalry in the general domestic setting, relationships among children to their parents, ethics of upbringing and other concerns such as discipline, hard work and politics at the domestic level are treated in topical poetry.

B) Political Topical Poetry

This comments on the political matters of the community. Political behavior and negation of the rules of governance in the society are condemned and satirized. Rulers and leaders of the people are occasionally ripped or praised depending on their political attitude. It is a platform for correcting political misdeeds. This poetic form may also be made up of invectives, assaults, warnings and political inuendos among political groups and rivals. It expresses the state of relationship among clans, ethnic groups and even larger communities, fighting on a piece of land or engaging in some age-long enmity. There may be some overlapping with praise poetry because individuals, groups or communities may even be positively acknowledged in this poetic form.

C) Social Topical Poetry

Issues and matters on friendship, social groups, communal relationships and interactions are the subject matter of this category. This type of topical poetry comments on fashions in vogue, styles, slangs and general social behavior and practices around.

Functions

We shall be able to shed more light on the nature of this form as we discuss its functions generally. Topical poetry does the following:

a) Comments generally on domestic, socio-cultural and political happenings in society.
b) Keeps records and relates the past to influence the present and the future.
c) Projects fashions and advertises ideas and social norms in vogue at a particular point in time.
d) Serves as a medium for disseminating information about the day-to-day affairs of the community. Performs the function of the modern electronic and print media.
e) Provides a forum for socialization, teaching and enforcing of beliefs, norms and ethics of the community. It provides outlet for teaching the code of conduct of the community as it relates to discipline, ethics of works and morality.
f) Aids social mobilization and communal solidarity.
g) Exposes the tension, rancour and acrimonies in the traditional settings.

ANALYSIS OF SAMPLES

i. Domestic Topical Poetry

Domestic topical poetry is chanted and performed by fathers, mothers and other adults in the society. It is made up of spontaneous rich poetic composition. Domestic topical poetry encourages the children to embrace the ethics and values of the society. Such songs

Topical, Lullaby, and Occasional Poetry

and chants deal with the knowledge of child rearing and upbringing. Children are educated to realize the value of hardwork, discipline, honesty and diligence. Through this medium, children are groomed to take after their parents' virtues and resourcefulness as indicated in the sample below:

>Omo Omo dá ìyá rè l'ójú
>Bí a bá lo sájò,
>Omo eni a w'olé d'eni
>Kàkà ká b'ógórùún òbùn
>Bí a bí'kan ògá, ó tó!
>Àpà òbùtà ràìràì
>Omo olórò ìsaájú
>Níí tàlèkè
>F'ómo olórò ìkehìn
>Níí f'owó m'emu
>Níí gb'ésin tà
>Níí f'owó mutí
>Níí gb'ówóò 'wòfà
>Fi sanwó f'éléran
>Níí lé erú re re re
>Láléè wògbé
>Erú bá wogbó, tolówó gbé
>Erú d'omo, eni lo
>Nélé ibikan dandan
>Eléèébú leebu ya
>Ení bíni là á jo
>B'ómo kò jo sòkòtò
>Omo á jo kíjìpá
>Tojú timú l'omo eni fíí joni

>The child
>The mother trusts her child
>Whenever one travels
>One's child looks after the house
>For us to have a hundred filthy children
>One decent child is enough
>The squanderer shall have enough to eat
>The first rich man's child
>Is he who sells the beads
>For the second rich man's child
>It is he who spends on palm-wine

> He sells away the (parent's) horse
> And spends the money on alcohol
> He robs the poor servant
> To pay the meat-seller
> He chases the servant away
> To the bush
> And the servant disappears and the riches disappear
> The servant becomes somebody in his home
> One whose curses bears his curse
> It is one's parents that one resembles
> If a child does not resemble the trousers
> He will resemble the wrapper
> With the face, with the nose does one's child resemble one.

As evident in the poetic composition, the focus is the child. The poet turns an educator and social philosopher. The target is not the child alone, parents are tactically robed in. For parents to expect good behavior from their children, they (parents) must show good examples. Another example which illustrates this goes thus:

> A gb'ójú l'ógún fi ra rè f'ósì ta
> Ìyá re lè lówó l'ówó
> Baba re lè l'ésin l'éèkàn
> Bóo bá gb'ójú lé won
> O té tán ni mo so fún o
>
> He who puts his hope on
> legacy has poverty awaiting him
> Your mother may be rich
> Your father may have horses in the stable
> If you rely on them
> You will suffer from disgrace

Songs that intend to project the traditional culture of the people are chanted in homes and other domestic settings, but such poetic compositions go all out for public consumption and entertainment. These songs in most cases have their roots in the philosophy, religion and cultural beliefs of the people. One of such relates to the norms of discipline in child-rearing among the Yorubas:

Topical, Lullaby, and Occasional Poetry

En-n-n-n-n
Èyin téè n wé rodorede
En-n-n-n-n
B'ómo bá yàgbé
Baba rè ní ó ko

En-n-n-n
Those of you who win immature child
En-n-n-n
When the child excretes
It is the father that will pack it

This simply explains the policy of family planning in the traditional African society. It is a re-affirmation of the cultural belief that a child should at least be three years before the parents prepare for another. This makes the child to be strong and healthy. Parents are expected to abstain from sexual intercourse while nursing a child. Sexual intercourse, it is believed, pollutes the milk fed to the child. A child fed through such milk becomes rickety, weak and unhealthy. This is a coherent system of traditional medical care, which the modern medicine has not been able to controvert. The song is a general criticism of immorality in the society.

Domestic topical poetry raises issues pertaining to the social well-being and survival of man. A housewife or even the husband may express fear and anxiety about the scarcity or inavailability of some essential farm products by raising alarm:

Àjànàkú ò jé a d'áko l'ónà jíjìn
Ewúré ò je ká d'áko etílé
En-en, bíyàn bá wòlú
Gbogbo ayé ní ó rí i

The elephant does not allow us to farm afar off
The goat does not allow us to farm near home
En-en, if there is famine
The whole world will see it

This type of topical poetry may have some other symbolic interpretations, depending on the suffering of the people in the society. The housewife in the contemporary society may as well use this song to criticize some excruciating economic programs like the Structural Adjustment Program (SAP) suffocating the life of many Nigerians.

World economic strains through the International Monetary Fund (IMF) or other globalization forces may have been criticized through this form of poetic composition. "The elephant" and "the goat" in the song are the inimical forces against human progress.

Also, some domestic topical songs reflect the day-to-day ethics and general routines of the people. Such songs project the communal customs, attitude to work and discipline that a family or the locality as a whole is noted for. A common song among housewives and children in Ìlorin can be cited for illustration:

>Àwa mò béè
>Àwa mò béè
>Nílé Akéwúsolá
>Nílé Akéwúsolá
>Nílé tí won n tànkárá
>Nílé tí won n tànkárá
>Òle ò le gbé'lùú wa
>Òle ò le gbé'lùú wa
>Aago méjo lòle n jí
>Aago méfà là wá n jí
>Ìrun àkópè là wá n jí
>Aago méfà la wá n jí

>We know it so
>We know it so
>In the house where we pride on Quranic knowledge
>In the house where we pride on Quranic knowledge
>In the house where they read (the Quran)
>In the house where they read (the Quran)
>The lazy one cannot live in our town
>The lazy one cannot live in our town
>The lazy one wakes up at 8 o'clock
>We wake up at 6 o'clock
>We wake up at the first-call-to-prayer
>We wake up at 6 o'clock

The attitude and manners in modern Ilorin community are even reflected in this poetry. These include: reading the Quran and early morning prayer, which reflect the Islamic practicaes in the city.

ii. Political Topical Poetry

Politics is a commonplace game in all the facets of human existence. Politics is played in the household among husbands, wives and children. Politics is played at work and at the playing ground. It is therefore a facet of human existence that provokes poetic composition in traditional and modern societies. Politics in the traditional set up may be at the domestic, neighborhood, inter-clans and inter-community levels. We think it is necessary for students to attempt philosophical definitions of politics with their teacher.

First, let us have discussions based on topical political poetry at the home front. There is competition for the first class position and recognition between or among wives in polygamous setting. There is the struggle to win the favor of the husband, co-wives, mother-in-law and other relatives of the husband. The husband must have a great sense of management, judgement and fairplay.

The political situation in every home, compound or neighborhood in African is known through this medium. Topical poetry of this category is chanted by the wives, grandmothers, mothers-in-laws, children and other members of the family. The relationships among these are reflected in the nature of the songs composed at any point in time. Let us consider the situation that has led to the composition of this:

> Èmi mo nìyá oko mi
> Èmi mo nìyá oko mi
> Bó wù mí ma yín l'órun
> Èmi moo,
> Emí mo nìyá oko mi o
> Bó wù mí ma yín l'órun
> K'orí ó pé

> I am the owner of my mother-in-law
> I am the owner of my mother-in-law
> If I like I can twist her neck
> Indeed, I am,
> I am the owner of my mother-in-law
> If I like I can twist her neck
> So, mind your business

The wife here, who is the poet, is at peace with her mother-in-law. It could even be that they have just settled a quarrel and so the wife wants to announce it to the world that she is in love and enjoys a mutual relationship with her mother-in-law. People are thus warned to keep away from insinuations and intrigues.

In polygamous homes, co-wives occasionally quarrel. Each wife displays her talent in the use of invectives, insults and biting satirical comments in form of songs. One does not need to pay attention to hear such songs in a neighboring house. The following illustrates this:

   K'éran má je'lé la fi se
   K'éran má je'lé la fi se
   Ìyáwo onfiranù
   K'éran má
   K'éran má je'lé la fi se o
   Ìyáwo onfiranù
   Koríopé

   We have kept her to ward off goats from the house
   We have kept her to ward off goats from the house
   The wayward wife
   We have kept
   We have kept her to ward off goats from the house
   The wayward wife
   So, mind your own business

Students should adduce the various reasons why these types of song are composed. They should also be able to identify the frame of reference that signals abuse in the poem. Consider the situation in a polygamous family and suggest the way the other wife being abused will react. Let us consider another example from a co-wife, who may be attacking or reacting to the insult of the other wife. She sings:

   Pelembe n sesè
   Pelembe n sesè
   Níbo ni pépéye n bò wá
   Pelembe n sesè

   She has flat legs
   She has flat legs
   Where is the duck coming
   She has flat legs

However, it must be stressed that the husband, who may be the central figure in the conflict, is not always left out in the tirades of these domestic poets. The nagging wife may then level her lance at the husband, who she thinks, favors the other wife. She ridicules the husband thus:

    E pèlé oko iyàwó, elépònon wáyà
    Bó bá sòpá,
    E sáà jé ká mò
    Ká lè já'wé lágbàlá
    Kéyìn ó nà

    Sorry, the husband with a wired testicle
    When you develop swollen testicle,
    Just let us know
    So that we can go for leaves at the backyard
    So as to straighten your backbone

Here, the neglected wife is mocking the husband, condemning his intimacy with the other wife. This is the aspect of the conflict painful to her. She may think that a frontal attack on the husband may lead to a change of relationship.

Topical political poetry goes beyond the domestic domain. Clans and communities involved in clashes over the crown, lands encroachment, etc., occasionally engage in verbal warfare, probably as a preliminary to real physical combat. In this case, the poets may be few men and later the whole of the community may be involved. They compose songs that show disregard for their rivals:

    Òkun ni wá o
    A ò f'omi olómi san'ra
    Igi ewúro ò fi t'òjò koròo
    E má torí wa lo gbóbè kaná o
    Ení torí wa lo gb'óbè kaná o
    Orí iná l'obè ó dànù sí o

    We are the ocean
    We are not fattened by other waters
    The bitter leaf tree is not bitter because of the rain
    Do not put soup on fire because of us
    He who puts soup on fire because of us
    The soup will pour away on the fire

The poets here are many, since it is the voice and force of the community. The emphasis is on the power of self-sustenance, without essentially relying on others. Warnings and threats are issued through such poetic compositions.

However, such a situation may deteriorate into open fracas and physical confrontation, producing a more fierce political poetry:

> Oká n lérí
> Olúfà n lérí
> Òní la ó m'ejò t'ó gùn jura won lo
>
> The adder is boasting
> The python is boasting
> It is today we shall know the snake that is longer.

Both the adder and python are snakes, but one is stronger than the other. Definitely the strength of the python will surpass that of the adder. The strong contrast draws the conflict between the rivals. The victory of the stronger is marked by another song:

> Àjé n lérí
> Osó tí n halè ojó pé
> Won p'òfo lónìí o
> Kì í s'àwàdà
> Ojú tì wón o
>
> The witch is boasting
> The wizard has been threatening for long
> They have lost today
> It is not a joke
> They are ashamed

Political wranglings also occur among members of the royal family. This may even escalate into inter and intra families' feuds. The individuals or the collective of a group assert their power of supremacy and the ability to survive the crisis and weather the tide. At times, such poetry is produced by musical accompaniments like "dundun" or "bata." These are Yoruba traditional drums. The song is always chorused by the peoples:

Onílù: Adébímpé, kínkín o gbodo gbin

Topical, Lullaby, and Occasional Poetry

> Iba Oromojogbo
> Adélakùn, omo Adébíopón
> Bó d'énú won, bí ò dúkùn won
> O s'egbèrún odún l'áyé
> Omo Adébíopón
> G'ésin ní késé
> Bó d'énú won, bí ò dékùn won
> O s'egbèrún odún l'áyé

> Adebimpe, the enemy must not breathe
> Homage to Oromojogbo
> Adelakun the son of Adébíopón
> Whether they are satisfied or not satisfied
> You will spend one thousand years on earth
> The son of Adébíopón
> Kick the horse
> Whether they are satisfied or not satisfied
> You will spend one thousand years on earth

The poet intimidates the enemies by invoking and digging the genealogical root reflected in the names of ancestors like "Oromojogbo" and "Adébíopón." The enemies are provoked and the war mood is signaled by the kicking of the horse, but the most important thing is that the poet will survive whether or not the enemies like it.

This type of political poetry is imitated raw in contemporary politics. In the political days of the Action Group (AG) and the National Council of Nigeria and Cameroun (NCNC) provoking topical poetry borrowed from traditions were always exchanged between party thugs. We have this example:

> Àwon wón ó fidà para won
> Àwon wón ó fidà para won
> Ìjàpá tí n fidàko pako
> Àwon wón ó fidà para won

> It is they that will kill themselves with the sword
> It is they that will kill themselves with the sword
> The tortoise hanging the sword on its own head
> It is they that will kill themselves with the sword

This has some relationship with incantatory poetry. Probably a member of one party casts a spell on the members of the other and they are fighting among themselves, the song would be chanted to heighten the tension. Opponents would sing such songs when there were intra-party wranglings. Our students should make organized research on this type of political poetry.

iii. Social Topical Poetry

Chidi Amuta is very right when he asserts that the reflection on socio-political matters of the day is the justification that traditional oral poets have for their creativity. The preoccupations of social topical poetry are derived from the poets' depiction of the social and political scenario of their settings. Poets turn social commentators and critics. At times, the poets acknowledge the positive values in some social norms. Most of the time, they detest the evil and malaise that plague the society.

We can cite the example of 'Dan Maraya's song "jawabin Aure" on the rampant cases of divorce. H.A. Daba[2] observes that 'Dan 'Maraya, a famous Hausa oral poet, thinks that the high rate of divorce among the Hausas is traceable to "some old idle mischievous women." Let us listen to the poet's composition on the evil of divorce:

>Maigida da uwargida
>In an yi fad'a don Annaabi
>Don Allah a bar saurin fita
>To amma in an bibiya,
>Watakila gidan da manafik'a
>Abin da maigida iyi
>Aje a gayawa uwargida
>Sannan ita ba ta bincike
>Abin da uwargida ta yi
>Aje a gayawa maigida
>Sannan shi ba ya bincike
>Sai ka ga hasuma ta hadu
>To daga nan kuma sai rabuwa ta zo

>Housemaster and the senior wife
>If you quarrel
>For the sake of Allah do not leave the house
>If the case is to be considered carefully,
>Hypocrites are to be found in the house
>Whatever the husband does
>Is narrated to the wife

> And she believes without investigation
> Whatever the wife does
> Is also taken to him
> And he believes without inquiring
> You see, within seven days
> Enmity will rise up (between them)
> And divorce occurs.

The poet's target is the domestic setting. The devil-woman identified in the song is an archetype of "la femme fatale." This devil archetype stirs confusion and bitterness among husbands and wives to cause divorce. The song emphasizes the ignorance of couples about the evil machinations of this devil incarnate. She gives distorted information to both the husband and wife. This type of poetry is to ensure the stability of the African homes and the community in general.

The traditional artist always appraises the social situation. He critizes anti-social behaviors. Such preoccupations of the traditional poet or singer are aptly reflected in the composition of Àyìnlá Omowúrà, who works within the traditional framework lie 'Dan Maraya. The sample to be studied is a bitter criticism of bleaching, rampant among old and young women in Nigeria. Art for the traditional poet like Omowúrà is for the defence of societal norms and declaration of war against such tendencies of acculturation. Omowúrà sings:

> Òrò kan wà nílè tí mo fé so
> Dúró b'Ólórun Oba se dá e
> Má b'awo jé f'éni bí e
> Ká má sì é mò torí afé ayé[3]

> I have a matter to discuss
> Accept the way God has created you
> Do not spoil your complexion for your parents
> Do not lose your complexion for worldly pleasure

Omowúrà condemns Africans who bleach their skin. This ironically causes a health crisis rather than pleasure. Omowúrà revisits the traditional African belief on creation. Tampering with the body structure means the abortion of the creative handiwork of Obàtálá and other African creation gods. To the artist, it is thus an abominatin and a sacrilege to bleach.

Introduction To African Oral Literature & Performance

At times, there are overlappings between social and political topical poetry. The poet may make compositions that are social comments targeted at the forces of oppression. We draw an example from a traditional Igbo song to illustrate this:

> Ochicha amaghi ngwe
> Mu Kwanyalu n'owhe
> O jee mee
> Owhe m onogolu!
> Mje Kpee Ochicha
> be Agudimgbo
> Whuye anyasi dawakwa
> Agudimgbo akuwalu
> Ochicha eke:
> Owhe m
> Mutenyelu azu
> Mu tenyelu ngwongwo
> Ochicha mee
> Owhe onogolu!

> Cockroach knows not the ingredients
> I put into the soup
> He went and made my soup his seat!
> I went and reported Cockroach
> To Wall-Gecko
> (But) At the fall of dusk
> Wall-Gecko beats a drum for Cockroach
> My soup
> Into which I put fish
> Into which I put diverse ingredients
> Cockroach made
> The soup his seat![4]

Cockroach in this composition symbolizes oppression and social injustice. The insect is the epitome of many fraudulent powerful individuals. The soup represents the sweat and labor of the oppressed now exploited by the marauder. Despite the complaints of the victim to a higher authority, Wall-Gecko, the oppression persists. Modern society is besieged by this parabolic nocturnal animal, Cockroach. In human guise they are politicians, religious leaders, businessmen and other social forces that cause social dysfunctionality. Students should explore this composition further and suggest its other possible interpretations.

Topical poetry is a very important poetic composition in Africa. This type of poetry permeates every sector of the society and communal relationships. They also probe the ills and evils of the society.

LULLABY INTRODUCTION

Lullabies are the songs used by mothers and traditional nurses to soothe and pet babies so as to make them stop crying, or sometimes, lure them to sleep. The African mother is a caring mother. She does anything: sing, dance, clap, fan, pet, beg, to make her child comfortable. A Yoruba proverb says *"Abiamo kì í gbo ekún omo rè kó sùn lo,"* "A nursing mother does not hear the cry of her child and continue to sleep." *Abiamo boja gberogboro.* The intimacy between the mother and the child derives from genetic and hereditary influence. The mother sees the child as the image of herself or that of the husband, or both. Hence, in most cases, lullaby contains the expression "Oko mi," my husband. This love can be traced to the archetypal Oedipal complex syndrome. The result of this intimacy is spontaneous poetic compositions to placate, improve the mood and feeling of the child.

Functions

It will be necessary for us to briefly itemize the functions of lullabies in general, they include:

a) Soothing the children to stop them from crying.
b) Luring the children to sleep.
c) Helping the mother to express her affection to her child.
d) Expressing cultural norms and communal attitudes, directly or indirectly introduced to children.
e) Inculcating in children a sense of creativity and perception through rhythms and musical patterns.
f) Encourage a deep sense of feeling and rapport between the child and the mother.
g) Helping children to cultivate the elements of the language of their community, thus aiding in the language learning process.
h) Introducing the children to some traditional occupations and activities, the performance of which necessitates this poetic composition.

Analysis of Samples

Mothers can read the psychology of their children. Every lullaby composed and performed is carefully picked to achieve an immediate purpose. Let us consider this one composed by Ijesha mothers among the Yorubas:

>Dáké o e e
>Omo Ògbóni
>Mére ni e kun
>Omo a jí bo bua
>Omo a fo ku a pa keke
>Dáké o okoò mi
>Dáké mó bíínú o
>Dáké o e e
>O káre omo Owá
>Omo Oni'kab teere olugberu ajojiko wese
>Àjèjì ò wesè níbè ebo ni arifise
>Baba re nìkàn ló wesè níbè
>À wè gbó wè tó
>Omo ekùn gòlò
>Dáké o e e
>Dáké o e e
>Dáké Olúkóredé
>Má fekuru já mi láyà
>Èyìn na gbémo o pòn
>Dáké o e e
>Oko mi

>Keep quiet my child
>The child of Ògbóni
>You who traditional necklace fits
>You who comes to life to behave well
>Some children cry and cry and others keep calm
>Keep quiet my husband
>Keep quiet don't be annoyed
>Keep quiet
>Well done Owá's child
>The child of a narrow spring named Ogbere
>Where strangers don't wash legs
>Stranger that washes his legs there becomes a meat for sacrifice
>Only your father washes his legs there

Topical, Lullaby, and Occasional Poetry

And lives longer
Child of tiger
Keep quiet
Keep quiet
Keep quiet, Olúkóredé
Don't hit my chest with mashed bean cake
It is on the back that we keep a child
Please keep quiet
My husband

The emphasis in this composition is an attempt to placate the child that is crying. Thus, there is the recurrence of the pleading note "Dáké o." The mother may be performing some domestic chores or she may be at her occupational base, working. The child feels a sense of neglect and begins to cry. In most cases, the melodious rendition of the mother is enough to soothe the child.

This song reminds us of praise poetry, which we discussed in Chapter Twelve. The mother-poet digs up the traditions to bring the mind of the child to rest. Lineage names are invoked as in the references to "the child of Ògbóni" and "the child of Owá." Besides, the heroic tradition of the lineages are invoked. Hence, he is praised as "the child of tiger." As we have mentioned, all these are methods of informal education of a child.

At times, we have songs of this type composed to really show the problem of the child. The child may be hungry, sick or he may just need the gentle touch of the mother. He may even be annoyed. Sometimes, the mother reaches the conclusion that the child is troublesome. The example just cited explains this. The mother cautions the child not to "hit my chest with mashed bean cake." The source of the child's anger or cry may be hunger. Hence, he can be pacified in this rendition:

Dáké o
Ta ní nà án o?
Eye ni, tutu si
Kó sá lo
Ta ní nà án o?
Ìyá è ni
Ó gb'ómú r'oko
Kò gbé e wálé mó

Introduction To African Oral Literature & Performance

> Keep quiet
> Who beats him
> It is the bird
> Beg to it run away
> Who beats him
> It is the mother
> Who takes the breast to the farm
> Who does not bring it home again

Here the mother finds a cunning way of placating the child, who was properly fed. The mother adduces that it is the bird that has beaten the child, but the real fact is that the mother does not want to feed him again, hence the pretence, "she takes the breast to the farm/ she does not bring it back home again." It is probably the melody rather than the mother's explanation that will placate the child.

"Mothering" or nursing a baby is an arduous responsibility that deserves patience. Mothers in African traditional settings think alike. The example below from the Igbo community shows this similarity.

> Nwannem ta kwuo onu, kwuo onu na nne gi loo
> Nne gara Uzo egbelu
> I gbu teregi ukpara ndo
> Onye ozo erighi ya
> Mu na gi ga eri ya
> Uh uh uh uh uh

> My little baby don't cry, don't cry
> That your mother will come
> Mother went to the farm
> To get fruit of life for you
> No other person will eat it
> We would eat it together
> Don't don't, don't don't don't

The interpretation of the last line may vary. It may be that the mother is mimicking the child's crying pattern. This may make the child to feel that the mother is playing with him, hence he will be quiet. However, it may backfire, irritating the child the more. We cite another example from the Ibgo community:

> Tata ndoo, ndoo, ndoo, ndoo
> Eweta Utera mu na gi eria

Topical, Lullaby, and Occasional Poetry

>Ndoo, ndoo, ndoo, ndoo
>Eweta ji mu na gi eria
>Ndoo, ndoo, ndoo, ndoo
>Eweta area na ni gi anvo
>Oponial tourom nwata uto o o o
>
>Baby don't cry, don't cry, don't cry
>If they bring eba we will eat
>Don't cry, don't cry, don't cry, don't cry
>If they bring yam we will eat
>Don't cry, don't cry, don't cry, don't cry
>If they bring breast milk, only you will drink

On some rare circumstances, this type of poetic form turns ritualistic. We are specifically referring to lullabies composed for twins. Twins are children defined as being sacred. Among the Yorubas, they are worshipped. They have images like those of other gods and goddesses, representing their supernatural being. Hence it is often chanted that:

>Kí ní ó fi'bejì se
>Kí ní ó fi'bejì se
>Babaláwo tí n kanrí ìbejì mónú
>Kí ní ó fi'bejì se
>
>What can he do to the twins
>What can he do to the twins
>Babalawo that begrudges the twins
>What can he do to the twins

"Babaláwo" who is highly revered in the science of magic and juju cannot do anything to the twins, because of their link with the supernatural forces.

Therefore when poetic renditions are made for the twins, they are more than mere lullabies. While such songs may be used to soothe and placate the twins, they are inherently loaded with metaphysical meanings. It is common among Yoruba mothers who give birth to twins to sing thus:

>Epo n be èwà n be o o
>Epo n be, èwà n be o o
>Àyà mi ò já, o ye e

Àyà mi ò já láti bí 'beejì o
Epo n be èwà n be o o.

There is palm oil, there is beans
There is palm oil, there is beans
I am not afraid, o yes
I am not afraid to give birth to twins
There is palm oil, there is beans

"Palm oil" and "beans" are objects used by their mother for sacrifices to the gods for their good health and survival. Some of these mothers become itinerant, going about to beg for the survival of the twins. It is believed at times, that it is a religious injunction that this must be done, but in a sense they become freelance poets.

On the whole, we can draw some relationship between African lullabies and what in the English tradition is called nursery rhymes. Probably, the logic is what the former initiates the children to the latter, which they themselves sing and peform. Children's songs and plays probably also receive their inspirations from lullabies, but how many of these songs do we hear today? You need to respond critically to this question to be able to initiate further discussions on this subject matter.

OCCASIONAL POETRY INTRODUCTION

In this section, we shall discuss briefly "Ekun-iyawo," which we translate as "The bride's poetry." "Ekun-iyawo" is very important because of its archetypal nature. Symbolically, marriage with this form of poetry is associated is an archetype of the rites of passage from immaturity to maturity. The lady, who has been with her parents and other relatives since her birth, will now assume a new status. This is the status that will make her start her own family. Let us examine the functions of the bride's poetry.

Functions

The bride's poetry allows for the following:

a) Dramatizes the archetypal ritual of passage of rites from immaturity to maturity.
b) Enables the bride to express her mixed feelings about her permanent departure from her generic setting and place of birth.
c) Depicts the emotional attachment and affection between parents and daughters of all often shed tears during the performance.

Topical, Lullaby, and Occasional Poetry

d) Serves as a forum for the daughter to acknowledge the moral upbringing, discipline and culture of survival she enjoyed from her parents.
e) Shows the ritualistic drama associated with this rite of passage and project the richness of African culture.
f) Serves as a forum for parents to bestow their blessings on the bride and to admonish her of responsibilities in her new socio-cultural setting.

Analysis of Samples

This period is always laden with tense emotions of love and affection. The sense of detachment from her source makes for occasional eruptions of tears. It is during this dramatic moment of separation for good that the bride renders this emotional poetic piece:

> Baba mi mo wá gbàre mi o
> Ìre mi pò, irìe mi kò kéré
> Bí ò té mi l'órùn mi ò lo
> Bí ò kúnnu gbájè
> A sì kúnnú ahá
> Àmó bí ò té mi lórùn mi ò lo
> Ire lónìí orí mi af ire
> U-u-uh, -u-u-uh, u-u-uh
> Ire, àní kí n má yà nísò àgàn
> Ábíkú l'elédèé bi
> Àbí gbìn ni tògèdè
> Orí ó má jé n bábìígbìn omo
> Bí mo b'ógún nílé
> Ání bí mo b'ógbòn lódèdè
> Orí ó mà ní se mí lágàn láàrin won
> Ire lónìí o orí mi àfi ire
> U-u-u-h, u-u-u-h, u-u-u-h
> Baba mi n ó yalé bàbá re
> Nílé Òpómúléró Mojaàlekàn
> Abímbésú ará ìlú Òyán
> Omo eké tó dá mi moja
> Té e ba n loolé Abímbésú onílé Òyán
> Òpómúléró Mojaàlekàn
> Òpómúléró Mojaàlekàn
> Baba mo wá gbàre mi kí n to lo

> My father, I have come for my blessings
> My blessings are many, my blessings are not small
> I shall not go until I am satisfied
> If it does not fill the *gbájè*
> It will fill *ahá*
> But if I am not satisfied I shall not go
> Fortune is mine today, nothing but fortune for me
> U-u-uh,-u-u-u-uh, u-u-u-uh
> Fortune, do not let me be in the company of barren women
> The pig bears its own to die
> The plantain bears its own for burial
> My head, do not leat me bear children for burial
> If I give birth to twenty in the room
> And if I give birth to thirty in the parlour
> My head do not make me barren among them
> Fortune is mine today, nothing but fortune for me
> U-u-uh, u-u-u-uh, u-u-uh
> My father, I want to pay homage to your ancestors
> In the lineage of Òpómúléró Mojaàlekàn
> Abimbesu from Òyán land
> The pillar of Mojalekan
> When you are going to the house of Abmbeésú at Òyán
> Òpómúléró Mojaàlekàn
> Òpómúléró Majaàlekàn
> My father, I have come for my blessings before I go

The central content of this poetry is the appeal for blessings from the parents and prayer for fortunes and luck in future. The poetry is repeated to the mother, taking into consideration her lineage cognomen, too. The bride also needs blessings so that she will be productive and not barren. A very important aspect of the poetry is the profuse reference to the lineage of her father. The implication is that the bride is not only invoking the blessings of the living, she is also invoking the ancestors for guidance in her new life. No wonder, the bride chants the praise poetry of the Òpómúléró lineage. This is a notable traditional ritual, which has been eroded by the marriage culture of imported religions. It will be of assistance if our students can investigate thoroughly into the routines of this archetypal ritual.

Stylistics and Nature of Performance

Having treated the subject matter of topical, lullaby and occasional poetry, we think it will be helpful to our students to discuss their stylistics and nature of performance under the same heading. This will allow for apt revision of the issues already discussed but via the aesthetics of rendition and performance. The arrangement will also make for a comparative study of the stylistics and nature of performance of these forms of poetry.

The stylistics and nature of performance of domestic, political and topical poetry are similar with slight differences. It is rare to have long poetic compositions for these forms. In most cases, they are brief, directly hitting the target. The spontaneity of the process of composition is partly responsible for this brevity. The domestic nature of the poetry is reflected in the composition and objects mentioned. Domestic items like calabash, grinding stone, water and food materials are used for creative effects. Some of these objects are used also as musical accompaniments to influence oral performance and the audience.

A very predominant stylistic feature of topical poetry is the use of invectives. Invectives are linguistic arrangements that contain insults, abuse, satire and cynicism. The emotional state of the poet provokes this stylistic device. Let us consider the line, "We have kept her to ward off goats from the house." The co-wife to which this is addressed is experiencing a demeaned personality. This implies that she is of no consequence. A direct abuse or insult is metted to a husband describing him as having wired and swollen testicle. Alternatively, we may wish to consider the reaction of a co-wife who is described as having flat feet like those of a duck. All these are common features of topical poetry. Students should be able to test the relevance of this stylistic device.

Generally, imagery and symbols are profusely used in this poetic form. We have already given the symbolic interpretations of the "elephant" and "goat" that do not allow for comfortable farming. "Cockroach" in the Igbo topical poetry conveys the same meaning. These are forces of reaction in the society. The poet who refers to herself/himself as "ocean" or "bitter leaf" expresses a symbol of independence, greatness and importance. He/she does not depend on others for existence. This is to deflate the personality of the person to whom the poem is directed. The imagery of the adder and python depicts a test of power and knowledge. The poet who by implication is a "python" in this case only shows that his enemy cannot compete with him or match him. The same inference can be drawn in the test of strength by both the witch and wizard. Maxims and witty sayings, loaded with metaphysical meanings are used as in the examples "It is they that will kill themselves with swords" and "The witch is boasting/The wizard is boasting."

Lullabies do not have any complex formation in terms of imagery and use of symbols. Occasionally imagery emerges when the mother employs the family or lineage poetry of the kid, but generally lullabies are constructed in simple language, reflecting the tender age, mind and psychology of the child, who is the main audience in this case. This poetrc form is typified by repetitions. Words, lines and a soothing tone are continuously repeated. The stylistic ploy works as a therapy on the child, who on hearing a recurrence of words, lines and tone may be consciously or unconsciously lurred to quietness. Students should make references to the samples used and their own fieldwork materials to detect these stylistic devices.

The stylistic composition of the occasional poetry, "bride-poetry" is always an amalgamation of the thematic and artistic contents of praise poetry already discussed in Chapter Four. It is necessary to emphasize the mythical and ritualistic artistic contents of the form. This is because it relies heavilty on the contents of lineage poetry, rituals and archetypes.

We shall briefly discuss the traditional performance of these various poetic genres. Domestic topical poetry grows from an atmosphere of conflict, hence its confrontational nature. The housewife rendering this type of poetry girds up her loins, claps her hands and modulates her voice to suit her emotion. She spits on the ground and makes derogatory dramatic gestures to provoke her enemy. Any domestic materials available are used as musical accompaniment to heighten the emotional tension involved in the rendition and performance. The enemy may decide to react in the same way or keep quiet depending on her emotional and moral disposition. The audience is constituted by neighbors who may decide to intervene, keep quiet or stand aloof enjoying the scene.

A lullaby is performed with the same domestic simplicity and aura. The nature of performance depends on where the mother or the nurse is. At home or elsewhere, she may decide to put the child on her back while dancing and making calculated movements to match the rhythm of the child's cry. This in most cases diverts the attention of the child, who may burst out laughing, keep quiet abruptly or doze off. A lullaby may have a touch of occupational poetry. A woman grinding, weaving or rolling clay pottery matches the lullaby with the occupational rhythm to placate the child. Occasionally when the child cannot be placated, neighbors intervene. This constitutes the rare additional audience on this occasion. The oral performance of occasional poetry is highly dramatic and ritualistic.

CONCLUSION

Our discussion of topical, lullaby and occasional poetry should have widened the outlook of our readers on the scope of oral poetry. These are forms of traditional poetry commonplace in the traditional societies, touching men and women, old and young. They express the crises of man in society and seek for amelioration. Topical poetry still persists in contemporary society but with a profound and gravity of the outlook of complex formalized societies. Lullabies are fast dying. Bride poetry is still observed in some traditional settings. The neglect of these poetic forms undoubtedly affects the generic moral outlook of contemporary societies.

EXERCISES AND FIELDWORK

1. Discuss at least two topical issues a traditional poet in your locality identifies in his poetry. Make a thorough study of his oral composition.
2. Compare a domestic topical poem of your choice with a contemporary public song, discussing their point of differences from the thematic and stylistic point of view.
3. Discuss the relevance of lullabies in children's development and acquisition of the traditional oral art in Africa.
4. Identify the philosophical and moral lessons contained in the bride's poetry collected during your fieldwork.
5. Make a comprehensive study of the performance techniques of topical poetry, lullabies and bride's poetry.
6. Discuss the impact of urbanization on the poetic forms studied in this chapter. Collect from your home or neighborhood samples of topical, lullaby and occasional poetry, and compare.

Further Reading and Work

(the audio material should help to compare to the transcribed ones, and should afford practice in performance of lullaby)

"African Lullaby" Sound Recording Music: Songs: Cassette tape 1 sound cassette (52 min., 25 sec.). Roslyn, NY : Ellipsis Arts, 1999.

Thomas, Joyce Carol and Brenda Joysmith. *Hush songs: African American lullabies.* New York: Jump at the Sun, 2000..

Seeger, Pete and Michael Hays. *Abiyoyo: based on South African lullaby and folk story.* New York: Macmillan, 1986.

Notes and References

1. See Chidi Amuta *The Theory of African Literature* (London: Zed Publishing Company, 1989) Abdul Rasheed Na'Allah also quotes and discusses social and topical poetry extensively in his paper "Odalaye Aremu: Partisanship, Politics and Traditional African Oral Art" (Unpublished Ms.)

2. H.B. Daba "The case of Dan Maraya Jos: A Hausa Poety" in *Oral Poetry in Nigeria* ed. Uchegbulan N. Abalogu (Lagos: Nigeria Magazine, 1981)

3. Ayinla Omowura, NEM (LP) 0344, 1978.

4. R.N. Egudu "The Igbo Experience: in *Oral Poetry in Nigeria* ed. Uchegbulan N. Abalogu. (Lagos: Nigeria Magazine, 1981)

 # Conclusion

Our concern and attempt to evolve a suitable pedagogy for the teaching and understanding of African oral literature and performance is emphasized in our Introduction and Chapter One. Up 'till now, oral literature and performance have been reduced to a mere classroom exercise in the Universities where it is largely taught. Our practical experience of fieldwork is an attempt to create innovation in this direction. We envision that a more viable empirical method and learning of oral literature and performance will emerge from this pedagogical approach.

Section II has comprehensively dealt with the content, style and performance of the various traditional poetic forms. It is evident that the traditional artist is imbued with great talent, versatile poetic mind and creative vision. The relevance of this poetic creativity to the socio-cultural and political life of the society cannot be overemphasized. Traditional oral narratives and drama are heavily complemented with poetry in forms of songs, chants, recitations and incantations.

Traditional poetry has heavy bearing on the liturgical systems or modes of worship of contemporary religions such as Islam and Christiantiy. Such bearing emerges in the invocation and evocation of traditional repertoires during worship in churches and mosques. Renditions of prayers are heavily loaded with the traditional spirit of incantations, invocations, supplication, admonition and divination, typical of oracular poetry. Modern worshippers invoke the spirit of African traditional poetry, by raising songs and performance with a traditional outlook. This is evident in services at the African Church on the African continent and in the Black Church in the African Diaspora.

Musical accompaniments, integral constituents of traditional religion, are now used in many modern religious settings. The traditional concepts of functions and aesthetics have found their ways into modern religions. We can then pose the question: Is this a process of de-acculturation or syncretism? This is a question to be answered by both traditionalists, modernists and even postmodernists in various disciplines.

Whatever the debate or argument, this situation creates a forum for negating the Eurocentric perceptions of some foreign scholars, who do not accept the functional-aesthetic relevance of African orature. African cultural aesthetics as we argue in Section 1 has a generic link with African cosmology. The aesthetics of African orature cannot be discussed without the functionality of the cosmic realm. It is therefore naive to reduce the analysis of cultural aesthetics and oral performance to a mere sociological or religious affair. We are in effect negating the thesis that practical exemplifications of African orature are mere "religious and sociological issues rather than literary ones."[1]

It is also necessary to highlight developments in contemporary poetic tradition in Africa that contaminates the invigorating force and voice in traditional poetry. Evidences abound that poetic habits in the present are seriously contaminated with the naive formalist view of "art for art's sake" and bourgeois concept of materialism. Even when the spirit of traditional poetry is evoked by modern practioners, it lacks the ritualistic and cognitive depth that characterizes the aura of the traditional setting.

We are thus restating our position that those modern poets who tag themselves professionals are merely freelancers begging for money. Constructive dialectics can emerge from the synthesis of the traditional and modern poetic forms for the moral and political upliftment of the society, rather than spiritual decay now engulfing modern set-ups.

The concern for material acquisition has influenced the tastes, fashions as well as inner and outer outlook of the African society of our global century. This is akin to what we refer to as pop or hip hop culture. Therefore, instead of the budding generation to generate a radical consciousness from traditional poetic forms, they become slaves of foreign cultures. It is a more viable teaching and practice of elements of oral literary traditions that can check this cultural crisis of our cyber generation.

Notes and References

1. Quoted from the Letter of Laura A. Winkiel, Managing Editor of *Religion and Literature*. Department of English, University of Notre Dame, Indiana to Abdul Rasheed Na'Allah, dated September 10, 1992.

Bibliography

Abu-Manga, Al-Amin. "The Concept of Woman in Fulani Narratives," *Nigeria Magazine,* Lagos: 1984.

Adéèkó, Adéléke. *Proverbs, Textuality, and nativism in African literature.* Gainesville: University Press of Florida, 1998.

"African Lullaby" Sound Recording Music: Songs: Cassette tape 1 sound cassette (52 min., 25 sec.). Roslyn, NY : Ellipsis Arts, 1999.

Ahmed, Sa'idu Babura. *Narrator as Interpreter: Stability and Variations in Hausa Tales.* Ibadan: Spectrum Books, 2002.

Ahmed, U.B. *Amina: Sarauniyar Zazzau* Zaria: Hudahuda Publishing Company, 1983.

Ajunwon, Bade. *Funeral Dirges of Yoruba Hunter.* New York: Nok Publishers International, 1982.

Akinlana, Obakunle and Myron Jackson. *Storyteller Obakunle Akinlana presents African folktales, stories, songs and music.* Tampa, FL.: Common Touch Studio, 2004.

Akínyemí, Akíntúndé. *Yorùbá royal poetry: a socio-historical exposition and annotated translation.* Bayreuth: Bayreuth University, 2004.

Akporobaro, F.B.O. *Introduction to African Oral Literature, a literary-descriptive Approach.* Lagos, Nigeria: Lighthouse Publishing Company, 2001.

Annan, Ivan. Ghana *Children at Play: Children Songs and Games.* Sound Recording:Music: Songs: Cassette tape 1 sound cassette. Washington D.C. : Smithsonian Folkways Records, 1991.

Anyidoho, Kofi, "Mythmaker and Mythbreaker: The Oral Poet as Earwitness" in *African Literature in its Social and Political Dimensions* ed. Eileen Julien & Mortimer Mildred & et.al. Washington: African Literature Association and Three Continents Press, 1983, 5-14.

Apter, Andrew. "Death and the King's Henchment: Ken Saro-Wiwa and the Political Ecology of Citizenship in Nigeria." *Ogoni's Agonies: Ken Saro-Wiwa and the Crisis in Nigeria*. Ed. Abdul-Rasheed Na'Allah. Trenton: AWP, 1998.

---. "The Pan-African Nation: Oil-Money and the Spectacle of Culture in Nigeria."*Public Culture* 8.3, 1996: 441-66.

Ardagh, Philip. African myths and legends. Parsippany, NJ : Dillon Press, 1999.

Arnoldi, Mary Jo. *Playing With Time: and and performance in Central Mali*. Bloomington: Indiana University Press, 1995.

Arnott, Kathleen. *African Myths and Legends*. New York: H.Z. Walk, 1963.

Awoonor, Kofi. *A study of the influences of oral literature on the contemporary literature of Africa*. Diss., State University of New York at Stony Brook; Ann Arbor, Michigan: University Microfilms International, 1978.

Babalola, S.A. *The Content and Form of Yoruba Ijala* Ibadan: Oxford University Press, 1976.

Bada, Samuel Ojo. *Iwe Itan Saki*. Saki: Ladepo Printing Press, 1937.

Barber, Karin. "Text and Performance in Africa" in *Bulletin of the School of Oriental and African Studies*. 66.3 (2003): 324-33.

---. "Obscurity and Exegesis in African Oral Praise Poetry" in *The Yoruba Artist: New Theoretical Perspectives on African Arts*. Washington, D.C.: Smithsonian, 1994. 150-60.

---. "Multiple Discourses in Yoruba Oral Literature." in *Bulletin of the John Rylands University Library of Manchester* (BJRL). 73-3 (1991): 11-24.

Beans, C. Wandell & Doly William C. ed. *Myths, Rites, Symbols: A Mircea Eliade Reader*. New York: Harder & Rex, 1976.

Besmer, Fremont E. *Hausa Performance*. New York, Garland Pub., 1998.

Bigsby, C.W.E. (ed) *Approaches to Popular Culture*. London: Edward Arnold, 1976.

Boadi, L. A. "Praise Poetry in Akan" in *Research in African Literatures*. Summer 1989, pp. 181-93.

Bodkin, Maud. *Archetypal Patterns in Poetry: Psychological Studies of Imagination*. London: New York & Toronto: Oxford University Press, 1934.

Bodunde, Charle. *Oral Traditions and Aesthetic Transfer: form and social vision in Black poetry*. Bayreuth: Baureuth University, 2001.

Boólájí, Emmanuel Bámidélé. *The Dynamics and Manifestations of Efe: The Satirical Poetry of the Yoruba Gelede Groups of Nigeria*. Ph.D. Dissertation: Center of West African Studies, University of Birmingham,1984.

Brisman, Heskel. *Uganda Lullaby: African Chant*. Bryn Mawr, PA : Elkan-Vogel, Inc., 1973.

Bibliography

Brown, Duncan. *Voicing the Text: South African Oral Poetry and Performance.* Cape Town and New York: Oxford University Press, 1998.

---. *Oral Literature and Performance in Southern Africa.* Athens: Ohio University Press, 1999.

Bryan, Ahsley. *The Night Has Eears: African Proverbs.* New York, NY: Antheneum Books for Young Readers, 1999.

Bundo, Daisuke. „Social Relationship embodied in singing and dancing performances among the Baka." *African Studies Monograph.* 26. 2001: 85-101.

Canonici, Noverino N. *Zulu Oral Traditions.* Durban, Zulu Language and Literature, University of Natal, 1996.

Chidi, Amuta. *The Theory of African Literature.* London and New Jersey: Zed Books Ltd., 1989.

Courlander, Harold. *A Treasury of Africak Folklore: the oral literature, traditions, myths, legends, epics, tales, recollections, wisdom, sayings, and humor of Africa.* New York: Marlowe & Company, 1996.

Daba, H.A. "The Case of Dan Maraya Jos: A Hausa Poet" in *Oral Poetry in Nigeria* (ed.) Uchegbulan N. Abalogu. Garba Ashiwaju & Regina Amadi - Tshiwala. Lagos: Nigeria Magazine, 1981.

Dandatti, A. "The Role of an Oral Singer in Hausa-Fulani Society: A Case Study of Mamman Shatta" Ph.D. Thesis, University of Indiana, 1975.

Dasylva, A.O. *Classification Paradigms in African Oral Narratives.* Ibadan: Atlantis Books, 1999.

Dorsch, T.S. trans & intro. *Aristotle, Horace, Longinus: Classical Literary Criticism.* Hammondsworth: Penguin Books Ltd., 1965.

Drewal, Margaret Thompson. *Yoruba Rituals: performance, play, agency.* Bloomington, Indiana University Press, 1992.

---. "The State of Research on Performance in Africa." *African Studies Review.* 34.3, 1991: 1-64.

---. "Ritual performance in Africa Today." In *Africa: Prophesy and Pupettry, weddings and worship, ritual, rivalry and opera.* Cambridge: MIT Press, 1988.

Ebron, Paulla A. *Performing Africa.* Princeton, NJ: Princeton University Press, 2002.

Egudu, R.N. "The Igbo Experience" in *Oral Poetry in Nigeria* (ed.) Uchegbulan N. Abalogu, Garba Ashiwaju & Regina Amadi-Tshiwala Lagos: Nigeria Magazine, 1981.

Eisner, Will. *Sundiata: a legend of Africa.* New York: NBM, 2003.

Fadahunsi, Ayo. "The Logic of Incantation." *Journal of African Philosophy and Studies.* Lagos 1 (1 & 2), 1988, pages 39-48.

Fagunwa, D.O. *Ogboju Ode Ninu Igbo Irunmole.* Apapa. Nelson, 1950.

Fieldman, B. & Richardson. *The Use of Modern Mythology.* Bloomington: Indiana University Press, 1972.

Finnegan, Ruth. *Oral Literature in Africa.* Nairobi: Oxford University Press, 1976.

Frost, Mary. *Zambian Oral Literature.* Zambia: University of Zambia, University of Chicago Photo Duplication Dept., 1981.

Gueye, Marame. *Wolof Wedding Songs: Women negotiating voice and space through verbal art.* Diss., State University of New York at Binghamton, 2004.

Hale, Thomas A. *Griots and Griottes: Masters of words and music.* Bloomington, Indiana University Press, 1998.

Hale, Thomas, et. al. *The Epic of Askia Mohammed.* Bloomington, Indiana University Press, 1996.

Idowu, Bolaji, *Olodumare.* London: Longmans, 1962.

Johnson, John Williams, et. al. *Oral epics from Africa: vibrant voices from a vast continent.* Bloomington, Indiana University Press, 1997.

Kabira, Wanjiku Mukabi. *Gikuyu Oral Literature.* Nairobi, Kenya: East African Educational Publciehrs, 1993.

Kamera, W.D. *Siswati Lesingakabhalwa: singeniso selucwaningo=Swazi Oral Literature, an introductory survey.* Manzini, Swaziland: Ruswanda Publication Bureau, 2001.

Kaschula, Russel. *African Oral Literature: functions in contemporary contexts.* London:NAE, 2001.

Knappert, Jan. *Epic Poetry in Swahili and Other African Languages.* E.J. Brill, 1983.

Knipp, R. Thomas, "Myth, History and the Poetry of Kofi Awoonor" in *African Literature Today* Vol. 11 ed. Jones Eldred. London: Heinemann, 1980.

Kunene, Daniel. *Heroic Poetry of the Basotho.* Oxford: Clarendon Press, 1971.

Kunene, Mazisi, *Anthems of the Decade: A Zulu Epic dedicated to the women of Africa.* London: Heinemann, 1981.

Ladipo, Duro. *Oba Koso*: (The King did not hand). Ibadan: Institute of African Studies, 1972.

Levi-Strauss, Claude. *Structural Anthropology* trans from French by Claire Jacobson & Brooke Grundfest Schoepf. New York, London; Basic Books, Inc., 1963.

Liyong, Taban lo. *Popular Culture of East Africa: Oral Literature.* Nairobi, Kenya: Longman, 1972.

Mbiti, J.S. *African Oral Literature.* Paris: Presence Africaine, 1971.

Bibliography

---. *African Religions and Philosophy*. London: Heinemann, 1969.

McLaughlin, Roberta. *Folk Songs of Africa*. Sound Recording: Music: Folk music: LP recording 1 sound disc (27 min.): + 1 song book. Glendale, Calif.: Bowmar Records, 1963.

Miruka, Simon Okumba. *Studying Oral Literature*. Nairobi: Acacia Stantex Publishers, 1999.

Mosley, Albert. "The metaphysics of Magic and Philosophical Implications" in *Second Order: An African Journal of Philosophy*. Vol. vii Nos. 1 & 2 Ile Ife: University of Ife Press, 1978.

Moyo, Steven Phaniso Chinombo, et. al. *Oral Traditions in Southern Africa*. Lusaka: Institute for Cultural Studies, University of Zambia, 1986.

Na'Allah, A. *Yoruba Folktales: cultural plurality and oral narratives*. Ph.D. Diss., University of Alberta. Ann Arbor: UMI Dissertation Services. 1999.

---. "Interpretation of African Orature: Oral Specifity and Literary Analysis." *Alif: Journal of Comparative Poetics*. 17 (1997): 125-42.

---. "Odolaiye Aremu: Partisanship, Politics and Tradition in African Oral Art." Unpublished paper: University of Ilorin, 1990.

Nandwa, Jane and Bukenya Austin. *African Oral Literature for Schools*. Nairobi: Longman, 1983.

Nketia, J. H. Kwabena. *Funeral Dirges of the Akan People*. New York: Negro University Press, 1969.

Nwoga, Donatus Ibe. *African Traditional Literature*. Enugu: Forth Dimension Publishers, 1980.

Obafemi, Olu, *A Night of Mystical Beast,* Benin: Adena Publishers, 1986.

Obiechina, E.N. *Culture, Tradition and Society in the West African Novel.* Cambridge: Cambridge University Press, 1975.

Ogede, Ode. *Art, Society and Performance: Igede Praise Poetry*. Gainesville: University Press of Florida, 1997.

---. "The Power of Word in Igede Incantatory Poetry." *Africana Marburgensia*. 27.1-2. 1994, 13-20.

Ogúndéjì, Philip Adédotun. *Introduction to Yoruba Oral Literature*. Ibadan: University of Ibadan, Ibadan External Studies Program, 1991.

Ogunjimi, Bayo & Abdul-Rasheed Na'Allah. *Introduction to African Oral Literature*, Vol. 1 – Prose. Ilorin: University of Ilorin Press, 1991.

Ogunjimi, Bayo. "Niyi Osundare. The Literary Evangelist Combs the World." *The Guardian*. June 5 & 12, 1993 Lagos, p. 19.

Ojiaku, Ezike I.P.A. "Igbo Divination Poetry" in *Abu Afa: An Introduction* No. 150, 1984, p. 37.

Ojo, S.O. *Iwe Itan Saki*. Saki

Okafor, Clement Abiazem. "Research Methodology in African Oral Literature." *Okike*, 16, 1979: 83-97.

Okereke, Augustine. *Oral Heroic Poetry of the Arondizuogu Igbos of Nigeria*. Berlin: Lagos, 1998.

Okpewho, Isidore. "Oral Literary Research in Africa" in *African folklore: an encyclopedia*. Ed. Philip M. Peek. New York: Routledge, 2004, Pp. 303-310.

---. "The Resources of the Oral Epic." *African Intellectual Heritage* Ed. Molefi Kete Asante and Abu S. Abarry. Philadelphia: Temple University Press, 1996. 119-130.

---. *African Oral Literature: backgrounds, character and continuity*. Bloomington, Indiana University Press, 1992.

---. *Oral Performance in Africa* Ibadan. Spectrum Books Ltd., 1990.

---. "The primacy of performance in oral discourse" in *Research in African Literatures*. 21.4 (1990): 121-28.

---. *Myth in Africa*. Cambridge: Cambridge Press, 1983.

---. *The Epic in Africa: Toward a Poetics of the Oral Performance*. New York: Columbia University Press, 1979.

Onuekwusi, Jasper. *Fundamentals of African Oral Literature*. Owerri, Nigeria: Alphabet Nigeria Publishers, 2001.

Opland, Jeff. "Praise Poetry: Praise Poetry of the Xhosa" in *African Folklore: An Encyclopedia*. New York: Routledge, 2004, pp. 361-62.

Osundare, Niyi. "Poems for Sale: Stylistic Features of Yoruba Ipolowo Poetry" in *African Notes* Vol. xv Nos 1 & 2, 1991, pp. 63-92.

Owomoyela, Oyekan. *Yoruba Proverbs*. Lincoln: University of Nebraska Press, 2005.

---. *Culture and Customs of Zimbabwe*. Westport, Conn.: Greenwood Press, 2002.

---. *Yoruba Trickster*. Lincoln, Nebraska: University of Nebraska Press, 1997.

---. *The African Difference: Discourses on Africanity and the Relativity of Cultures*. Johannesburg: Witwatersand University Press, 1996.

---. *A Kì í: Yorùbá Proscriptive and prescriptive proverbs*. Lanham, MD: University Press of America, 1988.

---. *Folklore and the Rise of Theater among the Yoruba* Ph.D. Diss., University of California, Los Angeles. Reproduction. Microfilm of typescript. Ann Arbor, Michigan: University Microfilms, 1971.

Parrinder, Edward Geoffrey. *African Mythology*. New York: P. Bedrick, 1986.

Bibliography

Plato. *The Republic of Plato* Trans Francis MacDonald Cornford. London: Oxford University Press. 1979.

Pongweni, Alec J. C. *Shona Praise Poetry as a Role Negotiation: The Battles of the Clans And the Sexes*. Gweru, Zimbabwe: Mambo Press, 1996.

Prahlad, Sw. Anand. *African-American Proverbs in context*. Jackson: University Press of Mississippi, 1996.

Preminger Alex, Frank &. & et.al *Princeton Encyclopedia of Poetry and Poetics*. London & Basingstoke, Macmillan Press Ltd., 1975.

Rotimi, Ola. *Kurunmi*. Ibadan; Oxford University Press, 1971.

Seeger, Pete and Michael Hays. Abiyoyo: based on South African lullaby and folk story. New York: Macmillan, 1986.

Sekoni, Ropo. *Folk poetics: a sociosemiotic study of Yoruba trickster tales*. Westport, Conn.: Greenwood Press, 1994.

---. "Literary Pragmatology in Postcolonial Nigeria" in *International Semiotics Spectrum:* a Publication of the Toronto Semiotic Circle, 1989.

---. "Toward a New Taxonomy of Yoruba Trickster Tales." *Artes Populares*. 2 (1984): 523-9.

Soyinka, Wole, *Death and the King's Horsemen*. London: Metheun, 1975.

Speed, Francis and Peggy Harper. *Kwa-Hir: Traditional Theatre of the Tiv People of Nigeria*. Addison, IL: KSH Video Productions, 1990.

Stone, Ruth M. *Music in West Africa: Expressing Music, Expressing Culture*. New York, Oxford University Press, 2004.

---. *Time in African Performance*. New York: Galand Pub., 1998.

Strand, Julie Lynn. *Style and Substance: Improvisational Trends in Madinka balafon Performance*. MA Thesis, Arizona State University, 2000.

---. *Myth, Literature and the African World*. Cambridge: Cambridge University Press, 1976.

Thomas, Joyce Carol and Brenda Joysmith. *Hush songs: African American lullabies*. New York: Jump at the Sun, 2000..

Thram, Diane Janell. Performance as ritual, performace as art: therapeutic efficacy of Dandanda song and dance in Zimbabwe. PhD. Diss., Indiana University Press, 201.

Uba-Mgbemena, Asonye, "Ifo Prose Narratives as Bearer of Beliefs of Traditional Igbo Society. A paper presented at the Second Annual Conference of the Folklore Society of Nigeria, Ilorin 1982.

Uzochukwu, Sam. *Traditional Funeral Poetry of the Igbo*. Lagos: Lagos University Press, 2001.

Whorf, Benjamin, "The Relation of Habitual Thought and Behavior to Language" in *Language, Culture and Society*. ed. Blount B.G. Cambridge Massachusettes: Winthrop Publishers, 1974.

Yai, Olabiyi Babalola. "Tradition and the Yoruba Artist" in *African Arts*. 32.1 (1999) 32-5.

---. "Fundamental Issues in African Oral Literature" in *Ife Studies in African-Literature and the Arts ISALA*. 1 (1982): 4-17.

Index

Ààlòò 21, 103
Aaro 39, 203
Abu-Manga, Al-Amin 78
Achebe, Chinua 85
Adereth, Max 36
Àdó 39, 180
African universe 9, 10, 12, 13, 16-19, 22, 32, 48, 55, 65, 88, 95, 107, 109, 125, 147, 155
Àló o 21, 103
Amadioha 10, 11, 131
Àmàó, Omoékeé 86
Amina, Queen 207, 209
Ancestor, ancestors 9, 12, 14, 21, 40, 43, 49, 52, 55, 63, 66, 88, 89, 91, 106, 107, 127, 128, 135, 165, 167, 184, 186-188, 201, 225, 236
Anyidoho, Kofi 56
Apter, Andrew 1
Archetypes 32, 34, 47-54, 238
Aremo Alaseju 90
Armah 50
Artistes, freelance 27, 28
Artistes, professional 26-28
Atilogwu dancers 26

Awon, Shao 52, 53, 58, 59, 102, 108, 202

Barber, Karin 2
Basaori 53, 59, 60, 102
Bayagida 51-53, 58, 102, 104, 108
Bayero, Alhaji Ado 180
Being, the supreme 10, 11, 62, 167
Betrayal 51, 52, 203
Bigsby, C.W.E. 36
Black Church 241
Bodkin, Maud 47
Borno 58, 104, 108
Borno, King of 104, 108
Brooks De Vita, Alexis 54

Chief priest 39, 142
Communal 13-15, 18, 26, 39, 52, 59, 76, 85, 87, 95, 127, 130, 135, 136, 142, 176, 185, 187, 192, 195, 196, 200-203, 206, 211, 216, 220, 229
Communication 14-17, 19, 39, 86, 97, 100
Community 5, 13-15, 23, 25-27, 34, 39, 56, 62, 72, 78, 80, 81, 85,

89, 97, 103, 106, 113, 135, 142, 144, 165, 166, 169, 170, 172-175, 180, 182, 185, 199, 200, 205-207, 209, 211, 215, 216, 220, 223, 224, 227, 229, 232

Cosmology 13, 60, 72, 76, 99, 100, 125, 144, 159, 242

Cowries 39, 142, 196

Cultural artifacts 13, 39, 40, 59, 125, 128

Dadakúàdà 41, 86
Deity, deities 143
Dùndún 39, 141, 194, 224
Durkheim, Emile 85

Egyptian 33
Eleburubon, Yemi 140
Electronic Classrooms 31
Eliade, Mircea 57
Epic 2, 12, 50, 66, 72, 135, 205, 206, 211, 212
Eré Olómooba 26, 173, 176
Èsù 10, 11
Etsu 171, 172, 180, 181
Euba, Femi 54
Eurocentric 2, 32, 91, 160, 206, 242

Fagunwa, D.O. 43, 206
FESTAC 1977 1
Fieldman, B. 66
Fieldwork 1, 2, 4, 31, 33-35, 37-43, 45, 53, 62, 72, 84, 92, 100, 109, 121, 129, 131, 132, 134, 137, 141, 144, 162, 181, 196, 205, 212, 238, 239, 241

Fieldwork, problems of 43
Fieldwork, techniques 37, 45

Fieldworker 34, 37-39, 41, 44, 45
Finnegan, Ruth 2, 162
Fulani, fulanis 23, 51, 78, 106, 173, 175

Gatanan Gatanan Ku 21

Heroic 3, 4, 12, 16, 19, 53, 65-67, 69, 71, 108, 185, 186, 188, 193, 195, 199, 201, 203, 205-207, 209, 211, 212, 231
Hip-hop 35, 36, 242

Idowu, Bolaji 56
Ìjàpá 225
Indigenous occupations 205
Individualism 18, 87, 206
ìrùkèrè 138

Jet age 37
Jeyifo, Biodun 143
Jung, Carl 34, 49, 54

Kábíyèsí 168, 169
Knappert, Jan 206
Knipps, Thomas 56
Kofoworola, Ziky O. 41
Kowa da nasa 18
Kunene, Mazisi 135
Kwa Hir performers 26

Ladipo, Duro
Legend 4, 50, 53, 65-67, 69-72, 103, 105, 106, 108, 113, 116, 132, 143, 205, 206, 209
Legend, Àsegbé 69
Legend, Crocodile 71, 72, 108
Levi-Straus, Claude 35

Index

Magic 11, 16, 32, 88, 147, 150, 160, 233
Mbiti, J.S. 13, 60, 149
Methodology, fieldwork 31-46
Methodology, oral literature 31-46
Morèmi 53, 70, 71, 105, 106, 108, 206
Musical accompaniment 23, 24, 28, 141, 142, 193, 194, 238
Myth 2, 4, 11, 51-53, 55, 56, 58-62, 65, 67, 88, 102-105, 108, 112, 113, 116, 128-130, 143, 183, 185
Myth, Awon 52, 53, 58, 59, 102, 108, 202
Myth, Basaori 53, 59, 60, 102
Myth, Emedike 51, 60, 61, 109, 116

Negritude 66, 186
Ngugi 56
Nok Culture 33, 204

Oath-taking 203
Obafemi, Olu 56
Obàtálá 10, 11, 127, 129, 133-135, 144, 227
Obiechina, E. N. 85
Odùduwà 67, 108
Oedipal complex 51, 52, 229
Ògún 10, 11, 48, 127-130, 140-143, 173, 174, 201
Olófin 51, 53, 67-69, 108, 116
Olúkòso 126, 131
Onoge, Omafume 36
Osé 39, 142, 150, 169
Osundare, Niyi 204

Palace 26, 27, 39, 41, 70, 96, 105-107, 111, 180, 194
Poetry 2, 12, 13, 16, 17, 19, 23-25, 28, 33-35, 38, 41, 68, 69, 86, 92, 119, 121, 125-129, 131-137, 139-144, 147-151, 153-162, 165-177, 179-197, 199-207, 209, 211, 212, 215-217, 219-221, 223-229, 231, 233-239, 241, 242
Patigi, Etsu of 171, 181
Philosophical belief 16
Plato 126
Pop culture 36, 37
Priest, Ifa 137, 139, 142

Richardson, R.J. 66

Sakí 51, 69, 102, 173, 174, 181
Sàngó 10, 11, 39-41, 69, 126, 127, 131-133, 135, 142, 143, 148, 150, 151
Scapegoating 50
Sèkèrè 39
Sekoni, Ropo 33, 101, 115
Senghor 186
Sharro 51
Society, modern 181, 228
Society, traditional 71, 89
Solomon 50
Sòpònná 10
Soyinka, Wole 61, 129
Spirits 11, 19, 21, 52, 55, 59, 75, 90, 106-108, 127, 128, 139, 153, 165, 167, 184, 204
Spontaneous improvisation 160
Spontaneous renditions 41, 125, 131, 233, 241
Storytelling 20, 22, 23, 28, 104, 115, 116

Taylor and Auguste Comte 13
Technological rationality 17
Tortoise 23, 48, 51, 52, 81-83, 111,
    117, 225
Trick 48
Trickster 48, 54

Uriah 50

woodcarver 204
Wood-carving 204

Yan Tauri 26
Yoruba mythology 10, 134